By the authors

Larry Chang

*Wisdom for the Soul: Five Millennia
of Prescriptions for Spiritual Healing*

Roderick Terry

*Brother's Keeper: Words of Inspiration
for African-American Men*

*One Million Strong: A Photographic
Tribute of the Million Man March*

*The lips of the wise are as the doors of
a cabinet; no sooner are they opened,
but the treasures are poured before you.
Like unto trees of gold arranged in
beds of silver, are wise sentences uttered
in due season.
~ Khemetic Wisdom ~*

Proverbs are full of poetry and twists. They are made up of words that have been molded for centuries, if not milleniums, until a minimum of words carry an extraordinary potential for meaning.
~ Gaston Kaboré ~

WISDOM
for the Soul
of Black Folk

Compiled & Edited by
Larry Chang

Contributing Editor
Roderick Terry

Wisdom is not like money, to be tied up and hidden.
~ Akan Wisdom ~

Ossie & Barbara,
in appreciation.
Larry Chang

GNOSOPHIA
WASHINGTON

Wisdom for the Soul Of Black Folk

Published by:
Gnosophia Publishers
P O Box 3183, Washington, DC 20010-0183, USA
http://www.wisdomforthesoul.org
orders@wisdomforthesoul.org

Publisher's Cataloging-in-Publication Data

Wisdom for the soul of Black folk / compiled & edited by
Larry Chang ; Roderick Terry, contributing editor. –
1st ed.
p. cm.
Includes bibliographical references and index.
LCCN 2007905212
ISBN-13: 9780977339150
ISBN-10: 0977339157

1. Blacks–Quotations. 2. African Americans–
Quotations. 3. Self-realization–Quotations, maxims,
etc. 4. Spiritual life–Quotations, maxims, etc.
I. Chang, Larry. II. Terry, Roderick.

PN6081.3.W57 2007   082'.08996
QBI07-600204

First edition

First printing 2007

Printed in USA

To the island and people of Jamaica who gave
me birth and shaped me; to the memory of
Nanny, Muriel Meredith, who nurtured me; to
Ruoji, wherever you are, who weaned me on
Anansi.

The spider is an iconic symbol of wisdom in many African
cultures. Its web, produced from within itself, represents the life-
giving nature of the sun and the interconnectedness of all life. In
Akan cosmology, Anansi, from the Twi word for spider, is the
son of Nyame, the sky god and Asase Ya, the earth goddess. He
is credited with creating the sun, moon, stars, night, day and was
the first man in whom Nyame breathed life. He originated
agriculture, weaving, construction and social organization. As
the keeper of stories, Anansi tried to hoard all of the world's
wisdom in a calabash. He soon realized the selfishness and
futility of this, so he released wisdom to the world.

GUIDE TO USAGE

NAMES : For the most part, authors are referred to
in the text by the names they are most widely
known, with birth and/or other names listed in the
index.

ABBREVIATIONS USED:

b.	born
BCE	Before the Common Era
c.	circa (about)
C.	Century
CE	Common Era
d.	died
fl.	flourished
Ibid.	from the same source
ed(s).	editor(s)
tr(s).	translator(s)

Give your ears, hear the sayings,
Give your heart to understand them;
It profits to put them in your heart.
~ Amenemope ~

Contents

*Why should I pester you with
quotations? – to shew you the depth of
my erudition, and strut like the fabled
bird in his borrowed plumage.*
~ Ignatius Sancho ~

Acknowledgments

Sandra "Cookie" Carmon for getting at me to finish this;
Namon Armstrong for unstinting support;
Roderick Terry for use of material from his unpublished work,
"Hope Chest"

Excerpts from
Letters of the Late Ignatius Sancho, An African.
In Two Volumes. To Which Are Prefixed,
Memoirs of His Life, Vols.1 & 2
© University of North Carolina at Chapel Hill

It is through other people's wisdom that we learn
wisdom; a single person's understanding does not
amount to anything.
~ Yoruba Wisdom ~

Nyansa, as wisdom, is an Akan word,
made up of *nya* and *nsa* meaning
"that which is obtained and is never exhausted."
~ N. K. Dzobo ~
"Knowledge and Truth: Ewe and Akan Conceptions,"
Person and Community: Ghanaian Philosophical Studies,
Kwasi Wiredu & Kwame Gyekye, eds.

Introduction

Another book of quotations? Indeed there are numerous excellent extant anthologies of quotations, but these tend to be very broad, with a bias toward canonical and well-known authors; those works which document the contributions of Black authors have tended to focus on African-Americans, considerable as their output is. Undeniable recognition of this prevalence is reflected in the title of the present volume which pays homage to W. E. B. Du Bois' classic work and in the preponderance of entries from American sources. Nevertheless, effort has been made to cast a wider net to capture under-represented and unfamiliar voices.

Much of African wisdom, originating in pre-literate cultures and colonial societies, has been conveyed orally. As the role and numbers of griots diminish, so have the surviving oralatures. Alex Haley notes, "When a griot dies, it is as if a library has burned to the ground." What remains is represented, exceptionally by the Ife Oracle commentaries, in secret society rituals, and in proverbs, tribal songs and folk tales, but this too is threatened by the inundation of digitized global culture. Replacement generations have increasingly become consumers of cultural products packaged elsewhere rather than participate as creators and agents in and of their own traditions. The irony is that now that we have the technological capability to record, preserve and transmit performative legacies, we lose them instead to the onslaught of canned entertainment with its emphasis on materialistic bling and egoistic gratification.

Despite this, with the flowering of national and ethnic consciousness, there is a post-colonial movement to speak the marvellous complexity and diversity of the Black experience into the record. In addition to creating and augmenting national literatures, to the extent even of writing in threatened and obscure languages to preserve and promote their continuity, to syncretizing and synthesizing the ethnic and ancestral with the contemporary, Black authors have inserted themselves into the mainstream of metropolitan literary output, reflecting back to those societies their multicultural actualities. This assertion has been succintly captured in the title, *The Empire Writes Back*, an anthology of post-colonial criticism. Indigenes, immigrants and their descendants, beneficiaries of tertiary education, are producing books, many of which have broken out of the confines of niche markets to become international bestsellers.

Khemetic texts preserved in papyri and stelae are the earliest literature to have survived, followed by the writings of North African Romans and Ethiopian philosophers and clerics, and the lately recovered Timbuktu manuscripts from their repositories in the desert sands of Mali. The Transatlantic slave experience gave rise to the slave narratives and abolitionist literature from both sides of the Atlantic, which expressions characterized the struggle of the 18th and 19th centuries. Post-Emancipation under colonial rule and white domination, Black poetry and prose emerged, adhering to prevailing standards, evidenced typically in the work of Phillis Wheatley and the sonnets of Claude McKay. With the Civil Rights and Black Power movements would come iconoclastic expressions of protest and identity. Today, global Black literature covers the entire gamut of genres from philosophy and science fiction to erotica and graphic novels. The proliferation of media affords us unprecedented access to the minds of diverse thinkers of African origin and descent through biographies, memoirs and interviews.

Fortunately for our purpose, there is a sizeable body of literature by Black authors who speak to universal values and eternal verities. This anthology of their work focuses on the inner life, on personal development and self-actualization. The quotations have been selected to inspire, enlighten and encourage; they have been arranged by category and by author in chronological order. The resulting timeline of thought in itself is useful and instructive as it demonstrates very clearly the evolution of consciousness evident in the contemporary thinking on particular subjects. One or more quotations in each classification will be sure to strike a responsive chord in the reader.

In the stress of modern life, we seek solutions, or at least some insight from whatever quarter, that may relate to or throw light on the challenges we may be facing. We can take some small comfort in realizing that there is no need to reinvent the wheel. We have a legacy of recorded thought spanning some five millennia in various world cultures that addresses every conceivable condition that has faced the individual. Somebody somewhere has probably been there, done that already. We can refer to what they have thought and said of the experience, and we can learn from them.

These selections indicate, not only that Black folk should be listening to themselves, but that the rest of humanity would do well to give an ear.

Jak Manduora mi no chuuz non.

Unfortunately, no one has yet found a way to make most scholarly texts interesting enough to entice laymen to read them – unless they are assigned by teachers with the power to inflict punishment. So it is left to the historical novelist and other nonacademic writers to popularize the complex issues of academia.
~ Playthell Benjamin ~

A wise man who knows his proverbs can reconcile difficulties.
~ Nigerian Wisdom ~

Table of Subjects

ABILITY

Man's greatness consists in his ability to do and the proper application of his powers to things needed to be done.
~ Frederick Douglass, 1817-1895 ~

The world cares very little about what a man or woman knows; it is what a man or woman is able to do that counts.
~ Booker T. Washington, 1856-1915 ~

Don't look at me as a color. Look at me as what I am capable of doing.
~ Eartha Kitt, b. 1927 ~
Interview by Blase DiStefano, "Eartha Kitt *Purr*-severes: The Feline Feminist Talks About Her Two Lives as the Child and the Woman," *OutSmart*

There is a bit of advantage in playing to be naïve. You know what you know and you know that you know. You keep quiet and you let your work do the talking for you.
~ Buchi Emecheta, b. 1944 ~
Interview by Zhana, 1966

We all have ability. The difference is how we use it.
~ Stevie Wonder, b. 1950 ~

Once I developed confidence in myself and began to believe that I was smart, then all of those innate abilities began to come out. Everybody has them, everybody who has a normal brain, because there is no such thing as an average human being. If you have a normal brain, you are superior. There's almost nothing that you can't do.
~ Benjamin Carson, b. 1951 ~
"Gifted Hands That Heal," Academy of Achievement Interview, 2002 June 7

Often the way I work is that I don't realize I'm going to want to do it. I just try to do it and then if it's possible, I figure I can do it.
~ Nalo Hopkinson, b. 1960 ~
Interview by Kellie Magnus, *Caribbean Review of Books*, Issue 73

ACCEPTANCE

Be content with your lot; one cannot be first in everything.
~ Aesop, fl. c. 550 BCE ~
"Juno and the Peacock"

He who cannot do what he wants must make do with what he can.
~ Terence, c. 190-159 BCE ~

Accept the weather as it comes and people as they are.
~ Haitian Wisdom ~
Wit & Wisdom of Africa: Proverbs from Africa & The Caribbean, Patrick Ibekwe, ed., 1998

Take what you get till you get what you want.
~ Jamaican Wisdom ~

The secret to success is to learn to accept the impossible, to do without the indispensable, and to bear the intolerable.
~ Nelson Mandela, b. 1918 ~

Only one thing can be guaranteed and that is the principle of accepting the challenges of life, of society in the same way as nature does.
~ Wole Soyinka, b. 1934 ~
Interview by John Agetua in *When the Man Died: Views, Reviews, and Interview on Wole Soyinka's Controversial Book*, 1975

In the few moments life has left me, I learned to let my heart gallop on the saddle of intense feelings, to live life, as they say, to let her be.
~ Patrick Chamoiseau, b. 1953 ~
Texaco, Rose-Myriam Réjouis & Val Vinokurov, trs., 1992

Most of my major disappointments have turned out to be blessings in disguise. So whenever anything bad does happen to me, I kind of sit back and feel, well, if I give this enough time, it'll turn out that this was good, so I shouldn't worry about it too much.
~ William A. Gaines, b. 1971 ~

Resistance causes pain and lethargy. It is when we practice acceptance that new possibilities appear.
~ Unknown ~

The more we accept change, the more we relax the mind, and the more we are able to let go of many of our attachments.
~ Marlene Jones ~
"Moving toward an End to Suffering," *Dharma, Color, and Culture*, Hilda Gutiérrez Baldoquín, ed., 2004

Recognition of one's weakness is the most essential step towards overcoming such weakness, just as the identification (diagnosis) of an ailment is always essential to the curing of the ailment.
~ Oliver Mbamara ~
"Will You Keep Your New Year Resolution?" *Cafe Africana*, 2003

There is no limit to truths. We should be prepared to master all of them. In being prepared to accept any and all truths ... just as it comes, without trying to change it to suit our needs, we become free of the anxiety that comes from the urge to change and control. By master I mean receive with our full minds, open and without resistance. It doesn't mean that you know everything. Rather, it means that you may not know anything at all in a situation, but you have become so open to the infinite possibilities that you can approach and accept anything. Even pain. We have to be just as willing to touch and acknowledge the pain as we are to feel the joy. Why? Because one doesn't exist without the other.
~ Angel Kyodo Williams ~
Being Black: Zen and the Art of Living with Fearlessness and Grace, 2000

Acceptance for who we are, just as we are, whatever that may be: funky attitude, arrogant, self-pitying, too fat, kinky-haired, pimpled, freckled, too tall, too short, not enough money, always late, high-strung, unmotivated, skinny as a rail, high yellow, chinky-eyed, Kunta Kinte-looking, half-breed, flat-nosed, dim-witted, still living with your momma, working at McDonald's, conceited, know you better than anyone else, Cuchifrita, Coconut, Spic, Negro ... So say to yourself, "Here I am, in the best way I can be at this moment." And that is all that should ever count.
~ Ibid.

Acceptance is the answer to all my problems today ... I can find no serenity until I accept that person, place, thing, or situation as being exactly the way it is supposed to be.
~ Alcoholics Anonymous ~

ACCOMPLISHMENT / ACHIEVEMENT / EXCELLENCE

Do you wish to be great? Then begin by being. Do you desire to construct a vast and lofty fabric? Think first about the foundations of humility. The higher your structure is to be, the deeper must be its foundation.
~ Augustine of Hippo, 354-430 ~

You are not judged by the height you have risen, but from the depth you have climbed.
~ Frederick Douglass, 1817-1895 ~

Strive to make something of yourself; then strive to make the most of yourself.
~ Alexander Crummel, 1819-1898 ~

The person who can do something that the world wants done will, in the end, make his way regardless of his race ... Excellence is to do a common thing in an uncommon way.
~ Booker T. Washington, 1856-1915 ~

Up you mighty race, you can accomplish what you will.
~ Marcus Garvey, 1887-1940 ~
UNIA motto

Those that don't got it, can't show it. Those that got it, can't hide it.
~ Zora Neale Hurston, 1891-1960 ~

Knowing that material and spiritual progress are essential to man, we must ceaselessly work for the equal attainment of both. Only then shall we be able to acquire that absolute inner calm so necessary to our well being.
~ Haile Selassie, 1892-1975 ~

There ain't no man can avoid being born average, but there ain't no man got to be common.
~ Satchel Paige, 1900-1982 ~

We build our temples for tomorrow, strong as we know how, and we stand on top of the mountain, free within ourselves.
~ Langston Hughes, 1902-1967 ~
in *Brother's Keeper: Words of Inspiration for African-American Men*, Roderick Terry, ed., 1996

Accomplishments have no color.
~ Leontyne Price, b. 1927 ~
in Brian Lanker, *I Dream a World: Portraits of Black Women Who Changed America*, 1989

If a man is called to be a street sweeper, he should sweep streets even as Michelangelo painted or Beethoven composed music or Shakespeare wrote poetry. He should sweep streets so well that all the hosts of heaven and earth will pause to say, here lived a great streetsweeper who did his job well.
~ Martin Luther King, Jr., 1929-1968 ~

Even the smallest victory is never to be taken for granted. Each victory must be applauded.
~ Audre Lorde, 1934-1992 ~

Achievement is a process, not an event ... we often create this notion that you do all of this stuff and there ... you have arrived. I don't think that's the way it goes. You get there only to use it as a platform, to go again. That new arrival, if it has any meaning at all, inspires you to take off again.
~ Johnnetta Cole, b. 1936 ~
"Spelman's First Female President," Academy of Achievement Interview, 1996 June 28

If you are going to achieve excellence in big things, you develop the habit in little matters. Excellence is not an exception, it is a prevailing attitude.
~ Colin Powell, b. 1937 ~
The Powell Principles, 2003

Excellence is the name of the game, no matter what color or what country you're from. If you are best at what you're doing, then you have my admiration and respect.
~ Judith Jamison, b. 1943 ~

It's really a matter of the mind-set and what one thinks. Achievement really has very little to do with some innate intellectual gift.
~ Benjamin Carson, b. 1951 ~
"Gifted Hands That Heal," Academy of Achievement Interview, 2002 June 7

For me it's the challenge – the challenge to try to beat myself or do better than I did in the past. I try to keep in mind not what I have accomplished but what I have to try to accomplish in the future.
~ Jackie Joyner-Kersee, b. 1962 ~

ACTION / EFFORT

The possession of knowledge, unless accompanied by a manifestation and expression in action, is like the hoarding of precious metals – a vain and foolish thing. Knowledge, like wealth, is intended for use.
~ Hermes Trismegistus ~
in *The Kybalion: A Study of the Hermetic Philosophy of Ancient Egypt and Greece*, 1908

Men must not only know, they must act.
~ W. E. B. Du Bois, 1868-1963 ~

The proof that one truly believes is in action.
~ Bayard Rustin, 1912-1987 ~

You don't make progress by standing on the sidelines, whimpering and complaining. You make progress by implementing ideas.
~ Shirley Chisholm, 1924-2005 ~

Words mean nothing. Action is the only thing. Doing. That's the only thing.
~ Ernest Gaines, b. 1933 ~
"The Sky Is Gray," 1963

The haves and have nots can often be traced to the dids and didn't dos.
~ William Raspberry, b. 1935 ~

Perhaps we should remind ourselves that the ultimate purpose of education is not to know but to act.
~ Johnnetta Cole, b. 1936 ~

A lot of lessons I learned ... are so important in the application in daily life. Things like creating in the moment, being in the moment, trusting your instincts, not being afraid to go outside the comfort zone.
~ Herbie Hancock, b. 1940 ~
in R. J. DeLuke, "Herbie Hancock: (New) Directions Included," *All About Jazz*

Both tears and sweat are salty, but they render a different result. Tears will get you sympathy; sweat will get you change.
~ Jesse Jackson, b. 1941 ~

ACTUALIZATION / FULFILLMENT

As you think so shall you become.
~ Khemetic Wisdom ~
Temt Tchaas: Egyptian Proverbs, Muata Ashaya Ashby, ed., 1994

Death neither alarms nor frightens one who has had a long career of fruitful toil. The knowledge that my work has been helpful to many fills me with joy and great satisfaction.
~ Mary McLeod Bethune, 1875-1955 ~

Your world is as big as you make it.
~ Georgia Douglas Johnson, 1886-1967 ~

We must look into ourselves, into the depth of our souls. We must become something we have never been and for which our education and experience and environment have ill-prepared us. We must become bigger than we have been: more courageous, greater in spirit, larger in outlook. We must become members of a new race, overcoming petty prejudice, owing our ultimate allegiance not to nations but to our fellow men within the human community.
~ Haile Selassie, 1892-1975 ~
Speech to UN General Assemby, 1963 October 4
Important Utterances Of H.I.M Haile Selassie, 1972

Talk about it only enough to do it. Dream about it only enough to feel it. Think about it only enough to understand it. Contemplate it only enough to be it.
~ Jean Toomer, 1894-1967 ~
Essentials: Definitions and Aphorisms, 1931

It is not your environment, it is you – the quality of your minds, the integrity of your souls and the determination of your will – that will decide your future and shape your lives.
~ Benjamin Mays, 1895-1984 ~

We have the ability to shape, change, accept or reject anything we want. Open our minds to positive thought and faith, and prosperity can become a reality for each of us.
~ Johnnie Colemon, b. 1921 ~

If you can take care of the internal, you can easily take care of the external. Then you can avoid the infernal and latch on to the eternal.
~ Joseph Lowery, b. 1924 ~

Your own need to be shines out of any dream or creation you can imagine.
~ James Earl Jones, b. 1931 ~
Voices and Silences, 1993

Champions aren't made in gyms. Champions are made from something they have deep inside them – a desire, a dream, a vision. They have to have the skill, and the will. But the will must be stronger than the skill.
~ Muhammad Ali, b. 1942 ~

Most of us did not learn when we were young that our capacity to be self-loving would be shaped by the work we do and whether that work enhances our well-being.
~ bell hooks, b. 1952 ~
All About Love: New Visions, 2000

Everything that happens to us, and every choice we make, is a reflection of what we believe about ourselves. We cannot outperform our level of self-esteem. We cannot draw to ourselves more than we believe we are worth. The things we believe and say about ourselves come back to us in many ways. Self-motivation comes from self-knowledge. We must inspire ourselves by believing we have the power to accomplish everything we set out to do. We must put faith in our ability to use mind and spirit and picture our lives the way we want them to be.
~ Iyanla Vanzant, b. 1953 ~
Acts of Faith: Daily Meditations for People of Color, 1993

To create a life is to create a life out of what the world has given you. Self-construction is a creative response to circumstances.
~ K. Anthony Appiah, b. 1954 ~
Interview by Neir Eschel, *Daily Princetonian*, 2003 December 11

If you come to a thing with no preconceived notions ... the whole world can be your canvas. Just dream it, and you can make it so. I believe I belong to wherever I want to be, in whatever situation or context I place myself.
~ Whoopi Goldberg, b. 1955 ~

ADVERSITY

Perils and misfortunes, and want, and pain, and injury, are more or less the certain lot of every man that cometh into the world. It behooveth thee, therefore, O child of calamity, early to fortify thy mind with courage and patience, that thou mayest support, with a becoming resolution, thy allotted portion of human evil.
~ Akhenaton, c. 1385-c. 1355 BCE ~

The troubles that chase you away also show the road.
~ Kigezi Wisdom ~

But they have no suffering from the assault of present evils who have confidence in future good things. In fact, we are never prostrated by adversity, nor are we broken down, nor do we grieve or murmur in any external misfortune or weakness of body: living by the Spirit rather than by the flesh, we overcome bodily weakness by mental strength. By those very things which torment and weary us, we know and trust that we are proved and strengthened.
~ Cyprian, 200-258 ~
Treatise V: Address to Demetrianus

To be under pressure is inescapable. Pressure takes place through all the world: war, siege, the worries of state. We all know men who grumble under these pressures and complain. They are cowards. They lack splendor. But there is another sort of man who is under the same pressure but does not complain, for it is the friction which polishes him. It is the pressure which refines and makes him noble.
~ Augustine of Hippo, 354-430 ~

The ability to thrive and live under adverse circumstances is the surest guaranty of the future.
~ Charles Chestnutt, 1858-1932 ~
The Marrow of Tradition, 1901

Making my peace and adjusting to being attacked has helped me to grow. It's given me a certain sense of obligation to other people, and it's given me a maturity as well as a sense of humor.
~ Bayard Rustin, 1912-1987 ~
"Black and Gay In The Civil Rights Movement: An Interview with Open Hands," *Time on Two Crosses: The Collected Writings of Bayard Rustin*, Devon W. Carbado & Donald Weise, eds., 2003

If life teaches us anything, it may be that it's necessary to suffer some defeats. Look at a diamond: It is the result of extreme pressure. Less pressure, it is crystal; less than that it is coal; and less than that, it is fossilized leaves or just plain dirt.
~ Maya Angelou, b. 1928 ~

The ultimate measure of a man is not where he stands in moments of comfort and convenience, but where he stands at times of challenge and controversy.
~ Martin Luther King, Jr., 1929-1968 ~
The Strength to Love, 1963

Life is not just pleasure ... Difficulty is stimulating, challenging, it's an element of the pulse of life.
~ Gilberto Gil, b. 1942 ~
"Gilberto Gil Hears the Future, Some Rights Reserved," *New York Times*, 2007 March 11

When you are in adversity for conscience's sake, you are not alone.
~ Peter J. Gomes, b. 1942 ~

Life's challenges are not supposed to paralyse you. They're supposed to help you discover who you are.
~ Bernice Johnson Reagon, b. 1942 ~

In every crisis there is a message. Crises are nature's way of forcing change – breaking down old structures, shaking loose negative habits so that something new and better can take their place.
~ Susan L. Taylor, b. 1946 ~

The first step to overcoming hardship has to be a change in attitude. Far too many people today have a victim's mentality. People with this focus get so overwhelmed by their hardship that they feel paralyzed and powerless. Then, since they aren't responsible for the seemingly insurmountable obstacles surrounding them, they assume little if any responsibility for tackling those problems.
~ Benjamin Carson, b. 1951 ~

All human beings are periodically tested by the power of the universe ... how one performs under pressure is the true measure of one's spirit, heart, and desire.
~ Spike Lee, b. 1957 ~
in *Brother's Keeper: Words of Inspiration for African-American Men*, Roderick Terry, ed., 1996

AFFIRMATION / APPROVAL

For no man can be blessed without the acceptance of his own head.
~ Yoruba Wisdom ~

Sweet peace of mind shall yield you a dignity – which kings have not power to confer: – then will you experience that the self-ennobled are the only true noble.
~ Ignatius Sancho, 1729-1780 ~
Letter LXXIV to Mr JWE, 1780 June 30 in *The Letters of the Late Ignatius Sancho, an African*, Vol. II, 1782

One of the greatest handicaps ... is that there is no love for self, nor love for his or her own kind. This not having love for self is the root cause of hate (dislike), disunity, disagreement, quarreling, betraying, stool pigeons and fighting and killing one another. How can you be loved, if you have not love for self?
~ Elijah Muhammad, 1897-1975 ~
Message to the Blackman in America

Our sense of self as black people is always under attack in this society, but it's reaffirmed and enhanced at the moment you take a stance.
~ Derrick Bell, b. 1930 ~
in Roderick Terry, *One Million Strong: A PhotographicTribute of the Million Man March*, 1996

We, each of us, need so much to be affirmed. For each of us has – gnawing away at the center of our being – a sense of insecurity, some more than others. And frequently, the more insecure, the more aggressive we become. The more we like to throw our weight about and say people should recognize us. If they don't recognize us for goodness, then they will recognize us for being stroppy (obstreperous).
~ Desmond Tutu, b. 1931 ~
"Forging Equality in South Africa," Academy of Achievement Interview, 2004 June 12

Love yourself, appreciate yourself, see the good in you, see the God in you, and respect yourself.
~ Betty Shabazz, 1934-1997 ~

We are forever looking outside ourselves, seeking approval and striving to impress others. But living to please others is a poor substitute for self-love,

for no matter how family and friends may adore us, they can never satisfy
our visceral need to love and honor ourselves.
~ Susan L. Taylor, b. 1946 ~
Lessons in Living, 1995

We can accept the compliments we receive when we give them to
ourselves first. We can build our confidence by celebrating our small
victories and successes. We can support the faith and trust others have in
us by supporting and having faith in ourselves. It all begins with our
willingness to acknowledge that we are really fine, just the way we are.
~ Iyanla Vanzant, b. 1953 ~
Acts of Faith: Daily Meditations for People of Color, 1993

You've got to love yourself enough, not only so that others will be able to
love you, but that you'll be able to love others.
~ Cornel West, b. 1954 ~

When existing history and culture do not acknowledge and address you –
do not see or talk to you – you must write a new history, shape a new
culture, that will.
~ Marlon Riggs, 1957-1994 ~

It's foolish to give what other people think about us so much credence. All
that matters is how you feel about yourself. Do you love yourself? Ask
yourself that question, right now, out loud and let the answer be *yes* …
Because what other people may have to say about you is simply their
opinion. It's not who you are. Their opinion about you is not reality.
Reality is what is inside you.
~ RuPaul, b. 1960 ~
Lettin It All Hang Out, 1995

I'm confident enough that I couldn't care less if somebody thinks I'm gay.
~ Dennis Rodman, b. 1961 ~

The greatest pleasure in life is being pleased with your own efforts.
~ Blair Underwood, b. 1964 ~

You can't rely on other people to tell you who you are. If you listen to
them, you'll have to believe the good and the bad. The only thing you can
really rely on is what I call the midnight owl, that voice you hear when
you're just alone … That's what will tell you when you've done good.
~ Cheryl L. West, b. 1965 ~
in Gary Dauphin, "Cheryl L. West: Controversial Playwright," *Essence*, 1994 May

AGE / AGEING

The harder we work to conceal our age, the more we reveal it.
~ Tertullian, c. 160-240 ~
De cultu feminarum

There is no difference between growing old and living.
~ Kikuyu Wisdom ~
Wit & Wisdom of Africa: Proverbs from Africa & The Caribbean, Patrick Ibekwe, ed., 1998

How old would you be if you didn't know how old you was?
~ Satchel Paige, 1900-1982 ~
in Carson Kanin, *It Takes Time to Become Young*, 1978

Age is a question of mind over matter. If you don't mind, it doesn't matter.
~ Paige ~

The secret to the fountain of youth is to think youthful thoughts.
~ Josephine Baker, 1906-1975 ~

Puberty causes the changing of considerably more than your sheets.
~ Bill Cosby, b. 1937 ~

You are never too old to set another goal or to dream a new dream.
~ Les Brown, b. 1945 ~

I've grown as old as I can possibly be; the aging has stopped here, and now
I just grow better.
~ Gloria Naylor, b. 1950 ~

Knowing means becoming old. To say someone is old is to say that this
person knows something, or has experienced something valuable.
Furthermore, the mature self is hardened in the field of experience by
awareness. In contrast, the word *young* refers not just to age but also to the
absence of awareness.
~ Malidoma Somé, b. 1956 ~
The Healing Wisdom of Africa, 1999

Age is no barrier. It's a limitation you put on your mind.
~ Jackie Joyner-Kersee, b. 1962 ~

ANGER

Indulge not thyself in the passion of anger; it is whetting a sword to wound thine own breast, or murder thy friend.
~ Khemetic Wisdom ~
Temt Tchaas: Egyptian Proverbs, Muata Ashaya Ashby, ed., 1994

As a whirlwind in its fury teareth up trees, and deforms the face of nature, or as an earthquake in its convulsions overturns whole cities, so the rage of an angry person throws mischief around them.
~ Ibid.

Bad temper kills its owner.
~ Twi Wisdom ~
Wit & Wisdom of Africa: Proverbs from Africa & The Caribbean, Patrick Ibekwe, ed., 1998

Anger is a weed; hate is the tree.
~ Augustine of Hippo, 354-430 ~

What I've learned about being angry with people is that it generally hurts you more than it hurts them.
~ Oprah Winfrey, b. 1954 ~
in Robert Waldron, *Oprah! A Day with Oprah*, 1987

You can't let the anger burn you up. You want to be mad, you don't want to lose it. Because when you lose the anger, you lose your force. But you don't want the anger to supplant the greatest force, which is love, and that's a benevolent force. That's the force where, instead of you concentrating on what somebody is not doing, you then are concentrating on what you can do to make the situation better.
~ Wynton Marsalis, b. 1961 ~
"Music's Jazz Maestro," Academy of Achievement Interview, 1991 January 8

But it is not the feeling of anger itself that will make changes. It is how you respond to it. You can take the anger that you feel and make it productive rather than raging. You can use it as a catalyst for addressing wrong with great energy and power.
~ Angel Kyodo Williams ~
Being Black: Zen and the Art of Living with Fearlessness and Grace, 2000

APPEARANCE / FORM

The way to gain a good reputation is to endeavor to be what you desire to appear.
~ Khemetic Wisdom ~
Temt Tchaas: Egyptian Proverbs, Muata Ashaya Ashby, ed., 1994

Outside show is a poor substitute for inner worth.
~ Aesop, fl. c. 550 BCE ~

Oranges are yellow but you don't know if they are sweet.
~ Guyanese Wisdom ~
Wit & Wisdom of Africa: Proverbs from Africa & The Caribbean, Patrick Ibekwe, ed., 1998

A silk dress doesn't mean clean under-garments.
~ Haitian Wisdom ~
Ibid.

Clothes cover character.
~ Jamaican Wisdom ~
Ibid.

Do not remove the kinks from your hair – remove them from your brain.
~ Marcus Garvey, 1887-1940 ~

None of us is responsible for the complexion of his skin. This fact of nature offers no clue to the character or quality of the person underneath.
~ Marian Anderson, 1902-1993 ~

The world tends to trap you in the role you play and it is always extremely hard to maintain a watchful, mocking distance between oneself as one appears to be and oneself as one actually is.
~ James Baldwin, 1924-1987 ~
Nobody Knows My Name: More Notes of a Native Son, 1961

If you're not feeling good about you, what you're wearing outside doesn't mean a thing.
~ Leontyne Price, b. 1927 ~
Interview, *Essence*, 1975 February

You don't know anything except what's there for you to see. An act. Lies. Device. Not the pure heart, the pumping black heart. You don't ever know that.
~ Amiri Baraka, b. 1934 ~
Dutchman, 1962

It's not as important what folk look like on the outside, as what folk really have as the texture of the soul inside of them.
~ Johnnetta Cole, b. 1936 ~
"Spelman's First Female President," Academy of Achievement Interview, 1996 June 28

When we look past the color of other people's skin, we're more likely to see that they are a lot like us.
~ Famous Amos, b. 1937 ~
Watermelon Magic, 1996

Attributes that are considered appealing today may be out of style tomorrow ... The danger of living in a society that reveres beauty and youth to the nth degree is that people judge others on their ornamental rather than inherent value.
~ Ibid.

People do not wish to appear foolish; to avoid the appearance of foolishness, they are willing to remain actually fools.
~ Alice Walker, b. 1944 ~
in *All the Women Are White, All the Blacks Are Men, But Some of Us Are Brave: Black Women's Studies*, Gloria T. Hull, Patricia Bell Scott, & Barbara Smith, eds., 1982

If you don't believe fully in yourself, others sense it, no matter how much you try to front it off.
~ Nathan McCall, b. 1955 ~
Makes Me Wanna Holler: A Young Black Man in America, 1994

We put so much emphasis on image, it's really not the real deal. The real deal is who's on the inside.
~ RuPaul, b. 1960 ~

Black people have earned the right to be suspicious of the images depicting black life. We have been so stereotyped and maligned in film and theater and television for years. Yet, that pressure can also have the effect of censoring ... what is true to your experience. It's a constant balancing act.
~ Cheryl L. West, b. 1965 ~
in "New Traditions Compendium Forums & Commentaries: 1992-96," 1994

APPRECIATION

Reflection is the business of humankind; a sense of their state is the first duty: but who remembereth themselves in joy? Is it not in mercy then that sorrow is allotted unto us?
~ Khemetic Wisdom ~
Temt Tchaas: Egyptian Proverbs, Muata Ashaya Ashby, ed., 1994

He who is carried on another's back does not appreciate how far the town is.
~ Nigerian Wisdom ~

A man dies before we appreciate him.
~ Jabo Wisdom ~

The back does not know what the shirt does for it until it is torn off.
~ Jamaican Wisdom ~

Those who wear pearls do not know how often the shark bites the leg of the diver.
~ Amharic Wisdom ~
Wit & Wisdom of Africa: Proverbs from Africa & The Caribbean, Patrick Ibekwe, ed., 1998

Unless we learn the lesson of self-appreciation and practice it, we shall spend our lives imitating other people and deprecating ourselves.
~ Aida Overton Walker, 1880-1914 ~

What little balance I have emotionally, physically, spiritually, is because I was raised on a farm. It gave me an appreciation for nature, for connecting with the earth.
~ James Earl Jones, b. 1931 ~

It dawned on me that there was something special and thrilling about my people: our style, our manner and speech. Being among whites made me appreciate black folks that much more.
~ Nathan McCall, b. 1955 ~
Makes Me Wanna Holler: A Young Black Man in America, 1994

ART

Art is not simply works of art; it is the spirit that knows beauty, that has music in its soul and the color of sunsets in its handkerchief, that can dance on a flaming world and make the world dance too.
~ W. E. B. Du Bois, 1868-1963 ~

Seek to be an artist! Cease to be a drudge!
~ Mary McLeod Bethune, 1875-1955 ~

The true work of art is a creation not of the hands, but of the mind and soul of the artist.
~ Nancy Prophet, 1890-1960 ~

The ultimate in art is self-expression, not escape.
~ Duke Ellington, 1899-1974 ~

An artist must be free to choose what he does, certainly, but he must also never be afraid to do what he might choose.
~ Langston Hughes, 1902-1967 ~

We look too much to museums. The sun coming up in the morning is enough.
~ Romare Bearden, 1914-1988 ~

If you're any kind of artist you make a miraculous journey and you can come back and make some statements in shapes and colors of where you were.
~ Bearden ~

Any form of art is a form of power; it has impact, it can affect change – it can not only move us, it makes us move.
~ Ossie B. Davis, 1917-2005 ~
in Jeanne Noble, *Beautiful, Also, Are the Souls of My Black Sisters: A History of the Black Woman in America*, 1978

Art does not have a racial consciousness. Art is the creation of the imagination, and the imagination is not noted by color of the skin.
~ Lloyd Richards, 1919-2006 ~
Interview by N. Graham Nesmith, *African American Review*, 2005 Fall

All art is a kind of confession, more or less oblique. All artists, if they are to survive, are forced, at last, to tell the whole story, to vomit the anguish up.
~ James Baldwin, 1924-1987 ~
Nobody Knows My Name: More Notes of a Native Son, 1961

Art is inseparable from life, and form and content are one.
~ Paule Marshall, b. 1929 ~

A genuine artist, no matter what he says he believes, must feel in his blood the ultimate enmity between art and orthodoxy.
~ Chinua Achebe, b. 1930 ~
Anthills of the Savannah, 1987

All art makes us more powerfully whom we wish to become.
~ Audre Lorde, 1934-1992 ~

Art is a way of possessing destiny.
~ Marvin Gaye, 1939-1984 ~

Progressive art can assist people to learn not only about the objective forces at work in the society in which they live, but also about the intensely social character of their interior lives.
~ Angela Davis, b. 1944 ~

Artistic aptitude is not a requirement ... the arts are a bridge to walk across to a new life.
~ Bill Strickland, b. 1947 ~
Sierra Club "Spirit in Nature" Address, 2004

Often, what we write, the music we write, and the pictures we paint are dialogues with our deepest consciousness.
~ Marita Golden, b. 1950 ~

Art has a way of opening us up and allows us to be vulnerable, to deal with our ambiguities and incongruities and contradictions, so that we can grow and mature and develop.
~ Cornel West, b. 1954 ~

The artist as an artisan of the sacred can cooperate in bringing the sacred to birth in this world ... There is only a thin line between the artist and the healer.
~ Malidoma Somé, b. 1956 ~
The Healing Wisdom of Africa, 1999

ATTENTION / AWARENESS

How many common things are trodden underfoot which, if examined carefully, awaken our astonishment.
~ Augustine of Hippo, 354-430 ~

Unawareness is the root of all evil.
~ Unknown Egyptian Monk ~

It seems that at least one of the components of "our" modernity is the spread of the awareness we have of it. The awareness of our awareness (the double, the second degree) is our source of strength and our torment.
~ Édouard Glissant, b. 1928 ~

I think it pisses God off if you walk by the color purple in a field somewhere and don't notice it.
~ Alice Walker, b. 1944 ~
The Color Purple, 1982

You are no longer innocent, you are condemned to awareness.
~ Michael Eric Dyson, b. 1958 ~

Awareness itself can see what we're doing and the effects of what we're doing right as it's happening. If we see things after they happen, it's too late. But as soon as we bring awareness itself to catch ourselves right when we're causing stress, yahman, then we can let go. There's some peace. That's wisdom – our sense of discernment. But it takes precision and relentless dedication.
~ Ralph M. Steele ~
"A Teaching on the Second Noble Truth," *Dharma, Color, and Culture*, Hilda Gutiérrez Baldoquín, ed., 2004

It's *your* life that you are living. Don't pick and choose when you'll be there. All of it is yours. No one else suffers more if you waste it than you. Be patient with yourself and make every effort to be fully attentive so that you don't waste any of it.
~ Angel Kyodo Williams ~
Being Black: Zen and the Art of Living with Fearlessness and Grace, 2000

ATTITUDE

I am convinced, that the disposition of the mind in a great measure forms either the heaven or hell in both worlds.
~ Ignatius Sancho, 1729-1780 ~
Letter XXVI to Mrs H, 1779 June 17 in *The Letters of the Late Ignatius Sancho, an African*, Vol. II, 1782

It's not the load that breaks you down, it's the way you carry it.
~ Lena Horne, b. 1917 ~

Life is a grindstone, but whether it grinds you down or polishes you up depends on what you are made of.
~ Robert E. Johnson, 1922-1996 ~

We are held back only by our beliefs. If you believe that where you are and what you have is the best you will ever do, then that's where you'll stay. If you believe that life can be better, then it will become better.
~ Famous Amos, b. 1937 ~
Watermelon Magic, 1996

How you perceive experience and how you handle it determine how your life turns out in the long run.
~ Bill Cosby, b. 1937 ~

Think positively. Attitude plays a tremendous role in our well-being, as well as our ability to fight disease.
~ Benjamin Carson, b. 1951 ~

The right mental attitude is more important than knowledge.
~ Dennis Kimbro, b. 1950 ~
Think and Grow Rich: A Black Choice, 1991

There is a fine line between success and failure. That line is defined by your attitude.
~ Michael Lee-Chin, b. 1951 ~
Address to NCU Graduation, in *Jamaica Observer*, 2007 August 18

The level of an individual's consciousness is reflected in the attitude and choices of that individual at each point in time.
~ Oliver Mbamara ~
"The Conflict of Retaliation Versus Forgiveness," *Cafe Africana*, 2005 November

AUTONOMY / CONTROL

The self-mastered man or woman sets himself or herself apart. He or she is like a tree grown in fertile ground. It grows green and doubles its yield of fruit.
~ *Book of Declarations of Virtues* ~
in *Kemet and the African Worldview*, Maulana Karenga and Jacob Carruthers, eds., 1986

Salvation is accomplished through the efforts of the individual. There is no mediator between man and his/her salvation.
~ Khemetic Wisdom ~
Temt Tchaas: Egyptian Proverbs, Muata Ashaya Ashby, ed., 1994

God and Nature first made us what we are, and then out of our own creative genius we make ourselves what we want to be. Follow always that great law.
~ Marcus Garvey, 1887-1940 ~
"African Fundamentalism," *Negro World*, 1925 June 6

Man in his authority is a sovereign lord ... So few of us can understand what it takes to make a man – the man who will never say die; the man who will never give up; the man who will never depend upon others to do for him what he ought to do for himself; the man who will not blame God, who will not blame Nature, will not blame Fate for his condition; but the man who will go out and make conditions to suit himself.
~ Garvey ~

It is far better to be free to govern, or misgovern yourself, than to be governed by anybody else.
~ Kwame Nkrumah, 1909-1972 ~

Fate is determined by what one does and what one doesn't do.
~ Ralph Ellison, 1914-1994 ~

In order for us to be effective political people, we must be in control of the personal.
~ Toni Cade Bambara, 1939-1995 ~

There are two things over which you have complete dominion, authority and control – your mind and your mouth.
~ Molefi Kete Asante, b. 1942 ~

To endure and prosper, one needs the understanding that we alone, and not an abstraction called "social forces," determines moment by moment our individual destinies and our happiness.
~ Charles Johnson, b. 1948 ~
"Reading the Eightfold Path," *Dharma, Color, and Culture*, Hilda Gutiérrez Baldoquín, ed., 2004

Can't nothin' make your life work if you ain't the architect.
~ Terry McMillan, b. 1951 ~

Self-activity is the only activity. If you want to change your situation you have to build independent institutions – social, cultural, political institutions – in order to advance your struggles.
~ Linton Kwesi Johnson, b. 1952 ~

It isn't until you come to a spiritual understanding of who you are – not necessarily a religious feeling, but deep down, the spirit within – that you can begin to take control.
~ Oprah Winfrey, b. 1954 ~

There is no higher authority on the planet, when it comes to deciding what's best for you, than you. Life is a banquet, so you should eat until you're full, and do as you please as long as you're not hurting anybody else … You can't get satisfaction living your life according to someone else's rules.
~ RuPaul, b. 1960 ~
Lettin It All Hang Out, 1995

If one can come to see that ethnic and racial identities are bequeathed and hence unchosen and that these identities have morally questionable features built into them (racism, ethnocentrism, and national chauvinism); if one can accept the fluidity of the self and its capacity for self-reinterpretation, then one recognizes self-ownership as a viable option.
~ Jason D. Hill, b. 1965 ~
Becoming a Cosmopolitan: What It Means to Be a Human Being in the New Millennium, 2000

AVOIDANCE / DENIAL / REFUSAL

Not to know is bad; not to wish to know is worse.
~ Wolof Wisdom ~
Wit & Wisdom of Africa: Proverbs from Africa & The Caribbean, Patrick Ibekwe, ed., 1998

You can outdistance that which is running after you, but not what is running inside you.
~ Rwandan Wisdom ~

You cannot fix what you will not face.
~ James Baldwin, 1924-1987 ~

I had a power, and the power that I had – the only power that I had – was to say no. I had no power to influence, I had no power to instruct. I only had the power to say no. And that was sufficient for me. I said, "No, I don't want to do that. No, I cannot do that. No, I'm not available for that."
~ Sidney Poitier, b. 1927 ~
in *Songs of Wisdom: Quotations from Famous African Americans*, Jay David, ed., 2000

A person can run for years but sooner or later he has to take a stand in the place which, for better or worse, he calls home, and do what he can to change things there.
~ Paule Marshall, b. 1929 ~

Black people and society as a whole have wanted to minimize the reality of trauma in black life. It has been easier for everyone to focus on issues of material deprivation as the reason for our continued collective subordinated status than to place the issue of trauma and recovery on our agendas.
~ bell hooks, b. 1952 ~
Rock My Soul: Black People and Self-Esteem, 2003

We prefer sometimes to cover our heads with our hands and pretend that things do not happen. Until we acknowledge things to be the way they are, we cannot own them, and we cannot control them.
~ Chimamanda Ngozi Adichie, b. 1977 ~
in Ike Anya, "In the Footsteps of Achebe: Enter Chimamanda Ngozi Adichie, Nigeria's Newest Literary Voice," 2003 October 10

BALANCE

Everything flows, out and in; everything has its tides; all things rise and fall; the pendulum-swing manifests in everything; the measure of the swing to the right is the measure of the swing to the left; rhythm compensates.
~ Hermes Trismegistus ~
in The Kybalion: A Study of the Hermetic Philosophy, 1908

One who is serious all day will never have a good time, while one who is frivolous all day will never establish a household.
~ Ptahotep, c. 2350 BCE ~
Maxims of Ptahhotep

The equilibrium you admire in me is an unstable one, difficult to maintain. My inner life was split early between the call of the Ancestors and the call of Europe, between the exigencies of black-African culture and those of modern life.
~ Léopold Senghor, 1906-2001 ~

Hearts tend to be large, squishy undiscerning sorts of things, the home of powerful feelings and emotions, but a thinking heart is one that deploys its passions carefully. It strikes me as a good formula for life, loving minds and thinking hearts, and I commend that notion of the self to you as you make your way.
~ Peter J. Gomes, b. 1942 ~
Sermon, Lafayette College 172nd Baccalaureate Service

A balanced life doesn't just happen. It is a state of grace we create by staying connected with our thoughts and feelings and consciously measuring what we do. Just as feeling fit and flexible demands physical exercise, just as expanding your mind requires intellectual effort, so bringing your life into balance and maintaining your spiritual equilibrium require focused awareness and daily retreat from the stresses of the world.
~ Susan L. Taylor, b. 1946 ~
Lessons in Living, 1995

I recognize more than ever that I am what I call an "in-between" person: Someone who walks and travels constantly between cultures, geographical regions, types of blacknesses, and political/historical realities.
~ Thomas Glave, b. 1964 ~
Interview by Alexis Deveaux, ArtVoice.com

BEGINNING / ENDEAVOUR

The beginning is the most important part of the work.
~ Igbo Wisdom ~
Wit & Wisdom of Africa: Proverbs from Africa & The Caribbean, Patrick Ibekwe, ed., 1998

The hard part is the first grinding; when that is done the rest is easy.
~ Hausa Wisdom ~
Ibid.

Start where you are with what you have, knowing that what you have is plenty enough.
~ Booker T. Washington, 1856-1915 ~

We have only started; we are just on our way; we have just made the first lap in the great race for existence, and for a place in the political and economic sun of men.
~ Marcus Garvey, 1887-1940 ~
Philosophy and Opinions of Marcus Garvey, Vol. II, Amy Jacques Garvey, ed., 1925

The end is in the beginning and lies far ahead.
~ Ralph Ellison, 1914-1994 ~
Invisible Man, 1952

Take the first step in faith. You don't have to see the whole staircase, just take the first step.
~ Martin Luther King, Jr., 1929-1968 ~

You start with what you can. You start here and now, from your local position. Because your feet are on the ground. You have to start from yourself, from your ground, not to be in the air. That's why struggle starts locally, and it expands, and it connects globally. You have to start locally from your soil, from your village, from your country, from your state. To liberate yourself.
~ Nawal el Saadawi, b. 1931 ~
Interview by Stephanie McMillan, 1999

It ain't nothing to find no starting place in the world. You just start from where you find yourself.
~ August Wilson, 1945-2005 ~

BEING / ESSENCE / SOUL

As the moon retaineth her nature, though darkness spread itself before her face as a curtain, so the Soul remaineth perfect even in the bosom of a fool.
~ Akhenaton, c. 1385-c. 1355 BCE ~

When the soul, in its gaze into heaven, has recognised its Author, it rises higher than the sun, and far transcends all this earthly power, and begins to be that which it believes itself to be.
~ Cyprian, 200-258 ~
Epistle to Donatus

As our body is a part of the universe, so also our soul is a part of the Soul of the universe … Souls are responsive to one another because they all come from the same soul.
~ Plotinus, 205-270 ~
Enneads, 250

In the world through which I travel, I am endlessly creating myself. I am part of Being to the degree that I go beyond it.
~ Frantz Fanon, 1925-1961 ~
Black Skin, White Masks, Charles Lam Markmann, 1967

Place cannot be circumvented and/or escaped, being is also inescapable. You cannot close being off. Today, we are relational beings, not rooted beings.
~ Édouard Glissant, b. 1928 ~
Interview by Michael Dash, *Renaissance Noire*, Hillina Seife, tr., 2006 March 22

What is a soul? It's like electricity – we don't really know what it is, but it's a force that can light a room.
~ Ray Charles, 1930-2004 ~

Remember, Jesus or Lord Buddha didn't share their visions to teach you who *they* were. They shared their vision to help teach you who *you* are. To help you understand the power that God has already blessed you with.
~ Russell Simmons, b. 1957 ~
Do You!: 12 Laws to Access the Power in You to Achieve Happiness and Success, 2007

BELIEF / RELIGION

The true believer begins with himself.
~ Berber Wisdom ~

One man's religion neither harms nor helps another man ... It is certainly no part of religion to compel religion.
~ Tertullian, c. 160-240 ~
Ad Scapulam, 2.2

You believe easily what you want to believe.
~ Haitian Wisdom ~
Wit & Wisdom of Africa: Proverbs from Africa & The Caribbean, Patrick Ibekwe, ed., 1998

There is no prospect that man will ever be without religion, but there is every prospect that he will soon be beyond our present religious beliefs.
~ William Pickens, 1881-1954 ~
Preachers Defend Hell, 1923

Since religion is dead, religion is everywhere. Religion was once an affair of the church; it is now in the streets, in each man's heart. Once there were priests; now every man's a priest.
~ Richard Wright, 1908-1960 ~
The Outsider, 1953

There is no heaven or hell in the sense that they are places one goes after death. The heaven or hell to which one goes is right there in the span of years that we spend in this body on earth.
~ Adam Clayton Powell, Jr., 1908-1972 ~

If the concept of God has any validity or use, it can only be to make us larger, freer and more loving. If God cannot do this, then it is time we got rid of Him.
~ James Baldwin, 1924-1987 ~
The Fire Next Time, 1962

Religion is not necessarily a good thing. It depends; religion can lead to great good, but it can equally lead to unspeakable evil and suffering.
~ Desmond Tutu, b. 1931 ~
"The Secular State and Religions," *The Wisdom of Desmond Tutu*, Michael Battle, ed., 1998

If we can put the names of our faiths aside for the moment and look at principles, we will find a common thread running through all the great religious expressions.
~ Louis Farrakhan, b. 1934 ~

How to die, we got that. But we were missing how to live. I do not recall any message of joy or love or happiness generated out of this experience. It was a confining, restricting mandate. I did not feel free to do anything other than what was presented to me as the way one must proceed; that whatever you do in this life has to be in preparation for that other life. So on balance, my church relationship was, without doubt, a very imprisoning kind of experience.
~ Barbara Jordan, 1936-1996 ~
in Barbara Jordan & Shelby Hearon, *Barbara Jordan: A Self Portrait*, 1979

Politics and church are the same thing. They keep people in ignorance.
~ Bob Marley, 1946-1981 ~

Many people – often people who consider themselves to be quite "religious" – believe that they have a monopoly on truth. Such a belief, however, can clearly be seen to limit one's flexibility and ability to learn. It greatly hampers even the possiblity for one to listen deeply to what is being said. Without such listening capability, no genuine dialogue can be had or progress made.
~ Jan Willis, b. 1948~

Most man-made religion is built on fear … the fear of judgment. The fear of retribution. Our fears come in all shapes and sizes … the fear of other religions, or other ways of thinking, and this one's at the root of all our problems.
~ Whoopi Goldberg, b. 1955 ~

Democracy demands that the religiously motivated translate their concerns into universal, rather than religion-specific, values. It requires that their proposals be subject to argument, and amenable to reason … accessible to people of all faiths, including those with no faith at all … At some fundamental level, religion does not allow for compromise. It's the art of the impossible. If God has spoken, then followers are expected to live up to God's edicts, regardless of the consequences. To base one's life on such uncompromising commitments may be sublime; to base our policymaking on such commitments would be a dangerous thing.
~ Barack Obama, b. 1961 ~
Speech, 2006 June 28, in *Washington Post*, 2006 July 2

BREAKTHROUGH / EPIPHANY / TURNING POINT

I had no idea history was being made. I was just tired of giving in.
~ Rosa Parks, 1913-2005 ~

There is a spirit and a need and a man at the beginning of every great
human advance. Each of these must be right for the particular moment of
history, or nothing happens.
~ Coretta Scott King, 1927-2006 ~
My Life with Martin Luther King Jr., Ch. 6, 1969

Occasionally in life there are those moments of unutterable fulfillment
which cannot be completely explained by those symbols called words.
Their meanings can only be articulated by the inaudible language of the
heart.
~ Martin Luther King, Jr., 1929-1968 ~

What seem to have been the turning points in my own life were all turning
points I recognized after the event. They were not intentional but they
were all connected with recognitions from outside of myself.
~ Stuart Hall, b. 1932 ~
Seminar, Program in the Comparative Study of Social Transformations (CSST), 1999 April 15

The laughter bubbled up, irrepressible. I saw the path to happiness and
liberation at a glance. It was inside myself.
~ Alice Walker, b. 1944 ~
"This Was Not an Area of Large Plantations," in *Dharma, Color, and Culture*, Hilda Gutiérrez
Baldoquín, ed., 2004

All human beings have the ability to change, but they all have their own
right moment; you have to be patient towards that historical individual
process. It is important.
~ Haile Gerima, b. 1946 ~
Interview, "Haile Gerima, Lion of Gondar," RastafariToday.com

All of us carry within ourselves something that is waiting for the right
moment when it can burst out and repair the particular separation that we
are experiencing. My own experience tells me a lot about exile and
nostalgia.
~ Malidoma Somé, b. 1956 ~
The Healing Wisdom of Africa, 1999

CAUSE

It is the heart which causes every completed concept to come forth, and it is the tongue which announces what the heart thinks. Thus all the gods were formed ... Indeed, all the divine order came into being through what the heart thought and the tongue commanded.
~ *Shabaka Text (Memphite Theology)*, c. 2700 BCE ~
in *Kemet and the African Worldview*, Maulana Karenga and Jacob Carruthers, eds., 1986

Every cause has its effect; every effect has its cause; everything happens according to law; chance is but a name for law not recognized; there are many planes of causation, but nothing escapes the law.
~ Hermes Trismegistus ~
in *The Kybalion: A Study of the Hermetic Philosophy of Ancient Egypt and Greece*, 1908

Everything we do is sowing, and all of our experiences are harvests.
~ Khemetic Wisdom ~
Temt Tchaas: Egyptian Proverbs, Muata Ashaya Ashby, ed., 1994

If we live good lives, the times are also good. As we are, such are the times.
~ Augustine of Hippo, 354-430 ~

Continue in right thinking, you will of course act well.
~ Ignatius Sancho, 1729-1780 ~
Letter I to Mr JWE, 1768 February 14 in *The Letters of the Late Ignatius Sancho, an African*, Vol. I, 1782

Destiny lies not in the stars, but in our hearts.
~ William Wells Brown, 1815-1884 ~

If you always do what you always did, you will always get what you always got.
~ Moms Mabley, 1894-1975 ~

It is not your environment, it is you – the quality of your minds, the integrity of your souls and the determination of your will – that will decide your future and shape your lives.
~ Benjamin Mays, 1895-1984 ~

Who plants a seed begets a bud,
Extract of that same root.
~ Countée Cullen, 1903-1946 ~
"Fruit of the Flower"

Man's chief delusion is his conviction that there are *causes other than his own state of consciousness*. All that befalls man – all that is done by him – all that comes to him – happens as a result of his state of consciousness. A man's consciousness is all that he thinks and desires and loves, all that he believes is true and consents to. That is why a change of consciousness is necessary before you can change your outer world.
~ Neville, 1905-1972 ~
The Power of Awareness, 1952

He who cannot change the very fabric of his thought will never be able to change reality, and will never, therefore, make any progress.
~ Anwar Sadat, 1918-1981 ~
in *Brother's Keeper: Words of Inspiration for African-American Men*, Roderick Terry, ed., 1996

I am the thinker that creates the thoughts that create the things.
~ Johnnie Colemon, b. 1921 ~

It works if you work it.
~ Johnnetta Cole, b. 1936 ~

The world we live in is first and foremost shaped by the mind.
~ Charles Johnson, b. 1948 ~

Negative thoughts and images undermine self-esteem more than any other factors. Our thoughts have the power to make us or to break us. How we feel about ourselves is more important than how others portray us. What really matters is our own interpretation of who we are.
~ Roderick Terry, b. 1964 ~
Brother's Keeper: Words of Inspiration for African-American Men, 1996

If you believe it is possible, you can make it happen. If you decide to become negative and believe that things will never be right, you will also have those results. So be very careful what thoughts you put in your mind. For good or bad, they will boomerang right back to you.
~ Beatryce Nivens ~
Success Strategies for African-Americans: A Guide to Creating Personal and Professional Achievement, 1998

CELEBRATION

Celebrate, then, the days of rejoicing and do not tire of them. For lo, none may take their goods with them and none who depart ever come back again.
~ *Book of Songs* ~
in *Kemet and the African Worldview*, Maulana Karenga and Jacob Carruthers, eds., 1986

Let's get together and celebrate something great. It is an opportunity to continue learning about ourselves. Growing up, there was none of this. Now we are so certain about what we have that we can have conferences and celebrate it.
~ Kamau Brathwaite, b. 1930 ~
in *Jamaica Daily Gleaner*, 2002 January 6

Identifying fully with the subjects of my study and the substance of their hope, I have freely allowed myself to celebrate. For I could not possibly remain silent and unmoved in the presence of the mysterious, transformative dance of the life that has produced the men and women, the ideas and institutions, the visions, betrayals, and heroic dreams renewed in blood that are at once the anguish and the glory of the river of our struggle.
~ Vincent Harding, b. 1931 ~
There is a River: The Black Struggle for Freedom in America, 1981

I find the idea of Carnival, its indigenous character, its embracing fellowship, its sense of celebration of art, of life, of creativity, worthy to be given the kind of appreciation reserved for religion.
~ Earl Lovelace, b. 1935 ~
Salt, 1997

let us celebrate
ourselves, all that is kind
and carnival, living
without goodbyes
without the acquiescences of grief
of ending
That small victory, only.
~ Dennis Scott, 1939-1991 ~
"Strategies," *Strategies*, 1989

Everything was so ordinary and itself, as if ordinariness might not
sometimes be worth celebrating, as if ordinariness could never be longed
for, as if ordinariness could never be missed, as if ordinariness was all there
was and anything else was an interruption.
~ Jamaica Kincaid, b. 1949 ~
Mr. Potter, 2002

It is not only the happy moments ... that should be talked about, but every
moment. All the moments that make up a human being have to be written
about, talked about, painted, danced, in order to really talk about life.
~ Rita Dove, b. 1952 ~
"The Possibility Poet," Academy of Achievement Interview, 1994 June 18

The more you praise and celebrate your life, the more there is in life to
celebrate.
~ Oprah Winfrey, b. 1954 ~
in Black Woman's Gumbo Ya-Ya, Terri L. Jewell, ed., 1993

Each day of our lives is meant to be a celebration of love and growth, filled
with adventure and new discoveries. However, it is mind-boggling how
many of us are willing to leave our lives hanging in the balance while we
wait for a special occasion or event to occur.
~ Roderick Terry, b. 1964 ~
"Hope Chest"

For most of us, what is worth celebrating is the fact that we are here, that
we against all the odds exist ... We are part of an endless circle, the
daughters of Anacaona.[1] We have stumbled, but have not fallen. We are
ill-favored, but we still endure. Every once in a while, we must scream this
as far as the wind can carry our voices.
~ Edwidge Danticat, b. 1969 ~
"We Are Ugly But We Are Here," The Caribbean Writer, Volume 10, 1996

It is the deep inner need to feel content that sets us out looking for
spiritual direction. We have to celebrate that, both as human beings and as
black people. We need to know and accept from the start that it is the
simple human desire to be happy that makes a spiritual path not only
fulfilling, but worth pursuing in the first place.
~ Angel Kyodo Williams ~
Being Black: Zen and the Art of Living with Fearlessness and Grace, 2000

---

[1] Hispaniola Taino queen

CENTERING

Life is like an anthill, built from within out.
~ Ewe Wisdom ~
in N. K. Dzobo, "The Image of Man in Africa," *Person and Community: Ghanaian Philosophical Studies,*
Kwasi Wiredu & Kwame Gyekye, eds.

We must accustom our minds to these new world structures, in which the
relationship between the center and the periphery will be completely
different. Everything will be central and everything will be peripheral.
~ Édouard Glissant, b. 1928 ~
Interview by Tirthankar Chanda, Label France, 2000 January, No. 38

At the end of the day, I haven't really tried to find my roots because I carry
them with me everywhere. The homeland is with me wherever I am.
~ Maryse Condé, b. 1937 ~
"One Day, People Are Going to Manage Simply to Say : I Am What I am," Interview by Catherine
Dana, *Africultures,* 2002 October 21

Exchange based on equality. I like the idea of a dance of centers that are
equidistant from the human center. They are in a circle. They all
contribute to and also draw from the center. Like spokes in a bicycle
wheel. But there is a difference. Human spokes must also borrow from one
another.
~ Ngugi wa Thiong'o, b. 1938 ~
Interview by Michael Alexander Pozo, St. John's University, 2004 August 16

The task could not be simpler, because there is nowhere to go, nothing to
do. To retreat, you need only be. How? By giving yourself to yourself before
you give yourself away.
~ Susan L. Taylor, b. 1946 ~
Lessons in Living, 1995

I learned early on that there's a place inside oneself that no one else can
violate, that no one else can enter, and that we have a right to protect that
place.
~ Kareem Abdul-Jabbar, b. 1947 ~
Kareem, 1990

You have to be able to center yourself, to let all of your emotions go ...
Don't ever forget that you play with your soul as well as your body.
~ Abdul-Jabbar ~

CHANGE

Change is Lord of the Universe … Nothing rests, everything moves; everything vibrates.
~ Khemetic Wisdom ~
Temt Tchaas: Egyptian Proverbs, Muata Ashaya Ashby, ed., 1994

Not everything that is faced can be changed; but nothing can be changed until it is faced … Most of us are about as eager to change as we were to be born, and go through our changes in a similar state of shock.
~ James Baldwin, 1924-1987 ~

Some women wait for something to change and nothing does change so they change themselves.
~ Audre Lorde, 1934-1992 ~

The world in which we are born is not the world in which we will die. Change is the only constant thing in life.
~ Famous Amos, b. 1937 ~
Watermelon Magic, 1996

Change is inherent in nature and human society – change actually is magic.
~ Ngugi wa Thiong'o, b. 1938 ~
Interview in *Socialist Worker*, 2006 November 4, No. 2025

Each person is constantly evolving, changing as he looks to the light he receives that helps him advance.
~ Djibril Diop Mambety, 1945-1998 ~
in N. Frank Ukadike, "The Hyena's Last Laugh: A Conversation with Djibril Diop Mambety," *Transition 78*, Vol. 8, No. 2, 1999

In one minute. Everything changes. The beauty is that change is a constant and, in one minute, everything can also get better … and that magnifies the power of individuals who challenge and change the course of events. Individuals in the right place at the right time.
~ Haile Gerima, b. 1946 ~
in Kalamu ya Salaam, "Haile Gerima in Ghana," Notes from PanaFest 1994

All that you touch
You Change
All that you Change
Changes you
The only lasting truth
Is Change.
~ Octavia Butler, 1947-2006 ~
Parable of the Sower, 1993

It is only normal that you will change, you grow up and carry on until you die. Until the day you die, you are growing up and changing.
~ Salif Keita, b. 1949 ~
Interview by Opiyo Oloya, *AfroDisc*, 1996 April 23

From where you are, from who you are in your everyday life, that's where you make change.
~ Toshi Reagon, b. 1964 ~

We gotta make a change. It's time for us as a people to start makin' some changes. Let's change the way we eat, let's change the way we live and let's change the way we treat each other. You see the old way wasn't working so it's on us to do what we gotta do, to survive.
~ Tupac Shakur, 1971-1996 ~
"Shorty Wanna Be a Thug"

Change is constant, and it is in the present that change is initiated, yet it is in the present that change comes to manifestation. What will be seen in the "future" is only the manifestation of what is created in the present. A sort of recognition of the finished creation.
~ Oliver Mbamara ~
"What Is Your Attitude of The Present?" *Why Are We Here?*, 2002

Change happens whether we want it to or not. We have always been changing and are always different in some ways than we were before ... The resistance to change comes from a fear deep inside of us that says *Maybe if I change, I won't recognize myself* ... Making changes in the way you see and handle life is not about giving up who you are.
~ Angel Kyodo Williams ~
Being Black: Zen and the Art of Living with Fearlessness and Grace, 2000

When we become aware of ourselves, we find the potential for radical transformation. If you want to change, that's where you have to start from. If you really wake up, if you really notice, it's inevitable that change will take place.
~ Ibid.

CHAOS / UNCERTAINTY

I have a great belief in the fact that whenever there is chaos, it creates wonderful thinking. I consider chaos a gift.
~ Septima Clark, 1898-1987 ~

People have a lot more
of the U N K N O W N
than the known in their minds.
The U N K N O W N is great,
it's like the darkness
Nobody made that
it just happens.
~ Sun Ra, 1914-1993 ~

When I say that our world is a chaos-world, I am not saying that it is an apocalyptic world, but rather a world that one can no longer predict or plan in advance. The "entanglements" at work have made the world complex. We now have to get used to the idea that we can live in the world without having the ambition to predict it or dictate to it.
~ Édouard Glissant, b. 1928 ~
Interview by Tirthankar Chanda, Label France, 2000 January, No. 38

We are told, and it is true, that everywhere things are disordered, disoriented, decrepit, have gone completely mad, blood, the wind. We see and experience this. But this is the whole world talking to you, in so many muzzled voices.
~ Glissant ~
Traité du Tout-monde – Poétique IV, 1997

When you struggle to reach for something you don't know, that's where the most interesting stuff is.
~ Herbie Hancock, b. 1940 ~

The best thing and the worst thing about life is that you don't know what is going to happen. The best thing and the worst.
~ John Edgar Wideman, b. 1941 ~
Interview by Laura Miller, *Salon*

CHARACTER

A man and his character – even rain cannot wash it off him.
~ Hausa Wisdom ~

Rain doesn't kill the strength of hot pepper.
~ Haitian Wisdom ~
Wit & Wisdom of Africa: Proverbs from Africa & The Caribbean, Patrick Ibekwe, ed., 1998

Driving away by means of character is better than driving away with a
stick.
~ Hausa Wisdom ~
Ibid.

Character is a god; according to the way you behave it supports you.
~ Yoruba Wisdom ~
Ibid.

Character, not circumstances, makes the man.
~ Booker T. Washington, 1856-1915 ~

When a man says to his character, "Stay here and wait for me," scarcely
has he turned his back than his character is close on his heels.
~ Birago Diop, 1906-1989 ~
Tales of Amadou Koumba, 1966

The only thing that endures is character. Fame and wealth – all that is
illusion. All that endures is character.
~ O. J. Simpson, b. 1947 ~
in *The Guardian*, 1995 October 30

Character, then, isn't what we think it is or, rather, what we want it to be.
It isn't a stable, easily identifiable set of closely related traits, and it only
seems that way because of a glitch in the way our brains are organized.
Character is more like a bundle of habits and tendencies and interests,
loosely bound together and dependent, at certain times, on circumstance
and context.
~ Malcolm Gladwell, b. 1963 ~
The Tipping Point: How Little Things Can Make a Big Difference, 2000

CHOICE / VOLITION

The power of choosing good and evil is within the reach of all.
~ Origen, c. 185-255 ~

To choose to go does not prevent one from returning.
~ Kikuyu Wisdom ~
Wit & Wisdom of Africa: Proverbs from Africa & The Caribbean, Patrick Ibekwe, ed., 1998

Every intersection in the road of life is an opportunity to make a decision.
~ Duke Ellington, 1899-1974 ~

To live is to choose. But to choose well, you must know who you are and
what you stand for, where you want to go and why you want to get there.
~ Kofi Annan, b. 1938 ~

You only have so much time in your life, and you only have so much
energy. So you have to select very carefully how you're going to spend that
time and how you're going to spend that energy. If you waste it spinning
your wheels on things that are not going to change, then it deprives you of
an opportunity of utilizing it on things that are going to change.
~ Benjamin Carson, b. 1951 ~
"Gifted Hands That Heal," Academy of Achievement Interview, 2002 June 7

What we choose, or fail to choose, and when we relegate our power of
choice to others, we have, with or without conscious intent, *chosen* to do
so.
~ Kathleen E. Morris, b. 1962 ~
"Without Exception or Limitation," in *Spirited: Affirming the Soul and Black Gay/Lesbian Identity*, G.
Winston James & Lisa C. Moore, eds., 2006

I am not interested whether somebody was good or bad, evil or not evil – I
am interested in the choices they made, and what they could have done
differently.
~ Chimamanda Ngozi Adichie, b. 1977 ~
in Henry Akubuiro, "My Love Life," Nigeria *Daily Sun*, 2007 January 14

We are all the same. The difference lies only in our choices. The ones we
have made and the ones we make.
~ Oliver Mbamara ~

COLLABORATION / SYNERGY

When spider webs unite, they can tie up a lion.
~ Ethiopian Wisdom ~

Sticks in a bundle are unbreakable.
~ Bondei Wisdom ~

If everyone helps to hold up the sky, then one person does not get tired.
~ Tshi Wisdom ~
Wit & Wisdom of Africa: Proverbs from Africa & The Caribbean, Patrick Ibekwe, ed., 1998

One hand can't tie a bundle.
~ Basa Wisdom ~

One hand cannot clap.
~ Jamaican Wisdom ~

It is in all things that are pure and social we can be as separate as the
fingers, yet one as the hand in all things essential to mutual progress.
~ Booker T. Washington, 1856-1915 ~
Cotton States Exposition Address, 1895 September 19

Living together is an art.
~ William Pickens, 1881-1954 ~
Address, 1932 November 2

If we must have justice, we must be strong; if we must be strong, we must
come together; if we must come together, we can only do so through the
system of organization.
~ Marcus Garvey, 1887-1940 ~

No organization can do everything. Every organization can do something.
~ A. Philip Randolph, 1889-1979 ~

The unity, the balance and the harmony of African civilization, of black
society, (is) based both on the *community* and on the *person*, and in which,
because it was founded on dialogue and reciprocity, the group (has)

priority over the individual without crushing him, but allowing him to blossom as a person.
~ Léopold Senghor, 1906-2001 ~
Négritude: a Humanism of the Twentieth Century, 1970

If you want to make peace with your enemy, you have to work with your enemy. Then he becomes your partner.
~ Nelson Mandela, b. 1918 ~
Long Walk to Freedom, 1994

We must either learn to live together as brothers or we are going to perish together as fools.
~ Martin Luther King, Jr., 1929-1968 ~
The Trumpet of Conscience, 1967

Change did not begin with you, and it will not end with you, but what you do with your life is an absolutely vital piece of that chain. The testimony of each of our daily lives is a vital missing remnant in the fabric of the future.
~ Audre Lorde, 1934-1992 ~
Commencement Address, Oberlin College, 1989 May 29

One man can be a crucial ingredient on a team, but one man cannot make a team.
~ Kareem Abdul-Jabbar, b. 1947 ~

It is a fact that in the right formation, the lifting power of many wings can achieve twice the distance of any bird flying alone.
~ Unknown ~

We got each other. We got our hearts and our brains and our hands, and if we work together we can do it, we can change the world.
~ Bill Strickland, b. 1947 ~
in John Brant, "What One Man Can Do," *Inc Magazine*, 2005 September

We have a stake in one another ... what binds us together is greater than what drives us apart, and ... if enough people believe in the truth of that proposition and act on it, then we might not solve every problem, but we can get something meaningful done for the people with whom we share this Earth.
~ Barack Obama, b. 1961 ~
Speech, 2006 December 1

COMMITMENT / DEDICATION

Commitment means that it is possible for a man to yield the nerve center of his consent to a purpose or cause, a movement or an ideal, which may be more important to him than whether he lives or dies.
~ Howard Thurman, 1889-1981 ~
Disciplines of the Spirit, 1963

It takes a deep commitment to change and an even deeper commitment to grow.
~ Ralph Ellison, 1914-1994 ~

I want to make something of my life? ... Work. There is no substitute for work. There is no substitute for commitment. You've got to commit to something that you love. Invest yourself in it. And trust it.
~ Lloyd Richards, 1919-2006 ~
"Broadway's Groundbreaking Director," Academy of Achievement Interview, 1991 February 15

To act is to be committed, and to be committed is to be in danger.
~ James Baldwin, 1924-1987 ~
"My Dungeon Shook," *The Fire Next Time*, 1962

You need to make a commitment, and once you make it, then life will give you some answers.
~ Les Brown, b. 1945 ~

If you have visibility, whether deserved or not, you need to use it to connect to a cause bigger than you.
~ Cornel West, b. 1954 ~

You have to stick to your plan ... very few people get anywhere by taking shortcuts. Very few people win the lottery to gain their wealth. It happens, but the odds certainly aren't with them. More people get it the honest way, by setting their goals and committing themselves to achieving those goals.
~ Michael Jordan, b. 1961 ~

Learning to love ourselves is not an easy process; instead it is a lifetime commitment that requires continuous nurturing. Like marriage vows, we must promise to love, cherish and accept every aspect of ourselves, for better or for worse, through good times and bad.
~ Roderick Terry, b. 1964 ~

COMMUNICATION

Evil communications corrupt good manners. I hope to live to hear that good communications correct bad manners.
~ Benjamin Banneker, 1731-1806 ~
Almanac Inscription

More and more as we come closer and closer in touch with nature and its teachings are we able to see the Divine and are therefore fitted to interpret correctly the various languages spoken by all forms of nature about us.
~ George Washington Carver, 1864-1943 ~
How to Search for Truth, 1930

If you love it enough, anything will talk with you.
~ Carver ~

What is the quality of your intent? ... Certain people have a way of saying things that shake us at the core. Even when the words do not seem harsh or offensive, the impact is shattering. What we could be experiencing is the intent behind the words.
~ Thurgood Marshall, 1908-1993 ~

If you talk to a man in a language he understands, that goes to his head. If you talk to him in his language, that goes to his heart.
~ Nelson Mandela, b. 1918 ~

In order to engage in meaningful dialogue we must come to the table respecting all participants equally and then we must do something that is quite difficult indeed: we must ourselves become as empty vessels, ready and available to receive. If we can't do this, we might as well not enter into discussion at all. To do so is only pretense.
~ Jan Willis, b. 1948 ~
"We Must ... Become as Empty Vessels," janwillis.net

The heartbeat of true love is the willingness to reflect on one's actions, and to process and communicate this reflection with the loved one.
~ bell hooks, b. 1952 ~
All About Love: New Visions, 2000

COMPARISON / COMPETITION

Scorn also to depress thy competitor by any dishonest or unworthy method; strive to raise thyself above them by excelling them; so shall thy contest for superiority be crowned with honor, if not with success.
~ Khemetic Wisdom ~
Temt Tchaas: Egyptian Proverbs, Muata Ashaya Ashby, ed., 1994

It is not necessary to blow out the other person's lantern to make yours shine.
~ Swahili Wisdom ~

Let us not try to be the best or worst of others, but let us make the effort to be the best of ourselves.
~ Marcus Garvey, 1887-1940 ~
"An Appeal to the Conscience of the Black Race to See Itself," 1923 August 14
Philosophy and Opinions of Marcus Garvey, Vol. II, Amy Jacques Garvey, ed., 1925

Until our Western need to compete begins to slow down and becomes a need to feel and love and express emotion and care for our inner selves as well as our outer selves ... if we can find a way to live in union with other people ... We have to love ourselves, love what we are doing, and find a way to express these things in unity with other people.
~ Katherine Dunham, 1910-2006 ~
in *New York Times*, 2006 May 23

There is nothing like returning to a place that remains unchanged to find the ways in which you yourself have altered.
~ Nelson Mandela, b. 1918 ~
Long Walk to Freedom, 1994

Black women and black men who recognize that the development of their particular strengths and interests does not diminish the other do not need to diffuse their energies fighting for control over each other.
~ Audre Lorde, 1934-1992 ~
Sister Outsider: Essays and Speeches, 1984

The healthiest competition occurs when average people win by putting in above average effort.
~ Colin Powell, b. 1937 ~
My American Journey, 1995

COMPASSION / EMPATHY / KINDNESS

Eat not bread while another stands by without extending your hand to him or her. As for food, it is always here; it is man and woman who do not remain.
~Khemetic Wisdom ~
Selections from the Husia: Sacred Wisdom of Ancient Egypt, Maulana Karenga, tr., 1984

No act of kindness, however small, is ever wasted.
~ Aesop, fl. c. 550 BCE ~
"The Lion and the Mouse"

Kindness effects more than severity.
~ Aesop ~
"The Wind and the Sun"

What does love look like? It has the hands to help others. It has the feet to hasten to the poor and needy. It has eyes to see misery and want. It has the ears to hear the sighs and sorrows of men. That is what love looks like.
~ Augustine of Hippo, 354-430 ~

If you know what hurts yourself you know what hurts others.
~ Malagasy Wisdom ~
Wit & Wisdom of Africa: Proverbs from Africa & The Caribbean, Patrick Ibekwe, ed., 1998

When the eye weeps the nose also becomes wet.
~ Duala Wisdom ~
Ibid.

Compassion … is preferable to cleanliness. Reflect that with a little soap I can easily clean my bed covers, but even with a torrent of tears I would never wash from my soul the stain that my harshness toward the unfortunate would create.
~ Martin de Porres, 1579-1639 ~

Life is just a short walk from the cradle to the grave – and it sure behooves us to be kind to one another along the way.
~ Alice Childress, 1920-1994 ~
A Short Walk, 1979

Compassion and nonviolence help us to see the enemy's point of view, to hear his questions, to know his assessment of ourselves. For from his view we may indeed see the basic weaknesses of our own condition, and if we are mature, we may learn and grow and profit from the wisdom of the brothers who are called the opposition.
~ Martin Luther King, Jr., 1929-1968 ~
The Words of Martin Luther King, Jr., Coretta Scott King, ed., 1983

Compassion is not just feeling with someone, but seeking to change the situation. Frequently people think compassion and love are merely sentimental. No! They are very demanding. If you are going to be compassionate, be prepared for action!
~ Desmond Tutu, b. 1931 ~
Interview, *Psychology Today*, 2005 March/April

As you seek the inner strength that helps you not only to endure but to overcome, do not look for what you can get, but for what you have been given, and for what you can give. We begin with calamity, but we end with compassion.
~ Peter J. Gomes, b. 1942 ~
Strength for the Journey: Biblical Wisdom for Daily Living, 2003

We are all prejudiced. We are all forming these judgments ... let's do some of these meditations that are specifically geared toward helping us recognize – become mindful of – prejudices and transform them. I want us to feel comfortable in our own skin. I think that's a starting place. Then we can see we're all human beings, and then maybe we can stand in each other's shoes.
~ Jan Willis, b. 1948~
in Lawrence Pintak, "Something Has to Change: Blacks in American Buddhism," *Shambhala Sun*, 2001 September

To love and nurture one another to become our best selves is the goal of community, not to battle against the natural divine connection we all share.
~ Conrad Pegues, b. 1964 ~
"Reflections Upon the Bambara Creation Myth," in *Spirited: Affirming the Soul and Black Gay/Lesbian Identity*, G. Winston James & Lisa C. Moore, eds., 2006

It's not enough to be gentle with those who are like us if we can't find it in ourselves to be kind with those who are less fortunate than we are. The true test of compassion lies in our ability to have concern for those least like ourselves.
~ Keith Boykin, b. 1965 ~
Respecting the Soul: Daily Reflections for Black Lesbians and Gays, 1999

COMPLACENCY

If you would attain to what you are not yet, you must always be displeased by what you are. For where you are pleased with yourself there you have remained. Keep adding, keep walking, keep advancing.
~ Augustine of Hippo, 354-430 ~

A sharp knife can become blunt.
~ Kikuyu Wisdom ~
Wit & Wisdom of Africa: Proverbs from Africa & The Caribbean, Patrick Ibekwe, ed., 1998

Just because it's near doesn't necessarily mean you'll get there.
~ Haitian Wisdom ~
Ibid.

Man, in his blindness, is quite satisfied with himself, but heartily dislikes the circumstances and situations of his life. He feels this way, not knowing that the cause of his displeasure lies not in the condition nor the person with whom he is displeased, but in the very self he likes so much.
~ Neville, 1905-1972 ~
"Fundamentals," *New Thought*, Summer 1953

Freedom brings its responsibilities and it is my earnest hope that the hurdle we have just cleared will not give rise within us to any complacency for what we have achieved, or any false illusions about the hard work that lies ahead.
~ Kwame Nkrumah, 1909-1972 ~
in *In Our Own Words*, Elza Dinwiddie-Boyd, ed., 1996

I know we have made some progress over the years, but I know we also have to continue. We can't be too satisfied, because we'll become complacent ... There is still racism among other people who haven't made up their minds that we're all human beings and we should be treated equally.
~ Rosa Parks, 1913-2005 ~
in *Songs of Wisdom: Quotations from Famous African Americans*, Jay David, ed., 2000

Complacency is the enemy of achievement.
~ Dennis Kimbro, b. 1950 ~
Think and Grow Rich: A Black Choice, 1991

COMPOSURE / PEACE / TRANQUILITY

As nature has blest me with a calm and tranquil mind, I shall be far happier in the dungeon ... than my persecutors, on their beds of down.
~ Robert Wedderburn, b. 1762 ~
Speech in court, 1820

Heaven is where you'll be when you are okay right where you are.
~ Sun Ra, 1914-1993 ~

Peace is not merely a distant goal that we seek, but a means by which we arrive at that goal.
~ Martin Luther King, Jr., 1929-1968 ~

If you cannot find peace within yourself, you will never find it anywhere else.
~ Marvin Gaye, 1939-1984 ~

For a future of peace to be possible, we must find methods for disarming our own hearts, ridding them of hateful stereotypes about others and of self-loathing and limiting views of ourselves.
~ Jan Willis, b. 1948 ~
Interview by Pam Kingsbury, "The Spiritual Journey of Jan Willis," *Southern Scribe*, 2002

I hope never to be at peace. I hope to make my life manageable, and I think it's fairly manageable now. But, oh, I would never accept peace. That means death.
~ Jamaica Kincaid, b. 1949 ~
in *Songs of Wisdom: Quotations from Famous African Americans*, Jay David, ed., 2000

When I relax and stop trying so hard to be what I am not, Buddha nature, or mindfulness and clarity, arise of their own accord. When I can simply accept whare I am at, make room for all my junk, and at the same time affirm the goodness already and always there, I touch peace and real freedom.
~ Sister Chan Chau Nghiem ~
"Coming Home," *Dharma, Color, and Culture*, Hilda Gutiérrez Baldoquín, ed., 2004

CONFIDENCE

In all thy undertakings, let a reasonable assurance animate thy endeavours; if thou despair of success, thou shalt not succeed.
~ Khemetic Wisdom ~
Temt Tchaas: Egyptian Proverbs, Muata Ashaya Ashby, ed., 1994

You must act as if it is impossible to fail.
~ Ashanti Wisdom ~

You at this time can only be destroyed by yourselves, from within and not from without. You have reached the point where victory is to be won from within and can only be lost from within.
~ Marcus Garvey, 1887-1940 ~
"The Sign by Which We Conquer," *Negro World*, 1923 September 22

My recipe for life is not being afraid of myself, afraid of what I think or of my opinions.
~ Eartha Kitt, b. 1927 ~

It's so important to believe in yourself. Believe that you can do it, under any circumstances. Because if you believe you can, then you really will. That belief just keeps you searching for the answers, and then pretty soon you get it.
~ Famous Amos, b. 1937 ~

One needs plenty of confidence, self-confidence, because if you don't believe in yourself, then you are going to find the task a lot harder. You need to believe that it's possible.
~ Trevor Rhone, b. 1940 ~
Interview by Kinisha O'Neill, *Jamaica Daily Gleaner*, 2003 March 31

The most important aspect is to be yourself and have confidence in yourself ... the triumph can't be had without the struggle.
~ Wilma Rudolph, 1940-1994 ~
in M. B. Roberts, "Rudolph Ran and World Went Wild," ESPN.com

One important key to success is self-confidence. An important key to self-confidence is preparation.
~ Arthur Ashe, 1943-1993 ~

Our greatest problems in life come not so much from the situations we confront as from our doubts about our ability to handle them.
~ Susan L. Taylor, b. 1946 ~

There is, of course, a very fine line between confidence and arrogance. Belief in one's own innate purity and power can easily be confused with an all-too-human pridefulness. The consequence of not understanding this crucial distinction, and of thereby going astray, is the creation of more suffering rather than the elimination of it.
~ Jan Willis, b. 1948 ~
Dreaming Me: An African American Woman's Spiritual Journey, 2001

An individual must believe in himself and his abilities. To do his best, one needs a confidence that says "I can do anything and if I can't do it, I know how to get help."
~ Benjamin Carson, b. 1951 ~

It is confidence in our bodies, minds and spirits that allows us to keep looking for new adventures, new directions to grow in, and new lessons to learn – which is what life is all about.
~ Oprah Winfrey, b. 1954 ~

I'm an actor so I simply act confident every time I hit the stage. I am consumed with the fear of failing. Reaching deep down and finding confidence has made all my dreams come true.
~ Arsenio Hall, b. 1955 ~

The ability to love and see the beauty in ourselves allows us to overcome feelings of inadequacy and insecurity. Self-love emboldens us with a greater sense of who we are. It gives us the confidence to be ourselves without seeking validation.
~ Roderick Terry, b. 1964 ~
"Hope Chest"

CONFLICT / OPPOSITION

If you meet a disputant who is more powerful than you, fold your arms and bend your back. Confrontation will not make them agree with you. Disregard their evil speech. Your self-control will match their evil utterances and people will call them ignoramuses.
~ Khemetic Wisdom ~
Temt Tchaas: Egyptian Proverbs, Muata Ashaya Ashby, ed., 1994

Imagine the vanity of thinking that your enemy can do you more damage than your enmity.
~ Augustine of Hippo, 354-430 ~

Only as we rise ... do we encounter opposition.
~ Frederick Douglass, 1817-1895 ~

If two refuse, no one fights.
~ Joaquim Machado de Assis, 1839-1908 ~
Esau and Jacob, 1965

Confronted with the impossibility of remaining faithful to one's beliefs, and the equal impossibility of becoming free of them, one can be driven to the utmost inhuman excesses.
~ James Baldwin, 1924-1987 ~

Each of us has the right to take pride in our particular faith or heritage. But the notion that what is ours is necessarily in conflict with what is theirs is both false and dangerous. It has resulted in endless enmity and conflict, leading men to commit the greatest of crimes in the name of a higher power.
~ Kofi Annan, b. 1938 ~
Nobel Lecture, Oslo, 2001 December 10

Every disagreement or misunderstanding we have with another person does not warrant a confrontation. Rather than get involved in a senseless debate over who is right or wrong, it is usually better to shrug if off. The ability to let go of a menacing encounter always provides a bridge to higher ground.
~ Roderick Terry, b. 1964 ~
"Hope Chest"

CONFORMITY

I would rather go to hell by choice than to stumble into heaven by following the crowd.
~ Benjamin Mays, 1895-1984 ~
in *Brother's Keeper: Words of Inspiration for African-American Men*, Roderick Terry, ed., 1996

It is very nearly impossible ... to become an educated person in a country so distrustful of the independent mind.
~ James Baldwin, 1924-1987 ~

Forget traditions! Forget conventionalisms! Forget what the world will say whether you're in your place or out of your place. Stand up and be counted. Do your thing, looking only to God – whoever your God is – and to your consciences for approval.
~ Shirley Chisholm, 1924-2005 ~

Few, if any, survive their teens. Most surrender to the vague but murderous pressure of adult conformity.
~ Maya Angelou, b. 1928 ~

Many people fear nothing more terribly than to take a position which stands out sharply and clearly from the prevailing opinion. The tendency of most is to adopt a view that is so ambiguous that it will include everything and so popular that it will include everybody. Not a few men who cherish lofty and noble ideas hide them under a bushel for fear of being called different.
~ Martin Luther King, Jr., 1929-1968 ~

Human salvation lies in the hands of the creatively maladjusted.
~ King ~

One has not only a legal but a moral responsibility to disobey unjust laws.
~ King ~

I have always been just me with no frame of reference to anything beyond myself ... I just don't fit in or belong anywhere and I tend to pride myself on not fitting in or belonging.
~ Bessie Head, 1937-1986 ~
in Gillian Stead Eilersen, "A Skin of Her Own," *New Internationalist*, No. 247, 1993 September

I don't give a damn what others say. It's okay to color outside of the lines.
~ Jimi Hendrix, 1942-1970 ~

I did learn music with griots, but I'm not one. But it's good sometimes to break tradition, when tradition prevents people from improving.
~ Salif Keita, b. 1949 ~
GlobalVillageIdiot.net

The hardest thing to be in this world, is someone who disagrees with popular people. To take unpopular stances in front of popular people. It's easy to be unpopular with unpopular people, but it's harder to be unpopular with popular people ... what I mean is the knowledge that it is okay to feel differently than the pack. That that is a fundamental right. That it's okay to disagree. It's better to be able to disagree and have a dialogue, than to go along with the pack and be truly unhappy.
~ Whoopi Goldberg, b. 1955 ~
"The One-Woman Show," Academy of Achievement Interview, 1994 June 17

I created my identity at the expense of who I really was and how I really felt. Even so, I was resolute in my deception. My façade was so thick that all the king's horses and all the king's men could not pull it away. I was determined not to reveal my true self. Naturally, my self-deception continued to manifest into my adult life. The older I got, the more time I spent perfecting and refining my exterior image ... whatever it took to make the right impression. I allowed how I looked on the outside to dictate how I felt inside. Eventually, after many years of silent suffering, empty feelings, failed relationships and introspection, I realized that I needed to get beyond my external self-image and focus on inner awareness.
~ Roderick Terry, b. 1964 ~
"Hope Chest"

When a culture suffers from an idiotic present in which a pathological and diseased frame of reference is the standard paradigm, it is the healthy individual who is seen as the freak, the one who is distorted, simply because he is trying to recover a universal human ethic.
~ Jason D. Hill, b. 1965 ~
Becoming a Cosmopolitan: What It Means to Be a Human Being in the New Millennium, 2000

CONGRUENCE / RESONANCE

If we live good lives, the times are also good. As we are, such are the times.
~ Augustine of Hippo, 354-430 ~

What you like in a book is you yourself.
~ Haitian Wisdom ~
Wit & Wisdom of Africa: Proverbs from Africa & The Caribbean, Patrick Ibekwe, ed., 1998

My slogan is if it don't fit don't force it. In other words, if you can't make
it, don't fake it. Let somebody else take it.
~ Moms Mabley, 1894-1975 ~

You don't get in life what you want; you get in life what you are.
~ Les Brown, b. 1945 ~

Womanhood has taught me how to discern the changes in the seasons of
my life, and to let the seasons be.
~ Renita Weems, b. 1954 ~

I don't have to explain myself. My frequency is very common and is open
to anybody who wants to tune in.
~ RuPaul, b. 1960 ~
"On Being Almost Seven Feet Tall Without Shoes," *New York Times*, 1993 July 11

When two people talk, they don't just fall into physical and aural harmony
... We imitate each other's emotions as a way of expressing support and
caring and, even more basically, as a way of communicating with each
other.
~ Malcolm Gladwell, b. 1963 ~
The Tipping Point: How Little Things Can Make a Big Difference, 2000

When people from groups who have historically found themselves socially,
economically and politically outside the margins hear that the Buddha
taught liberation, nothing more needs to be said.
~ Hilda Gutiérrez Baldoquín ~
in *Colorlines Magazine*, 2005 Spring

CONNECTION / INTERBEING / INTERDEPENDENCE

We are people because of other people.
~ Sotho Wisdom ~
Wit & Wisdom of Africa: Proverbs from Africa & The Caribbean, Patrick Ibekwe, ed., 1998

There are no bonds so strong as those which are formed by suffering together.
~ Harriet Jacobs, 1813-1897 ~
Incidents in the Life of A Slave Girl, 1861

We never know we are beings till we love. And then it is we know the powers and the potentialities of human existence, the power and potentialities of organic, conscious, solar, cosmic matter and force. We, together, vibrate as one in harmony with man and with the cosmos.
~ Jean Toomer, 1894-1967 ~
in Cynthia Kerman & Richard Eldridge, *The Lives of Jean Toomer*, 1987

There are roads out of the secret places within us along which we must all move as we go to touch others.
~ Romare Bearden, 1914-1988 ~

Life is to be lived, not controlled; and humanity is won by continuing to play in face of certain defeat. Our fate is to become one, and yet many – this is not prophecy, but description.
~ Ralph Ellison, 1914-1994 ~
Invisible Man, 1952

I commune with feelings more than prayer
For there is nothing else to ask for
That companionship is
And it is superior to any other is.
~ Sun Ra, 1914-1993 ~
"The Differences"

We are each other's harvest:
we are each other's business:
we are each other's magnitude and bond.
~ Gwendolyn Brooks, 1917-2000 ~
"Paul Robeson," *Family Pictures*, 1970

Remember you didn't get there by yourself.
~ Haitian Wisdom ~
Wit & Wisdom of Africa: Proverbs from Africa & The Caribbean, Patrick Ibekwe, ed., 1998

Each person's humanity is ideally expressed through his or her relationship with others, and theirs in turn, through a recognition of that person's humanity.
~ Nelson Mandela, b. 1918 ~
in *Brother's Keeper: Words of Inspiration for African-American Men*, Roderick Terry, ed., 1996

You can't walk alone. Many have given the illusion but none have really walked alone. Man is not made that way. Each man is bedded in his people, their history, their culture, and their values.
~ Peter Abrahams, b. 1919 ~
Return to Goli, 1953

If you can examine and face your life, you can discover the terms with which you are connected to other lives, and they can discover them, too – the terms with which they are connected to other people.
~ James Baldwin, 1924-1987 ~
"An interview with James Baldwin" by Studs Terkel, 1961
in *Conversations With James Baldwin*, 1989

I can never be what I ought to be until you are what you ought to be. This is the way our world is made. No individual or nation can stand out boasting of being independent. We are interdependent.
~ Martin Luther King, Jr., 1929-1968 ~

God created us so that we should form the human family, existing together because we were made for one another. We are not made for an exclusive self-sufficiency but for interdependence, and we break the law of being at our peril.
~ Desmond Tutu, b. 1931 ~

My existence is caught up and inextricably bound up with yours ... A solitary human being is a contradiction in terms.
~ Tutu ~
Morehouse Medical School Commencement Address, *The Wisdom of Desmond Tutu*, Michael Battle, ed., 1998

I would not know how to be a human being at all, except I learned this from other human beings. We are made for a delicate network of relationships, of interdependence. Not even the most powerful nation can be completely self-sufficient.
~ Tutu ~

Ubuntu. The essence of being human. We say a person is a person through other persons. I can't be human in isolation. I need you to be all you can be so that I can become me and all that I can be.
~ Tutu ~
Interview by Amy Goodman, *Democracy Now*

Difference must not be merely tolerated, but seen as a fund of necessary polarities between which our creativity can spark like a dialectic. Only then does the necessity for interdependence become unthreatening. Only within that interdependency of different strengths, acknowledged and equal, can the power to seek new ways of being in the world generate, as well as the courage and sustenance to act where there are no charters.
~ Audre Lorde, 1934-1992 ~
Sister Outsider: Essays and Speeches, 1984

The amazing thing is that, when you go searching for yourself, you find others, other selves who are similar to you, and who are also there with their own secrets.
~ Sonia Sanchez, b. 1934 ~
Interview by Susan Kelly, *African American Review*, Winter 2000

You never know how much you need it until you're deprived of it. You say to yourself when you are at liberty how desperate you are for your solitude, you love your periods of solitude, you scramble for it, you find ways of being by yourself so you can do what you want with yourself and your mind. But when you're deprived of it for a lengthy period then you value human companionship.
~ Wole Soyinka, b. 1934 ~
Interview by Harry Kreisler, 1998 April 16

Human relationships do not occur in a vacuum. They develop in the context of ecology, economics, politics, culture, and psyche. All these aspects of our society affect those relationships profoundly. These aspects are inseparable. They are connected. The most intimate is connected with the most earthly ... The material of life opens out into the spirituality of human life.
~ Ngugi wa Thiong'o, b. 1938 ~
Interview by Michael Alexander Pozo, St. John's University, 2004 August 16

If we lived a life that valued and protected trees, it would be a life that also valued and protected us – and gave us great joy. A way of life that kills trees, our present way of life, kills us too, body and soul.
~ Wangari Maathai, b. 1940 ~

Humanism starts not with identity but with the ability to identify with others. It asks what we have in common with others while acknowledging the internal diversity among ourselves. It is about the priority of a shared humanity.
~ Henry Louis Gates, Jr., b. 1950 ~

We are social in many ways and for many reasons: because we desire company, because we depend on one another for survival, because so much that we care about is collectively created.
~ K. Anthony Appiah, b. 1954 ~
"Liberalism, Individuality, and Identity," *Critical Inquiry* 27.2, Winter 2001

What we're all striving for is authenticity, a spirit-to-spirit connection.
~ Oprah Winfrey, b. 1954 ~
in *O Magazine*

Human beings long for connection, and our sense of usefulness derives from the feeling of connectedness. When we are connected – to our own purpose, to the community around us, and to our spiritual wisdom – we are able to live and act with authentic effectiveness.
~ Malidoma Somé, b. 1956 ~
The Healing Wisdom of Africa, 1999

… the intensity of human connection and attention … What would it be like if that intensity of human connection could be found here, in addition to all the material wealth that is available? If the human wealth could match the material wealth, what would happen? Heaven could be created, right here.
~ Ibid.

No matter what uniform we may be wearing, underneath it all we are all the same – unique individuals, alone, aching to belong. Ultimately, we all have more in common with each other than we don't have in common.
~ RuPaul, b. 1960 ~
Lettin It All Hang Out, 1995

The intention to communicate is more important than communication itself. When you decide to talk to the Other, a loving gesture has been made. If somebody wants to speak to me, it means I exist in their eyes.
~ Abderrahmane Sissako, b. 1961 ~
Interview by Olivier Barlet, *Africultures*, 2003 April 18

CONSCIENCE

A clear conscience is a soft mat.
~ Swahili Wisdom ~
Wit & Wisdom of Africa: Proverbs from Africa & The Caribbean, Patrick Ibekwe, ed., 1998

Clear conscience sleeps through thunder.
~ Jamaican Wisdom ~
Ibid.

Whenever conflict arises between material and spiritual values, the conscience plays an important role, and anyone who suffers from a guilty conscience is never free from this problem until he makes peace with his conscience.
~ Haile Selassie, 1892-1975 ~

Cowardice asks the question, "Is it safe?" Expediency asks the question, "Is it politic?" Vanity asks the question, "Is it popular?" But, conscience asks the question, "Is it right?" And there comes a time when one must take a position that is neither safe, nor politic, nor popular, but one must take it because one's conscience tells one that it is right.
~ Martin Luther King, Jr., 1929-1968 ~

It's the black bourgeoisie, it's the upper middle class, it's the rich black people who have sold their consciences at the price of silence in the face of denial of opportunity for their lesser-well-off brothers and sisters.
~ Michael Eric Dyson, b. 1958 ~
Interview by Amy Goodman, *Democracy Now*, 2007 July 18

Truth is a peacemaker and a healer. It makes it possible for us to negotiate the world with a clear conscience and a pure heart. We also have a moral obligation to be honest with those around us.
~ Roderick Terry, b. 1964 ~
"Hope Chest"

There has to be a guard at the gate, when you manifest yourself wholly ... That vessel is integrity, conscience and character. That guard of integrity usually gets killed, or fired. It's your conscience.
~ Lauryn Hill, b. 1975 ~
in Claude Grunitzky, "The Prophet," *Trace*

CONTINUITY

Man decays, his corpse becomes dust and all his relatives die. But a book causes him to be remembered ... Better is a book than a well-built house ... or a stela in a temple.
~ *Book of Songs* ~
in *Kemet and the African Worldview*, Maulana Karenga & Jacob Carruthers, eds., 1986

Whatever the sea has washed away, the heaven burned down, the earth undermined, the sword shorn down, reappears at some other time by the turn of compensation.
~ Tertullian, c. 160-240 ~
De Pallio, 2.6., S. Thelwall, tr., 1869

This Eternity how dreadful, how delightful!
~ Phillis Wheatley, 1753-1784 ~
Letter to JohnThornton, 1773 December 1

Out of the sighs of one generation are kneaded the hopes of the next.
~ Joaquim Machado de Assis, 1839-1908 ~
Education of a Stuffed Shirt

Believe in life! Always human beings will live and progress to greater, broader and fuller life.
~ W. E. B. Du Bois, 1868-1963 ~
"Last Message to the World," 1957

The most precious things are never totally won. It's like love. It's never totally won. It has to be worked at in order to be maintained ... There are certain eternals, and you have to struggle to keep those eternals fresh, alive, and there for the next generation.
~ Lloyd Richards, 1919-2006 ~
"Broadway's Groundbreaking Director," Academy of Achievement Interview, 1991 February 15

Death is not the end for someone who has faith.
~ Desmond Tutu, b. 1931 ~
in *Brother's Keeper: Words of Inspiration for African-American Men*, Roderick Terry, ed., 1996

To acknowledge our ancestors means we are aware that we did not make ourselves, that the line stretches all the way back, perhaps to God, or to Gods. We remember them because it is an easy thing to forget; that we are not the first to suffer, rebel, fight, love, and die. The grace with which we embrace life, in spite of the pain, the sorrow, is always a measure of what has gone before.
~ Alice Walker, b. 1944 ~
"In These Dissenting Times," *Revolutionary Petunias*, 1970

Life only *appears* to begin with birth and end with death. The flow of life is in fact continuous and eternal, birth and death are merely transformations.
~ Susan L. Taylor, b. 1946 ~
Lessons in Living, 1995

What is modern today will become tradition in a hundred years. There is a very deep dialectic relation between all that we invent today and what it will become tomorrow. We use yesterday's energy and fuel to invent what is modern ... Those moments that we seized, that will take on the value of eternity tomorrow.
~ Gaston Kaboré, b. 1951 ~
Masterclass with Gaston Kaboré, Cannes Film Festival 2007, Céline Dewaele, tr.

All life cannot be wiped off the face of the Earth. That is man's imagination. The Earth was always here and the Earth will always be here, whether it is in the form of man life, woman life, animal life, but there was never a time when there was nothing ... Man cannot destroy the Earth. Man may destroy what it is to make him live on the Earth, but just because him dead, him is not the only life. Man is not the supreme life on Earth, is man believe that. Every life is as important as man life, is just man take it upon him head and feel like him more important than everything else.
~ Mutabaruka, b. 1952 ~
Interview by Carter Van Pelt, 1998

One theory I believe is that when people die the spirit flies from them and fragments, and goes into people who are just coming into being ... the circle doesn't break, it just reinvents.
~ Whoopi Goldberg, b. 1955 ~
"The One-Woman Show," Academy of Achievement Interview, 1994 June 17

CONVICTION / PRINCIPLE

Be thou incapable of change in that which is right, and men will rely upon you. Establish unto thyself principles of action; and see that thou ever act according to them. First know that thy principles are just, and then be thou inflexible in the path of them.
~ Khemetic Wisdom ~
Temt Tchaas: Egyptian Proverbs, Muata Ashaya Ashby, ed., 1994

In every human Breast, God has implanted a Principle, which we call Love of Freedom; it is impatient of Oppression, and pants for Deliverance ... that same Principle lives in us.
~ Phillis Wheatley, 1753-1784 ~
Letter to Samson Occom, 1774 February 11

When you are in doubt as to which you should serve, forsake the material appearance for the invisible principle, for this is everything.
~ Alexandre Dumas, père, 1802-1870 ~
Twenty Years After, 1845

No man is really free who is afraid to speak the truth as he knows it is, or who is too fearful to take a stand for that which he knows is right.
~ Benjamin Mays, 1895-1984 ~
in Roderick Terry, *One Million Strong: A PhotographicTribute of the Million Man March*, 1996

Mix a conviction with a man and something happens.
~ Adam Clayton Powell, Jr., 1908-1972 ~
"Minimum Living – Minimum Religion," *Keep the Faith, Baby*, 1967

The human body has an enormous capacity for adjusting to trying circumstances. I have found that one can bear the unbearable if one can keep one's spirits strong even when one's body is being tested. Strong convictions are the secret of surviving deprivation; your spirit can be full even when your stomach is empty.
~ Nelson Mandela, b. 1918 ~
Long Walk to Freedom, 1994

The man who stands for nothing will fall for anything.
~ Malcolm X, 1925-1965 ~

Shallow understanding from people of good will is more frustrating than absolute misunderstanding from people of ill will. Lukewarm acceptance is much more bewildering than outright rejection.
~ Martin Luther King, Jr., 1929-1968 ~

Victory is often a thing deferred, and rarely at the summit of courage ... What is at the summit of courage, I think, is freedom. The freedom that comes with the knowledge that no earthly thing can break you; that an unbroken spirit is the only thing you cannot live without; that in the end it is the courage of conviction that moves things, that makes all change possible.
~ Paula Giddings, b. 1947 ~

Now is the best time to start thinking about the legacy you are going to leave behind and build the best reputation, because that will be your passport for life. In building a good reputation, you must state clearly what you stand for, demonstrate consistent behavior and walk the talk every day.
~ Michael Lee-Chin, b. 1951 ~
Address to NCU Graduation, in *Jamaica Daily Gleaner*, 2007 August 13

I remain more interested in what people, myself included, are actually willing to do: are we prepared to put everything we believe on the line in order to achieve something in which we passionately believe? Are we prepared to assay a radical assessment of our prejudices in order to move toward a radical improvement of ourselves and the lives of others?
~ Thomas Glave, b. 1964 ~
Interview by Alexis Deveaux, ArtVoice.com

Our first obligation is to be true to ourselves. Like the flow of our blood, every thought we think, word we speak and choice we make should come from the heart, the source of all truth.
~ Roderick Terry, b. 1964 ~
"Hope Chest"

If everyone is a product of this society, who will say the things that need to be said, and do the things that need to be done, without compromise? Truth will never start out popular in a world more concerned with marketability than righteousness. It will initially suffer ridicule and even violence – yet ultimately it is undeniable. All of humanity is living in a dream world, but suffering real consequences.
~ Lauryn Hill, b. 1975 ~
"The Middle Man," 2003

COST

What is the pay for titles, but flattery? How doth man purchase power but by being a slave to him who giveth it?
~ Akhenaton, c. 1385-c. 1355 BCE ~

There is no cure that does not cost.
~ Kenyan Wisdom ~

Nothing in the universe is attained by doing nothing. You must always give something to get something.
~ Cuban Wisdom ~

If you want roast corn, your fingers have to burn.
If you want good, your nose has to run.
~ Jamaican Wisdom ~

However humble I may be as a member of society, and whatever efforts may be made to degrade me and render me contemptible in the eyes of the world, I have nevertheless the pride, and the ambition, to flatter myself, that even my simple exertions will one day or other be of no mean importance to the cause I am embarked in, which is that of Religious Liberty and the Universal Right of Conscience. If we would obtain the privileges to which we are entitled, neither death nor dungeons must terrify us.
~ Robert Wedderburn, b. 1762 ~
Brief to court, 1820 May 9

I am resolved it is better to die than be a white man's slave.
~ Joseph Cinqué, 1813-c. 1879 ~
in *The New York Sun*, 1839

Men may not get all they pay for in this world; but they must pay for all they get. If we ever get free from all the oppressions and wrongs heaped upon us, we must pay for their removal. We must do this by labor, by suffering, by sacrifice, and, if needs be, by our lives, and the lives of others.
~ Frederick Douglass, 1817-1895 ~
Address on West India Emancipation, 1857 August 4

A man who will not labor to gain his rights is a man who would not if he had them prize and defend them.
~ Douglass ~

Many times I wondered whether my achievement was worth the loneliness I experienced, but now I realize the price was small.
~ Gordon Parks, 1912-2006 ~

People pay for what they do, and still more for what they have allowed themselves to become. And they pay for it very simply; by the lives they lead.
~ James Baldwin, 1924-1987 ~
Nobody Knows My Name: More Notes of a Native Son, 1961

When you go in search of honey you must expect to be stung by bees.
~ Kenneth Kaunda, b. 1924 ~

Human progress is neither automatic nor inevitable ... Every step toward the goal of justice requires sacrifice, suffering, and struggle; the tireless exertions and passionate concern of dedicated individuals.
~ Martin Luther King, Jr., 1929-1968 ~

Freedom has always been an expensive thing. History is fit testimony to the fact that freedom is rarely gained without sacrifice and self-denial.
~ King ~
The Words of Martin Luther King, Jr., Coretta Scott King, ed., 1983

Sometimes you got to hurt something to help something. Sometimes you have to plow under one thing in order for something else to grow.
~ Ernest Gaines, b. 1933 ~
A Gathering of Old Men, 1983

It is better to die for an idea that will live, than to live for an idea that will die.
~ Steve Biko, 1946-1977 ~

To get the desired results out of life, we have to make certain sacrifices and choices. Whether it is controlling our appetite, spending habits or how much time we spend watching television, we have to commit ourselves to doing what is necessary to achieve our goals.
~ Roderick Terry, b. 1964 ~
"Hope Chest"

COURAGE

As a rock on the sea shore, stand firm and let not the dashing of the waves disturb you. Raise your head like a tower on a hill, and the arrows of fortune drop at your feet. In the instant of danger, the courage of your heart will sustain you, and the steadiness of your mind beareth you through.
~ Khemetic Wisdom ~
Temt Tchaas: Egyptian Proverbs, Muata Ashaya Ashby, ed., 1994

Fear is nothing, the real thing is courage.
~ Ndebele Wisdom ~

Fortune favors the brave.
~ Terence, c. 190-159 BCE ~

If a ram is brave, its courage comes from its heart; its courage is from its heart not from its horns; its courage is from its heart and not from its head.
~ Tshi Wisdom ~
Wit & Wisdom of Africa: Proverbs from Africa & The Caribbean, Patrick Ibekwe, ed., 1998

To continue one's journey in the darkness with one's footsteps guided by the illumination of remembered radiance is to know courage of a peculiar kind – the courage to demand that light continue to be light even in the surrounding darkness.
~ Howard Thurman, 1889-1981 ~
in *Brother's Keeper: Words of Inspiration for African-American Men*, Roderick Terry, ed., 1996

I learned that courage was not the absence of fear, but the triumph over it. The brave man is not he who does not feel afraid, but he who conquers that fear.
~ Nelson Mandela, b. 1918 ~
Long Walk to Freedom, 1994

One isn't necessarily born with courage, but one is born with potential. Without courage, we cannot practice any other virtue with consistency.
~ Maya Angelou, b. 1928 ~

Courage faces fear and thereby masters it. Cowardice represses fear and is thereby mastered by it. Courageous men never lose the zest for living even

though their life situation is zestless; cowardly men, overwhelmed by the uncertainties of life, lose the will to live. We must constantly build dykes of courage to hold back the flood of fear.
~ Martin Luther King, Jr., 1929-1968 ~
The Strength to Love, 1963

For me courage is fear – it's the same energy, channelled by the alchemy of faith and passion into helping us to put ourselves at risk for the greater good.
~ Derrick Bell, b. 1930 ~
Ethical Ambition: Living A Life of Meaning and Worth, 2002

Courage is the power of the mind to overcome fear. It is one of the most supreme virtues that a man can possess ... We must have the courage to surmount our fears ... The problems and issues that face us are not new. There is no reason for us to be afraid. Others before us have already tested the waters and mastered their currents ... Courage gives us the strength to overcome in spite of obstacles set before us. We must also have the courage to question authority and not always blindly and passively submit to the pressures and dictates of the system. We must be self-possessed and, more than anything else, have the unyielding courage to stand alone.
~ Roderick Terry, b. 1964 ~
Brother's Keeper: Words of Inspiration for African-American Men, 1996

Self-love and trust in who we are, is what gives us the courage to be ourselves.
~ Terry ~
"Hope Chest"

Courage allows us to respond to fear. It does not require the absence of fear but rather working through fear. In those times when fear gets the better of you, your courage can help get you to do what you fear you must.
~ Keith Boykin, b. 1965 ~
Respecting the Soul: Daily Reflections for Black Lesbians and Gays, 1999

I grew up in ... an environment in which death invited itself without end. A virus, a bacterium, a parasite, a drought, a famine, a civil war, soldiers, torturers: death could take all forms and hit anyone, anytime. When I had malaria, I got well again. When I was circumcised, my wound transformed into scar tissue, and I survived. When my Qur'an teacher fractured my skull, doctors saved me. A bandit put the blade of his knife against my throat: I'm still alive, and more of a rebel than ever before.
~ Ayaan Hirsi Ali, b. 1969 ~
in Le Figaro, 2006 November 18

CREATIVITY / DISCOVERY / INNOVATION

Do not follow the path. Go where there is no path and begin the trail.
~ Ashanti Wisdom ~

Do a common thing in an uncommon way.
~ Booker T. Washington, 1856-1915 ~
Daily Resolves

Let us rejoice at the many unexplored fields in which there is unlimited
fame and fortune to the successful explorer.
~ George Washington Carver, 1864-1943 ~

Create, and be true to yourself, and depend only on your own good taste.
~ Duke Ellington, 1899-1974 ~
in *Brother's Keeper: Words of Inspiration for African-American Men*, Roderick Terry, ed., 1996

It is the unquestioning acceptance of the already existing that keeps people
from being creative.
~ Unknown ~

Everyone's got to be different. You can't copy anybody and end up with
anything. If you copy, it means you're working without any real feeling.
And without feeling, whatever you do amounts to nothing.
~ Billie Holiday, 1915-1959 ~
Lady Sings the Blues, 1956

We have only to think of the massive popular creativity of African
Americans in their world of social exclusion and segregation: their Negro
spirituals, the black church with its sustaining spirituality, its inspired and
influential musical forms, its foundations for oral expressiveness and
invention, its inspiration for literature; and then the blues, jazz and now
rap, and the constant inventiveness in language, dance, music, art, style
and fashion. This creativity, provides a praxis of transculturation, profound
in its world impact and interaction among the peoples of our planet. (It)
provides a different apprehension of social exclusion beyond the negative
function of social death.
~ John La Rose, 1927-2006 ~
"Unemployment, Leisure and the Birth of Creativity," *The Black Scholar*, Volume 26, No.2

I've always had this idea from the day I started to play music: that not only is it alive, but that it's endless and has no ego in it. There's something about creativity that every human being gets an equal share.
~ Ornette Coleman, b. 1930 ~

This is one of the glories of man, the inventiveness of the human mind and the human spirit: whenever life doesn't seem to give an answer, we create one.
~ Lorraine Hansberry, 1930-1965 ~

The power to create and innovate remains the greatest guarantee of respect and recognition.
~ Rex Nettleford, b. 1933 ~
Mirror, Mirror: Identity, Race and Protest in Jamaica, 1970

We must recognize and nurture the creative parts of each other without always understanding what will be created.
~ Audre Lorde, 1934-1992 ~

People who never believed that they even possessed the gift of self expression become creative and this in turn activates other energies within the individual. I believe the creative process is the most energizing. And that is why it is so intimately related to the process of revolution within society.
~ Wole Soyinka, b. 1934 ~
Interview in In Person – Achebe, Awoonor, and Soyinka at the University of Washington, 1975

Facing economic ruin when there is creative joy in your soul is usually just a temporary thing, for very soon you're going to fly and if you don't fly, that creative joy you feel will be stimulation enough to keeping pushing you on.
~ Trevor Rhone, b. 1940 ~
Interview by Kinisha O'Neill, Jamaica Daily Gleaner, 2003 March 31

How to develop without losing your identity, while reinventing yourself each day? ... This fear of losing ourselves is perhaps what gives us this touch of genius that makes us want to create each day.
~ Gaston Kaboré, b. 1951 ~
Masterclass with Gaston Kaboré, Cannes Film Festival 2007, Céline Dewaele, tr.

CRITICISM / JUDGMENT

Of little worth is the recommendation which has for its prop the defamation of another.
~ Tertullian, c. 160-240 ~
Adversus Marcionem, IV.15.5

You who judge others, at some time be also a judge of yourself. Look into the recesses of your own conscience.
~ Cyprian, 200-258 ~
Treatise V: Address to Demetrianus

If two friends ask you to judge a dispute, don't accept, because you will lose one friend; on the other hand, if two strangers come with the same request, accept because you will gain one friend.
~ Augustine of Hippo, 354-430 ~

Too much sharpness cuts the sharpener.
~ Kikuyu Wisdom ~
Wit & Wisdom of Africa: Proverbs from Africa & The Caribbean, Patrick Ibekwe, ed., 1998

Censure is dealt out by wholesale – while praise is very sparingly distributed – nine times in ten mankind may err in their blame – but in its praises the world is seldom, if ever, mistaken.
~ Ignatius Sancho, 1729-1780 ~
Letter LX to Mrs IWE, 1780 January 5 in *The Letters of the Late Ignatius Sancho, an African*, Vol. II, 1782

Judge not thy brother!
There are secrets in his heart that you might weep to see.
~ Leo Martin, 1859-1887 ~
"Judge Not Thy Brother," *Poetical Works*, 1883

It is very easy to sit in judgment upon the behavior of others, but often difficult to realize that every judgment is a self-judgment.
~ Howard Thurman, 1889-1981 ~

It is easier to light a match than it is to curse the darkness.
~ Paul Robeson, 1898-1976 ~

If a man look upon any other man and estimates that man as less than himself, then he is stealing from the other. He is stealing the other's birthright – that of equality.
~ Neville, 1905-1972 ~

Young men and women are so caught by the way they see themselves. Now mind you. When a larger society sees them as unattractive, as threats, as too black or too white or too poor or too fat or too thin or too sexual or too asexual, that's rough. But you can overcome that. The real difficulty is to overcome how you think about yourself. If we don't have that we never grow, we never learn, and sure as hell we should never teach.
~ Maya Angelou, b. 1928 ~

It is not a sign of weakness, but a sign of high maturity, to rise to the level of self-criticism.
~ Martin Luther King Jr., 1929-1968 ~

When you starts measuring somebody, measure him right ... Make sure you done taken into account what hills and valleys he come through before he got to wherever he is.
~ Lorraine Hansberry, 1930-1965 ~
Raisin in the Sun, 1959

A belief in one's self is not the same thing as arrogance. A belief in one's self is not the same thing as ceasing to care what others believe. But if you really know yourself, if you believe in who you are, it's amazing how much criticism you can withstand.
~ Johnnetta Cole, b. 1936 ~
"Spelman's First Female President," Academy of Achievement Interview, 1996 June 28

If we are to learn to improve the quality of the decisions we make, we need to accept the mysterious nature of our snap judgments.
~ Malcolm Gladwell, b. 1963 ~
Blink: The Power of Thinking Without Thinking, 2005

Of all the judgments you pass in life, the ones you pass against yourself are the most harmful. Relinquish the need to judge others and yourself. Judgment is a disguise used to deflect a fear of inadequacy. Accepting others without judgment is essential for personal growth and building strong relationships.
~ Roderick Terry, b. 1964 ~
"Hope Chest"

DANCE / MOVEMENT

Nothing rests; everything moves; everything vibrates.
~ Hermes Trismegistus ~
in *The Kybalion: A Study of the Hermetic Philosophy*, 1908

Jungle jazzing. Orient wrigging, civilized stepping. Shake that thing. Sweet dancing thing of primitive joy, perverse pleasure, prostitute ways, many adored variations of the rhythm, savage, barbaric, refined – eternal rhythm of the mysterious magical, magnificent – the dance divine of life. Oh, shake that thing.
~ Claude McKay, 1889-1948 ~
Banjo, 1929

We are the men of the dance, whose feet draw new strength pounding the hardened earth.
~ Léopold Senghor, 1906-2001 ~
"Prayer to Masks," *Selected Poems*, John Reed and Clive Wake, trs., 1964

There is a need in the body to express itself. Every culture has its own form of physical expression. An unfortunate thing about today – about Western dance – is it's too competitive in *feeling*. I don't dance because I can do this movement better than you. I do it because it's what I feel, and want to do.
~ Katherine Dunham, 1910-2006 ~
in *Washington Post*, 2006 May 23

There is a purifying process in dancing.
~ Dunham ~

The dance is strong magic. The dance is a spirit. It turns the body to liquid steel. It makes it vibrate like a guitar. The body can fly without wings. It can sing without voice. The dance is strong magic.
~ Pearl Primus, 1919-1994 ~

Rhythm is the soul of life. Every cell in your body moves in a constant rhythm. When we get out of rhythm, that is when we get into trouble.
~ Babatunde Olatunji, 1927-2003 ~
in *Hartford Courant*, 2001

dance your anger and your joys.
dance the guns to silence.
dance, dance, dance ...
~ Ken Saro-Wiwa, 1941-1995 ~

Dance and movement – the athleticism of a sport, or of dancing ... that
music that drives the dance, and the voice, singing ... I get some of the
greatest peace, some of the greatest contentment in my life from those.
~ John Edgar Wideman, b. 1941 ~
in Lisa Baker, "Storytelling and Democracy," *African American Review*, 2000 Summer

We've all been dancing since the beginning of time. We're always in
motion, even if we think we're not. If you feel static, then you've got a
problem.
~ Judith Jamison, b. 1943 ~
Dancing Spirit: An Autobiography, 1993

All movement is accompanied by a sense. I like wind very much. Wind is
music, just as music is wind ... Wind, like music, is the breath of movement
and life. It has to do with stimulation.
~ Djibril Diop Mambety, 1945-1998 ~
in N. Frank Ukadike, "The Hyena's Last Laugh: A Conversation with Djibril Diop Mambety,"
Transition 78, Vol. 8, No. 2, 1999

Dancing symbolizes the rhythmic, patterned movements of life itself. Music
and dance amplify and make manifest to our senses the unheard tones and
unseen waves that weave together the matter of existence. Even when we
are sitting most still or resting in deepest sleep, the atoms, molecules, cells,
tissues, organs, and systems of our bodies dance in astounding harmony
and exchange the ambient energies from air, water, food, and invisible
electromagnetic radiation.
~ Yaya Diallo, b. 1946 ~
in Yaya Diallo & Mitchell Hall, *The Healing Drum: African Wisdom Teachings*, 1989

My job is to be resilient. That's why I call life a dance.
~ Bill T. Jones, b. 1952 ~

There's nothing like the dance, there's nothing like tap dancing. It's a gift
that's given. You just have it: You can make music with your feet.
~ Dulé Hill, b. 1975 ~
"Dulé Hill of 'The West Wing'", CNN.com, 2000 December 6

DARING / CHALLENGE

What is left by the trembling one is taken by the one who climbs the tree.
~ Ovambo Wisdom ~
Wit & Wisdom of Africa: Proverbs from Africa & The Caribbean, Patrick Ibekwe, ed., 1998

If you like honey, fear not the bees.
~ Wolof Wisdom ~
Ibid.

Your daring has to be backed up with a willingness to lose that point. To make a bigger point, you might have to lose.
~ Katherine Dunham, 1910-2006 ~

The guy who takes a chance, who walks the line between the known and unknown, who is unafraid of failure, will succeed.
~ Gordon Parks, 1912-2006 ~
in *Brother's Keeper: Words of Inspiration for African-American Men*, Roderick Terry, ed., 1996

Living on the edge, living in and through your fear, is the summit of life ... people who refuse to take that dare condemn themselves to a life of living death.
~ John Harold Johnson, 1918-2005 ~
in *Brother's Keeper: Words of Inspiration for African-American Men*, Roderick Terry, ed., 1996

To act is to be committed, and to be committed is to be in danger.
~ James Baldwin, 1924-1987 ~
"My Dungeon Shook," *The Fire Next Time*, 1962

Challenges make you discover things about yourself that you never really knew. They're what make the instrument stretch, what make you go beyond the norm.
~ Cicely Tyson, b. 1933 ~

If those who made it did not have the courage and vision and made that "imaginary leap into the darkness," nothing would have happened. It is time we take creative risks.
~ Trevor Rhone, b. 1940 ~
in *Jamaica Sunday Gleaner*, 2001

If you run, you might lose. If you don't run, you're guaranteed to lose.
~ Jesse Jackson, b. 1941 ~

He who is not courageous enough to take risks will accomplish nothing in life.
~ Muhammad Ali, b. 1942 ~

Be determined to handle any challenge in a way that will make you grow.
~ Les Brown, b. 1945 ~

Even if you commit the enviable error of falling flat on your face because you dared to risk everything in the face of mockery, envy, and ever-lurking laughter ... remain undaunted, unhampered by fear; and always, always strive to be noble in that act of imagining which is now utterly yours: the supreme gift, and its accountability to your fellow travelers, and to all of us, and to the soul.
~ Thomas Glave, b. 1964 ~
"Fire & Ink: Toward a Quest for Language, History, and a Moral Imagination," 2002 Conference Address

We need to be more daring in our approach to life. Life has much more to offer than the same daily routine of least resistance and complacency. We must dare to take risks, face the unknown, go against the odds.
~ Roderick Terry, b. 1964 ~
Brother's Keeper: Words of Inspiration for African-American Men, 1996

Every risk we take is an opportunity for growth, a step toward self-discovery. Risks reveal to us a greater understanding of who we are by forcing us to exceed our usual limits ... Life is about taking chances and being able to express our creativity and individuality. It is healthy to break away from the usual modes of thinking or expectation.
~ Terry ~
"Hope Chest"

I told myself if I had one opportunity to make a significant impact, I would fly around the world to show kids that I did it and it didn't matter where I came from ... I went from washing planes to owning an aircraft worth $600,000. I also dared to follow my dream when everyone said I was too young and would not be able to afford it.
~ Barrington Irving, b. 1984 ~
Interview by Xavier Murphy, Jamaicans.com

DEATH / DYING

Death comes when the purpose of living is fulfilled; death shows what the reason for living was.
~ Khemetic Wisdom ~
Temt Tchaas: Egyptian Proverbs, Muata Ashaya Ashby, ed., 1994

If Death has come and killed your father and your mother, do not weep, saying, "My father and my mother are dead," but weep and say, "I and my father and my mother will go with you."
~ Ashanti Wisdom ~
Wit & Wisdom of Africa: Proverbs from Africa & The Caribbean, Patrick Ibekwe, ed., 1998

You must be willing to die in order to live.
~ Yoruba Wisdom ~

There is no such thing as dead matter: every being, every thing – be it only a grain of sand – radiates a life force, a sort of wave-particle.
~ Léopold Senghor, 1906-2001 ~
Négritude: a Humanism of the Twentieth Century, 1970

One realises one's heading for death. But that gives one a sense of deep possibilities.
~ Wilson Harris, b. 1921 ~
in Maya Jaggi, "Redemption Song," *The Guardian*, 2006 December 16

If you're afraid to die, you will not be able to live.
~ James Baldwin, 1924-1987 ~

Death is always close by. And what's important is not to know if you can avoid it, but to know that you have done the most possible to realize your ideas.
~ Frantz Fanon, 1925-1961 ~

What is there possibly left for us to be afraid of, after we have dealt face to face with death and not embraced it? Once I accept the existence of dying as a life process, who can ever have power over me again?
~ Audre Lorde, 1934-1992 ~
The Cancer Journals, 1980

Death's power is in our fear of it. Death's dominion is exercised not after the grave but before the grave.
~ Peter J. Gomes, b. 1942 ~

Once you're dead, you're made for life.
~ Jimi Hendrix, 1942-1970 ~

I do not know the end of my living and the beginning of my dying, for they – living and dying – are both mixed up.
~ Jamaica Kincaid, b. 1949 ~
Mr. Potter, 2002

The difference we normally place – to differentiate this existence from that one, dead from alive – is not a concern ... The boundaries are movable, they're exchangeable, they're equally symbolic.
~ Dionne Brand, b. 1953 ~
"She's A Wanderer," Interview by Suzanne Methot, Quill & Quire, 1999 April

Death results in simply a different form of belonging to the community. It is a lesson from nature that change is the norm, that the world is defined by eternal cycles of decline and regeneration ... Death is not a separation but a different form of communion, a higher form of connectedness with the community, providing an opportunity for even greater service.
~ Malidoma Somé, b. 1956 ~
The Healing Wisdom of Africa, 1999

Death is a natural part of life, spiritually speaking ... when you accept death, you accept life in all its simplicity, a life without all the trappings, life with its ups and downs, a happiness that comes and goes.
~ Abderrahmane Sissako, b. 1961 ~
Interview by Olivier Barlet, Africultures, 2003 April 18

Death has no power over the dead. It is only the living who fear it. When we learn to face the inevitable not grudgingly but joyfully, then we start to overcome our fear of death. By overcoming the fear, we learn the meaning of life.
~ Keith Boykin, b. 1965 ~
Respecting the Soul: Daily Reflections for Black Lesbians and Gays, 1999

Perhaps it was because I attended so many funerals that I have such a strong feeling that death is not the end, that the people we bury are going off to live somewhere else. But at the same time, they will always be hovering around to watch over us and guide us through our journeys.
~ Edwidge Danticat, b. 1969 ~
"We Are Ugly But We Are Here," The Caribbean Writer, Volume 10, 1996

DECISION / DECISIVENESS

Beware of irresolution in the intent of thy actions, beware of instability in the execution; so shalt thou triumph over two great failings of thy nature.
~ Khemetic Wisdom ~
Temt Tchaas: Egyptian Proverbs, Muata Ashaya Ashby, ed., 1994

Indecision is like the step-child: if he doesn't wash his hands he is called dirty; if he does, he is wasting water.
~ Madagascan Wisdom ~

When one's mind is made up, this dimishes fear; knowing what must be done does away with fear.
~ Rosa Parks, 1913-2005 ~
Quiet Strength, 1994

The longer I live, the more deeply I'm convinced that the diference between the successful person and the failure, between the strong and the weak, is a decision.
~ Willie E. Gary, b. 1947 ~

Truly successful decision making relies on a balance between deliberate and instinctive thinking.
~ Malcolm Gladwell, b. 1963 ~
Blink: The Power of Thinking Without Thinking, 2005

We control our destiny by the choices we make ... Our choices define who we are; each decision we make is an opportunity for personal growth and a deliberate step toward understanding our true essence.
~ Roderick Terry, b. 1964 ~
"Hope Chest"

Deciding to follow my own inner callings, deciding to just not be cowed by all the different sociopolitical scripts that I'd been raised with and not to succumb to the fear that had a lot to do with meeting the right person and my maturation process ... all of those things paved the way for my choice to proceed with fate.
~ Rebecca Walker, b. 1970 ~
Interview, Memoirville, Smith Magazine, 2007

DEFEAT

Your failures in life come from not realizing your nearness to success when you give up.
~ Yoruba Wisdom ~

Never let your head hang down. Never give up and sit and grieve. Find another way.
~ Satchel Paige, 1900-1982 ~

I prefer victorious bastards to legitimate people who give in!
~ Ousmane Sembène, 1923-2007 ~
Fespaco Press Conference, 2001 February 27

There is no better than adversity. Every defeat, every heartbreak, every loss, contains its own seed, its own lesson on how to improve your performance the next time.
~ Malcolm X, 1925-1965 ~

The encountering (of defeats) may be the very experience which creates the vitality and the power to endure.
~ Maya Angelou, b. 1928 ~

Never accept the negative thought, "I can't make it because I'm black." You can't concede defeat before you even start.
~ James Earl Jones, b. 1931 ~

It's easy to do anything in victory. It's in defeat that a man reveals himself.
~ Floyd Patterson, b. 1935 ~
in *The Boxing Book of Quotations*, Henry Mullan, ed., 1988

Defeat is not bitter unless you swallow it.
~ Joe Clark, b. 1939 ~

Winning is great, sure, but if you are really going to do something in life, the secret is learning how to lose. Nobody goes undefeated all the time.
~ Wilma Rudolph, 1940-1994 ~

You may not be responsible for getting knocked down, but you're certainly responsible for getting back up.
~ Jesse Jackson, b. 1941 ~

It might be true that all love is doomed to be unrequited or unfulfilled, because you never can consume or fully experience another person. Something will always elude you. That's what keeps you coming back, in a way.
~ John Edgar Wideman, b. 1941 ~
Interview by Laura Miller, *Salon*

Only a man who knows what it is like to be defeated can reach down to the bottom of his soul and come up with the extra ounce of power it takes to win when the match is even.
~ Muhammad Ali, b. 1942 ~

You must think of failure and defeat as the springboards to new achievements or to the next level of accomplishment.
~ Les Brown, b. 1945 ~

Just because Fate doesn't deal you the right cards, it doesn't mean you should give up. It just means you have to play the cards you get to their maximum potential.
~ Brown ~

You won't win until you learn how to lose … Along with everything else, you have to acquire the ability to accept defeat. No one makes it without stumbling.
~ Kareem Abdul-Jabbar, b. 1947 ~
Kareem, 1990

You can take from every experience what it has to offer you. And you cannot be defeated if you just keep taking one breath followed by another.
~ Oprah Winfrey, b. 1954 ~
"What I Know For Sure,," O *Magazine*, 2004 January

If you give up on your dream and stop right where you are, you never know what's around that corner.
~ Tyler Perry, b. 1970 ~
in "Talking the Dream, Growing the Brand," *New York Times*, 2007 June 6

DEFERMENT / DELAY

Indeed it is better to postpone, lest either we complete too little by
hurrying, or wander too long in completing it.
~ Tertullian, c. 160-240 ~

Soon come.
~ Jamaican Wisdom ~

What happens to a dream deferred?
Does it dry up like a raisin in the sun?
Or fester like a sore – and then run?
Does it stink like rotten meat?
Or crust and sugar over – like a syrupy sweet?
Maybe it just sags like a heavy load.
Or does it explode?
~ Langston Hughes, 1902-1967 ~
"Harlem," *Montage of a Dream Deferred*, 1951

We are now faced with the fact that tomorrow is today. We are confronted
with the fierce urgency of *now*. In this unfolding conundrum of life and
history there is such a thing as being too late. Procrastination is still the
thief of time. Life often leaves us standing bare, naked, and dejected with a
lost opportunity.
~ Martin Luther King, Jr., 1929-1968 ~
The Words of Martin Luther King, Jr., Coretta Scott King, ed., 1983

The waiting period is a time of comforting emptiness; thoughts that do not
necessarily have anything to do with the sickness of despair come and go
leaving nothing painful behind them.
~ Ayi Kwei Armah, b. 1939 ~
The Beautyful Ones Are Not Yet Born, 1968

Rather than live in the moment and enjoy life as it unfolds, we delude
ourselves into believing that the occurrence of some future act will
eventually make life worth smiling about.
~ Roderick Terry, b. 1964 ~
"Hope Chest"

DELUSION

Who is it that affirms most boldly? Who is it that holds his opinion most obstinately? Ever they who hath most ignorance; for they also have most pride.
~ Khemetic Wisdom ~
Temt Tchaas: Egyptian Proverbs, Muata Ashaya Ashby, ed., 1994

Beware lest you lose the substance by grasping at the shadow.
~ Aesop, fl. c. 550 BCE ~
"The Dog and the Shadow"

Two kinds of blindness are easily combined so that those who do not see really appear to see what is not.
~ Tertullian, c. 160-240 ~

Man aspires to know truth and the hidden things of nature, but this endeavor is difficult and can only be attained with great labor and patience ... Hence people hastily accept what they have heard from their fathers and shy from any (critical) examination.
~ Zara Yacob, 1599-1692 ~
The Treatise of Zara Yacob, Claude Sumner, tr., 1985

The illusion which exalts us is dearer to us than ten thousand truths.
~ Aleksandr Pushkin, 1799-1837 ~

A universal stupidity is the belief that our neighbor's success is the cause of our failure.
~ Charles V. Roman, 1864-1934 ~
"What the Negro May Reasonably Expect of the White Man," *American Civilization and the Negro*, 1916

If prejudice could reason, it would dispel itself.
~ William Pickens, 1881-1954 ~
The New Negro, 1914

Through a sort of protective social mimicry forced upon him by the adverse circumstances of dependence ... the Negro has been more of a formula than a human being ... The thinking Negro even has been induced to share this same general attitude, to focus his attention on controversial issues, to see himself in the distorted perspective of a social problem. His shadow, so to speak, has been more real to him than his

personality ... Little true social or self-understanding has or could come from such a situation.
~ Alain Locke, 1886-1954 ~
The New Negro, 1925

The resort to stereotype is the first refuge and chief strategy of the bigot.
~ Bayard Rustin, 1912-1987 ~

Nobody is more dangerous than he who imagines himself pure in heart, for his purity, by definition, is unassailable.
~ James Baldwin, 1924-1987 ~
Nobody Knows My Name: More Notes of a Native Son, 1961

Nothing in all the world is more dangerous than sincere ignorance and conscientious stupidity.
~ Martin Luther King, Jr., 1929-1968 ~

Once you begin to explain or excuse all events on racial grounds, you begin to indulge in the perilous mythology of race.
~ James Earl Jones, b. 1931 ~

We have been raised to fear the yes in ourselves.
~ Audre Lorde, 1934-1992 ~

In the process of overcoming those images which others project on me, I have an enormous responsibility not to project myths on others in turn ... what we're experiencing now calls on each of us to respect difference, not to assume that incorrect notions about gender are the possession of men alone, or to assume that it's only white folk who can project notions of bigotry and hatred. This is something we all better check ourselves out on.
~ Johnnetta Cole, b. 1936 ~
"Spelman's First Female President," Academy of Achievement Interview, 1996 June 28

Words can be webs, making us think in terms of essences; language is all concept, but things in the world are devoid of essence, changing as we chase them. Life must always be greater than our ideas about life.
~ Charles Johnson, b. 1948 ~
"Reading the Eightfold Path," *Dharma, Color, and Culture*, Hilda Gutiérrez Baldoquín, ed., 2004

When you start thinking that your way of thinking of stuff is the world thinking of it, then you fall into a type of narcissism that leads to real decline. Because then you shut off the possibility that you might be wrong, and you never really know if what you are thinking is not correct.
~ Wynton Marsalis, b. 1961 ~
"Music's Jazz Maestro," Academy of Achievement Interview, 1991 January 8

DEPENDENCE

A person who depends on others is not himself or herself but really the subject of others.
~ Marcus Garvey, 1887-1940 ~

Oh, how disgusting life becomes when on every hand you hear people (who bear your image, who bear your resemblance) telling you that they cannot make it, that fate is against them, that they cannot get a chance. If 400,000,000 Negroes can only get to know themselves, to know that in them is a sovereign power, is an authority that is absolute, then in the next twenty-four hours we would have a new race, we would have a nation, an empire, resurrected not from the will of others to see us rise, but from our own determination to rise, irrespective of what the world thinks.
~ Garvey ~

Don't depend on other people to be responsible for you. Don't make yourself stressed out over nonsensical things like material things.
~ Eartha Kitt, b. 1927 ~
Interview by Blase DiStefano, "Eartha Kitt *Purr*-severes: The Feline Feminist Talks About Her Two Lives as the Child and the Woman," *OutSmart*

You can't base your life on other people's expectations.
~ Stevie Wonder, b. 1950 ~

If you don't trust yourself to be involved in transforming that which needs to be changed, then you end up waiting for someone else to come along and do the work for you. This leads to a constant state of dependence on some external authority, when the means to achieving what you want sits within yourself.
~ Malidoma Somé, b. 1956 ~
The Healing Wisdom of Africa, 1999

DEPRESSION / DESPAIR / DISTRESS

To destroy an undesirable rate of mental vibration, concentrate on the opposite vibration to the one to be suppressed ... What is the source of sadness but feebleness of the mind? What gives it power but the want of reason? Rouse yourself to the combat, and it quits the field before you strike.
~ Khemetic Wisdom ~
Temt Tchaas: Egyptian Proverbs, Muata Ashaya Ashby, ed., 1994

Do not prefer death in misfortune out of despair.
~ Khemetic Wisdom ~
Wit & Wisdom of Africa: Proverbs from Africa & The Caribbean, Patrick Ibekwe, ed., 1998

Brooding deepens despair.
~ Shona Wisdom ~
Ibid.

It's when you're down that you learn about your faults.
~ Claude McKay, 1889-1948 ~

One has to go on. If one refuses to survive, if one refuses to "manage", one has given in to despair. And I don't think anybody has a right to despair, because it is not possible for any one person to have all the variables to give an answer to a particular situation. So we do the best we can and move on from day to day.
~ Ama Ata Aidoo, b. 1942 ~
in Adeola James, Interview with Aidoo, *In Their Own Voices: African Women Writers Talk*, 1990

One can be totally destitute, and yet it is in that state of destitution that one finds human dignity, fundamental values.
~ Abderrahmane Sissako, b. 1961 ~
"A Screenplay Is Not A Guarantee," Interview by Kwame Anthony Appiah

Recognizing that I had had a history of depression and being active in addressing that and resolving for myself that I didn't have to repeat some of those things that I had grown up with, all of those things paved the way for my choice to proceed with fate.
~ Rebecca Walker, b. 1970 ~
Interview, Memoirville, *Smith Magazine*, 2007

DESIRE

We would often be sorry if our wishes were gratified.
~ Aesop, fl. c. 550 BCE ~
"The Old Man and Death"

The desire is thy prayers; and if thy desire is without ceasing, thy prayer will also be without ceasing. The continuance of your longing is the continuance of your prayer.
~ Augustine of Hippo, 354-430 ~

One who chooses is never without desire.
~ Swahili Wisdom ~

Desires tie.
~ Kikuyu Wisdom ~
Wit & Wisdom of Africa: Proverbs from Africa & The Caribbean, Patrick Ibekwe, ed., 1998

The want of a thing is more than its worth.
~ Jamaican Wisdom ~

Our visions begin with our desires.
~ Audre Lorde, 1934-1992 ~

Decide that you want it more than you are afraid of it.
~ Bill Cosby, b. 1937 ~

Repression of your will and desire are the cornerstones of stress. When you believe, or are led to believe, you are unable to act upon the greatest desires of the soul, the result is mental and spiritual enslavement.
~ Iyanla Vanzant, b. 1953 ~
Acts of Faith: Daily Meditations for People of Color, 1993

Very much like people, desires need to be noticed. Under scrutiny, a lot of desires will just fizzle, whether it's things … or people. When we actually pay attention to them, we begin to notice that so many of our cravings just don't hold water.
~ Angel Kyodo Williams ~
Being Black: Zen and the Art of Living with Fearlessness and Grace, 2000

DETACHMENT

The purpose of practicing detachment is to separate us from our present reactions to life and attach us to our aim in life. This inner separation must be developed by practice. At first we seem to have no power to separate ourselves from undesirable inner states, simply because we have always taken every mood, every reaction, as natural and have become identified with them. When we have no idea that our reactions are only states of consciousness from which it is possible to separate ourselves, we go round and round in the same circle of problems – not seeing them as inner states but as outer situations. We practice detachment, or inner separation, that we may escape from the circle of our habitual reactions to life. That is why we must formulate an aim and constantly notice ourselves in regard to that aim.
~ Neville, 1905-1972 ~
"Fundamentals," *New Thought*, Summer 1953

Looking at life's situations from a distance is the first step toward finding a solution and preventing them from happening again. By separating yourself from your experiences, you are able to move on with your life. If you don't, you're stuck in the puddle of the past without a paddle.
~ Famous Amos, b. 1937 ~
Watermelon Magic, 1996

Avoid having your ego so close to your position that when your position falls, your ego goes with it.
~ Colin Powell, b. 1937 ~

Being detached in order to see better is not the same thing as pessimism ... All societies have talked of prophets who had to withdraw into the wilderness or into the mountains to meditate ... These are the seers.
~ Ngugi wa Thiong'o, b. 1938 ~
Interview by Michael Alexander Pozo, St. John's University, 2004 August 16

Between having desires and allowing them to consume us is the difference between attachment and detachment. People who are detached don't *not* want anything. It's that they can still live and function and flow when they don't get what they want, or when things don't work out as they wish.
~ Angel Kyodo Williams ~
"A Revolutionary Practice," Interview by Jenny Kinscy, beliefnet.com

DETERMINATION / PERSISTENCE / RESOLVE

As a camel beareth labor, and heat, and hunger, and thirst, through deserts of sand, and fainteth not; so the fortitude of a man shall sustain him through all perils.
~ Akhenaton, c. 1385-c. 1355 BCE ~

We will either find a way, or make one.
~ Hannibal, 247-183 BCE ~

To fall and rise up again is the journey of this world.
~ Igbo Wisdom ~
Wit & Wisdom of Africa: Proverbs from Africa & The Caribbean, Patrick Ibekwe, ed., 1998

The persistent drop rots the spot on which it falls.
~ Ugandan Wisdom ~
Ibid.

The quick one may not win; the enduring one will.
~ Tswana Wisdom ~
Ibid.

If you're hungry, tired, sick, or scared; if you can't make another step –
keep-a-goin!
~ Harriet Tubman, c. 1822-1913 ~

Lose not courage, lose not faith, go forward.
~ Marcus Garvey, 1887-1940 ~
Philosophy and Opinions of Marcus Garvey, Vol. I, Amy Jacques Garvey, ed., 1923

You keep trying! You never give up; you always have an optimistic viewpoint ... It's not so much confidence as it is curiosity and knowing that the capability is there – if you try. If you fail, you fail. But nothing is better than a good try.
~ Gordon Parks, 1912-2006 ~

The greatest glory in living lies not in never falling, but in rising every time we fall.
~ Nelson Mandela, b. 1918 ~
Long Walk to Freedom, 1994

As long as I can stand it, God, I'll keep on keeping on.
~ Ray Charles, 1930-2004 ~

There's probably little in life that matters more than first believing in one's ability to do something, and then having the sheer grit, the sheer determination, the perseverance to carry it through.
~ Johnnetta Cole, b. 1936 ~
"Spelman's First Female President," Academy of Achievement Interview, 1996 June 28

Wherever you are tonight, you can make it. Hold your head high; stick your chest out. You can make it. It gets dark sometimes, but the morning comes. Don't you surrender.
~ Jesse Jackson, b. 1941 ~

When life knocks you down, try to land on your back. Because if you can look up, you can get up. Let your reason get you back up.
~ Les Brown, b. 1945 ~

Making your mark on the world is hard. If it were easy, everybody would do it. But it's not. It takes patience, it takes commitment, and it comes with plenty of failure along the way. The real test is not whether you avoid this failure, because you won't. It's whether you let it harden or shame you into inaction, or whether you learn from it; whether you choose to persevere.
~ Barack Obama, b. 1961 ~
Speech, 2006 July 12

You have to realize that if you have an idea or passion for something, if people reject it, don't think it's not good enough. When you have a dream, when you have a goal, you have to pursue it because not everyone is going to see it. You can't let anyone limit you. Take advantage of your education. Take advantage of your opportunity.
~ Barrington Irving, b. 1984 ~
Address, CUNY Aviation Institute, 2007 March 26

Although one may try and fail sometimes in the bid to attain a positive goal, the will and determination to try again remains an essential element of survival and progress in an individual's life, whether material or spiritual.
~ Oliver Mbamara ~
"When One Door Closes," Why Are We Here?, 2003

DIFFERENTIATION / DIVISION / SEPARATION

Gender is in everything; everything has its masculine and feminine principles; gender manifests on all planes.
~ Hermes Trismegistus ~
in *The Kybalion: A Study of the Hermetic Philosophy*, 1908

I know the dark delight of being strange,
The penalty of difference in the crowd,
The loneliness of wisdom among fools.
~ Claude McKay, 1889-1948 ~
"My House"

Men often hate each other because they fear each other; they fear each other because they do not know each other; they do not know each other because they cannot communicate; they cannot communicate because they are separated.
~ A. Philip Randolph, 1889-1979 ~

The emotional, sexual, and psychological stereotyping of females begins when the doctor says: "It's a girl."
~ Shirley Chisholm, 1924-2005 ~

Freedom and justice cannot be parceled out in pieces to suit political convenience.
~ Coretta Scott King, 1927-2006 ~

Just because you are different does not mean that you have to be rejected.
~ Eartha Kitt, b. 1927 ~
Interview by Blase DiStefano, "Eartha Kitt *Purr*-severes: The Feline Feminist Talks About Her Two Lives as the Child and the Woman," *OutSmart*

The diaspora experience ... is defined, not by essence or purity, but by the recognition of a necessary heterogeneity and diversity; by a conception of "identity" which lives with and through, not despite, difference; by *hybridity*. Diaspora identities are those which are constantly producing and reproducing themselves anew, through transformation and difference.
~ Stuart Hall, b. 1932 ~
"Cultural Identity and Diaspora," *Colonial Discourse & Postcolonial Theory: A Reader*, Patrick Williams & Laura Chrisman, eds., 1990

It is not our differences that divide us. It is our inability to recognize,
accept and celebrate those differences.
~ Audre Lorde, 1934-1992 ~

The sharing of joy, whether physical, emotional, psychic, or intellectual,
forms a bridge between the sharers which can be the basis for
understanding much of what is not shared between them, and lessens the
threat of their difference.
~ Lorde ~

If folk can learn to be racist, then they can learn to be anti-racist. If being a
sexist ain't genetic, then, dad gum, people can learn about gender equality.
~ Johnnetta Cole, b. 1936 ~

Your intellect feels discontent
With having and not labelling …
To fix in one quick-drying definition.
You must not try to cram us all
Into your little box;
Your definition must perforce be false
Or we are dead.
~ Mervyn Morris, b. 1937 ~
"To a West Indian Definer"

The effort to separate ourselves whether by race, creed, color, religion, or
status is as costly to the separator as to those who would be separated …
The task that remains is to cope with our interdependence – to see
ourselves reflected in every other human being and to respect and honor
our differences.
~ Melba Beals, b. 1941 ~
Warriors Don't Cry, 1994

Colorism, like colonialism, sexism, and racism, impedes us.
~ Alice Walker, b. 1944 ~

The "differences" between "I" and "other" are merely the illusory uniforms
worn by the invisible and indivisible, in order to experience the illusory
play of separateness.
~ Mooji, b. 1954 ~

For most ... the stark visibility of the seen world affects their perception of the unseen world. Discrimination begins when you say that you can touch this and that, and therefore the tangible begins to supercede the reality of the intangible.
~ Malidoma Somé, b. 1956 ~
The Healing Wisdom of Africa, 1999

Gender has very little to do with anatomy. It is purely energetic. In that context, a male who is physically male can vibrate female energy, and vice versa. Anatomic differences are simply there to determine who contributes what for the continuity of the tribe.
~ Somé ~
"Gay Guardians of the Gate," Interview by Bert H. Hoff, in *M.E.N. Magazine*, 1993

It's no longer enough, if it ever was, to critique interlocking systems of oppression without offering affirming alternatives of how society should and can reconstitute itself. As we move into the inevitably more demanding multilingual, multicultural environment – both nationally and globally – of the next century, our greatest task will be an inversion of the commonly assumed equivalence between difference and disunity. We must re-write this equation, demonstrating again and again that unity does not require unanimity, that unity – that is, a sense of social cohesion, of community – can and does derive from the expression, comprehension, and active nurturing (and not merely tolerance or fetishization) of difference.
~ Marlon Riggs, 1957-1994 ~
Introduction, *Standards*, V5N1, 1992

A club involves membership – some people are in it and some people are out of it. There you have at the very inception ... a notion of dissonance between belonging and not belonging ... Obviously, that does involve conformity to some extent, but it's pushed quite early and quite vigorously right at the inception, beyond mere conformity.
~ Caryl Phillips, b. 1958 ~
Conversation with Alastair Niven, "English Literature and Empire Exhibition," British Library

We are all the same. The difference lies only in our choices. The ones we have made and the ones we make.
~ Oliver Mbamara ~

DILIGENCE

Be diligent as long as you live, always doing more than is commanded of you.
~Khemetic Wisdom ~
Selections from the Husia: Sacred Wisdom of Ancient Egypt, Maulana Karenga, tr., 1984

If you are a man who leads, a man who controls the affairs of many, then seek the most perfect way of performing your responsibility so that your conduct will be blameless.
~ Ptahotep, c. 2350 BCE ~
in *The Teachings of Ptahhotep: The Oldest Book in the World*, Asa Hilliard, Larry Williams & Nia Damali, eds., 1987

Do not speak falsely for you are great; do not act lightly for you have weight; be not untrue for you are the balance and do not swerve, for you are the standard.
~ *Book of Khun-Anup (The Eloquent Peasant)* ~
in *Kemet and the African Worldview*, Maulana Karenga & Jacob Carruthers, eds., 1986

Be industrious, let thine eyes be open, lest thou become a beggar, for the man that is idle cometh not to honor.
~ Khemetic Wisdom ~
Temt Tchaas: Egyptian Proverbs, Muata Ashaya Ashby, ed., 1994

Nothing is so difficult that diligence cannot conquer it.
~ Malagasy Wisdom ~
Wit & Wisdom of Africa: Proverbs from Africa & The Caribbean, Patrick Ibekwe, ed., 1998

People, in their rashness and ignorance, like to condemn things that are difficult and obscure, rather than ... learn their meaning by diligent painstaking.
~ Origen, c. 185-255 ~
De Principiis, Book 3

How much easier it is to preach than to do – but stop – we know good from evil; and, in serious truth, we have powers sufficient to withstand vice, if we will choose to exert ourselves. In the field, if we know the strength and situation of the enemy, we place out-posts and sentinels – and take every prudent method to avoid surprise. In common life we must

do the same; – and trust me, my honest friend, a victory gained over passion, immorality, and pride, deserves *Te Deums,* better than those gained in the fields of ambition and blood.
~ Ignatius Sancho, 1729-1780 ~
Letter VII to Mr M, 1770 March 21 in *The Letters of the Late Ignatius Sancho, an African,* Vol. I, 1782

Do what is required of you and remain a slave. Do more than is required and become free.
~ Marcus Garvey, 1887-1940 ~
in Roderick Terry, *One Million Strong: A PhotographicTribute of the Million Man March,* 1996

The only place success comes before work is in the dictionary.
~ Satchel Paige, 1900-1982 ~

If you want to continue living in poverty without clothes and food, then go and drink in the shebeens. But if you want better things, you must work hard. We cannot do it all for you; you must do it yourselves.
~ Nelson Mandela, b. 1918 ~
Long Walk to Freedom, 1994

If you want to be the best, Baby, you've got to work harder than anybody else.
~ Sammy Davis, Jr., 1925-1990 ~

There is no obstacle in the path of young people who are poor or members of minority groups that hard work and preparation cannot cure.
~ Barbara Jordan, 1936-1996 ~

When a job is once begun, never stop until it's done.
Be the job large or small, do it right or not at all.
~ Carol Moseley-Braun, b. 1947 ~

My philosophy is that not only are you responsible for your life, but doing the best at this moment puts you in the best place for the next moment.
~ Oprah Winfrey, b. 1954 ~

Doing our best is a self-contained principle, which can only be measured by personal standards. Doing our best means using all of our talents and abilities to the fullest potential, being able to recognize our weaknesses and maximize our strengths, and living up to our own standards. In any situation, as long as we do our best, we never have to worry about the end result of our efforts.
~ Roderick Terry, b. 1964 ~
"Hope Chest"

DIRECTION

Radiance is still there, as before,
but we don't face the right direction.
~ *Prophecies of Nefer-Rohu* ~
Khemetic Text, 2000 BCE
in *Desert Wisdom: Sacred Middle Eastern Writings from the Goddess Through the Sufis*, Neil Douglas-Klotz, tr., 1995

While the minds of most of us, black and white, have thus burrowed in the trenches ... the actual march of development has simply flanked these positions, necessitating a sudden reorientation of view. We have not been watching in the right direction; set North and South on a sectional axis, we have not noticed the East till the sun has us blinking.
~ Alain Locke, 1886-1954 ~
The New Negro, 1925

It isn't where you came from; it's where you're going that counts.
~ Ella Fitzgerald, 1917-1996 ~
in Stuart Nicholson, *Ella Fitzgerald*, 1994

One must know when you blaze trails that some of them are going to go in the wrong direction. And you're going to have to come back and go another way.
~ Lloyd Richards, 1919-2006 ~
Interview by St. Clair Bourne, 1999

A mountain can never be climbed looking down. The direction should always be onward and upward, and with faith, focus, discipline, dedication and hard work, our dreams will be realized.
~ Leontyne Price, b. 1927 ~

No man can know where he is going unless he knows exactly where he has been and exactly how he arrived at his present place ... Each of us has the right and the responsibility to assess the roads which lie ahead, and those over which we have travelled, and if the future road looms ominous or unpromising, and the roads back uninviting, then we need to gather our resolve and, carrying only the necessary baggage, step off that road into another direction.
~ Maya Angelou, b. 1928 ~

The line of progress is never straight. For a period of movement may follow a straight line and then it encounters obstacles and the path bends.
~ Martin Luther King, Jr., 1929-1968 ~

To be black and female in a society which is both racist and sexist is to be in the unique position of having nowhere to go but up!
~ Rosemary Brown, 1930-2003 ~

Why don't you study your grandmother and work back to Timbuktu? You can't make this leap over there to those African kingdoms without understanding who you are. You don't have to go to Africa to be an African. Africa is right here ... You don't need to make that leap across the ocean.
~ August Wilson, 1945-2005 ~
Interview by Bonnie Lyons & George Plimpton, *Paris Review*, No. 153, Winter 1999

Look inside to find out where you're going, and it's better to do it before you get out of high school.
~ Prince, b. 1958 ~

A word I've been talking about for ten years – diversity. I refuse to be going in just one direction. I have the possibility to touch different directions, and it's great for me.
~ Youssou N'Dour, b. 1959 ~
Interview by Banning Eyre and Sean Barlow, Afropop.org, 2004 May

(We) have to make some decisions that relate to the next 10 or 15 years. Because that's just life and we all have to make that walk ... and life is only a quick minute here.
~ Walter Beasley ~
Interview by Baldwin "Smitty" Smith, JazzMonthly.com

If there ever comes a time when you feel like you have to go someplace to find a better you and you're going any farther than the mirror, don't take another step. As long as you are looking toward anything but yourself, you'll always be headed in the wrong direction.
~ Angel Kyodo Williams ~
Being Black: Zen and the Art of Living with Fearlessness and Grace, 2000

DISCIPLINE

If you do not rise when you do not want to, you will not arrive when you want to.
~ Fulani Wisdom ~
Wit & Wisdom of Africa: Proverbs from Africa & The Caribbean, Patrick Ibekwe, ed., 1998

Discipline of the mind is a basic ingredient of genuine morality, and therefore of spiritual strength.
~ Haile Selassie, 1892-1975 ~

We must practice separating ourselves from our negative moods and thoughts in the midst of all the troubles and disasters of daily life. No one can be different from what he is now unless he begins to separate himself from his present reactions and to identify himself with his aim. Detachment from negative states and assumption of the wish fulfilled must be practiced in the midst of all the blessings and cursings of life. The way of true metaphysics lies in the midst of all that is going on in life. We must constantly practice self-observation, thinking from our aim, and detachment from negative moods and thoughts if we would be doers of truth instead of mere hearers.
~ Neville, 1905-1972~
"Fundamentals," *New Thought*, Summer 1953

To get where you want to go you can't only do what you like.
~ Peter Abrahams, b. 1919 ~
Tell Freedom, 1954

I punish myself more than anybody else does if I am stupid about my actions in public or whatever, and therefore I suffer, really suffer. I am not saying this in a bad way, because I learn from these things. And I analyze myself and I have to exorcise that feeling out of me. So, my exercise and being outdoors will exorcise me from doing that to a great extent.
~ Eartha Kitt, b. 1927 ~
Interview by Blase DiStefano, "Eartha Kitt *Purr*-severes: The Feline Feminist Talks About Her Two Lives as the Child and the Woman," *OutSmart*

I become something different when I don't attend to the little things … I feel that especially when it's chores I don't want to do, like taking out the garbage or doing my laundry. It's in the act of having to do things that you

don't want to that you learn something about moving past the self. Past the
ego.
~ bell hooks, b. 1952 ~
Interview by John Perry Barlow, *Shambhala Sun*

I have no discipline. I have no habits beyond avoidance of work. I describe
my process as throwing myself at the computer often enough that writing
happens.
~ Nalo Hopkinson, b. 1960 ~
Interview by Kellie Magnus, *Caribbean Review of Books*, Issue 73

I believed in studying just because I knew that education was a privilege.
And it wasn't so much necessarily the information that you were studying,
but just the discipline of study, to get into the habit of doing something
that you don't want to do, to receive the information, and then eventually
you start to like it.
~ Wynton Marsalis, b. 1961 ~
"Music's Jazz Maestro," Academy of Achievement Interview, 1991 January 8

By eliminating idle and unproductive behavior, self-discipline helps us to
concentrate on more worthwhile pursuits. When we are disciplined, we are
more likely to follow through with our dreams and aspirations ... it is vital
to control our thinking. A disciplined mind is a precursor to personal
growth.
~ Roderick Terry, b. 1964 ~
"Hope Chest"

Discipline does not just mean restraint. Rather, it can actually give you
more freedom as you learn to live without some things. You learn to
simplify your life and eliminate artificial needs. You learn to focus your
energy on the things that are important to you and avoid the diversions
that distract you from your goals.
~ Keith Boykin, b. 1965 ~
Respecting the Soul: Daily Reflections for Black Lesbians and Gays, 1999

DISCLOSURE / VERACITY

Words cannot give wisdom if they stray from the truth.
~ Khemetic Wisdom ~
Temt Tchaas: Egyptian Proverbs, Muata Ashaya Ashby, ed., 1994

Say not unto thyself, Behold, truth breedeth hatred, and I will avoid it;
dissimulation raiseth friends, and I will follow it. Are not the enemies made
by truth, better than the friends obtained by flattery?
~ Akhenaton, c. 1385-c. 1355 BCE ~

Do not bear witness with false words,
So as to brush aside a man by your tongue.
~ Amenemope, c. 11th C. BCE ~
The Instruction of Amenemope, Ch. 1, Miriam Lichtheim, tr.

Do not separate your mind from your tongue.
~ Khemetic Wisdom ~
Wit & Wisdom of Africa: Proverbs from Africa & The Caribbean, Patrick Ibekwe, ed., 1998

One who loves you does not spare you the truth.
~ Kigezi Wisdom ~
in *Black Woman's Gumbo Ya-Ya*, Terri L. Jewell, ed., 1993

Better a refusal than deception.
~ Malinke Wisdom ~

Truth keeps the hands cleaner than soap.
~ West African Proverb ~

Bitter truth is better than sweet falsehood.
~ Swahili Wisdom ~

Tell the truth and shame the devil.
~ African-American Wisdom ~

The end of an ox is beef and the end of a lie is grief.
~ Madagascan Wisdom ~

There are rare instances when truth is best served by silence.
~ Gordon Parks, 1912-2006 ~
in Roderick Terry, *One Million Strong: A PhotographicTribute of the Million Man March*, 1996

Truth-tellers are not always palatable. There is a preference for candy bars.
~ Gwendolyn Brooks, 1917-2000 ~
"Song for Winnie"

Whenever truth is spoken there is somewhere an increase of understanding and faith.
~ Pearl Bailey, 1918-1990 ~

Once you speak against the popular version of the truth, then you must be willing to pay the price for doing so.
~ Louis Farrakhan, b. 1934 ~
Speech at The Kennedy Center, 1985 July 22

In becoming forcibly and essentially aware of my mortality, and of what I wished and wanted for my life, however short it might be, priorities and omissions became strongly etched in a merciless light, and what I most regretted were my silences. Of what had I ever been afraid? To question or to speak as I believed could have meant pain, or death. But we all hurt in so many different ways, all the time, and pain will either change or end. Death, on the other hand, is the final silence. And that might be coming quickly, now, without regard for whether I had ever spoken what needed to be said, or had only betrayed myself into small silences, while I planned someday to speak, or waited for someone else's words. And I began to recognize a source of power within myself that comes from the knowledge that while it is most desirable not to be afraid, learning to put fear into perspective gave me great strength.
~ Audre Lorde, 1934-1992 ~
Sister Outsider: Essays and Speeches, 1984

People who have suffered from the wanton cruelty of others prefer the truth at all times, no matter what it might cost them.
~ Bessie Head, 1937-1986 ~
A Question of Power, 1973

Speak truth to power.
~ Marion Wright Edelman, b. 1939 ~
The Measure of Our Success, 1992

A wise person speaks carefully and with truth, for every word that passes between one's teeth is meant for something.
~ Molefi Kete Asante, b. 1942 ~
"Nija: The Way," *Afrocentricity*, 1988

If it pleases you, or it doesn't please you, you tell the truth. Never say the opposite.
~ Salif Keita, b. 1949 ~
"Bobo"

A lie is a temporary solution to a permanent problem.
~ Terry McMillan, b. 1951 ~

When nobody speaks your name, or even knows it, you, knowing it, must be the first to speak it.
~ Marlon Riggs, 1957-1994 ~

And so my own truth telling, as far as I'm able to muster up the courage to say what needs to be said, and that thing is on a continuum because all of us are made cowards by the realization that ultimately we have never said everything we're supposed to say.
~ Michael Eric Dyson, b. 1958 ~
"Some of Us Are in First Class, But The Plane Is in Trouble," Unvarnished Truth Awards, 2005

This impulse to speak is important for it is often activated by a moral impulse to tell the truth and avoid the tyranny of silence.
~ Caryl Phillips, b. 1958 ~
"Finding Oneself at Home," *The Guardian*, 2006 January 21

Some things must be said, and there are times when silence becomes an accomplice to injustice.
~ Ayaan Hirsi Ali, b. 1969 ~
Infidel, 2007

Coming out and telling my truth as I lived it and not being afraid of the consequences has been very liberating for me and I would say I'm healthier for it ... I'm a much healthier human being as a result of being able to tell the truth and not have unrealistic expectations.
~ Rebecca Walker, b. 1970 ~
Interview, Memoirville, *Smith Magazine*, 2007

DISPATCH

Better the small deed of the quick than the large one of him who delays.
~ Khemetic Wisdom ~
Wit & Wisdom of Africa: Proverbs from Africa & The Caribbean, Patrick Ibekwe, ed., 1998

The ox that runs ahead is the one who drinks clear water.
~ Haitian Wisdom ~
Ibid.

This is our chance. We must act now. Tomorrow may be too late and the opportunity will have passed.
~ Kwame Nkrumah, 1909-1972 ~
I Speak of Freedom: A Statement of African Ideology, 1961

A wise man who has the moment in his hand should not let the moment slip.
~ Nelson Mandela, b. 1918 ~
in Roderick Terry, One Million Strong: A Photographic Tribute of the Million Man March, 1996

If you think there is something that needs to be done, do it; don't talk about it. I've gone through endless talk about all the same issues, and they repeat themselves cyclically. At some point you say: "I'm not going around that circle again. I've been there."
~ Lloyd Richards, 1919-2006 ~
in Sharon Fitzgerald, "The Griot Wears a Watch," American Visions, 1998 August-September

You must take action now that will move you towards your goals. Develop a sense of urgency in your life.
~ Les Brown, b. 1945 ~

The way to overcome procrastinating is to take immediate action. Often, too much contemplation or waiting for the right time can be counter-productive. The present is always ripe for meaningful and positive change.
~ Roderick Terry, b. 1964 ~
"Hope Chest"

DISTRACTION / DIVERSION

To busy oneself with what is futile when one can do something useful, to attend to what is simple when one has the mettle to attempt what is difficult, is to strip talent of its dignity. It is a sin not to do what one is capable of doing.
~ José Martí, 1853-1895 ~
Martí Pensamientos, Carlos Ripoll, ed.

Perhaps the whole root of our trouble, the human trouble, is that we will sacrifice all the beauty of our lives, will imprison ourselves in totems, taboos, crosses, blood sacrifices, steeples, mosques, races, armies, flags, nations, in order to deny the fact of death, which is the only fact we have.
~ James Baldwin, 1924-1987 ~
The Fire Next Time, 1962

I never learned to stop at the skin. If I looked at a man or a woman, I wanted to see inside. Being distracted by shading or coloring is stupid. It gets in the way. It's something I just can't see.
~ Ray Charles, 1930-2004 ~
Brother Ray, 1978

Many times in life we are faced with challenging situations that take away our commitment to be the best we can. We forget some positive promise or resolution we may have made. It could be for a moment, a day, a month or years, but the bottom line is that the situation makes us forget who we are or some positive thing we have promised to be doing. Yet Life being so kind, brings us to the spot where we are reminded of who we are and given the chance to express the divinity in us.
~ Oliver Mbamara ~

For very good historical, political, and socio-economic reasons we are fixated on instant gratification ... Feeding our desires is very much a part of our culture here, and part of the culture we have created in order to have some sense of equality with our white counterpart. But that has also led to a dearth of spiritual sensibility.
~ Angel Kyodo Williams ~
"A Revolutionary Practice," Interview by Jenny Kinscy, beliefnet.com

DIVERSITY / MULTIPLICITY

The tongues are diverse in speech,
Their forms likewise and their skins are distinguished.
~ Akhenaton, c. 1385-c. 1355 BCE ~
in James H. Breasted, *Development of Religion and Thought in Ancient Egypt*

There are as many opinions as there are people: each has his own point of view.
~ Terence, c. 190-159 BCE ~

Manhattan is not merely the largest Negro community in the world, but the first concentration in history of so many diverse elements of Negro life. It has attracted the African, the West Indian, the Negro American; has brought together the Negro of the North and the Negro of the South; the man from the city and the man from the town and village; the peasant, the student, the businessman, the professional man, artist, poet, musician, adventurer and worker, preacher and criminal, exploiter and social outcast. Each group has come with its own separate motives and for its own special ends, but their greatest experience has been the finding of one another.
~ Alain Locke, 1886-1954 ~
The New Negro, 1925

Cultural pluralism: it's the air we breathe; it's the ground we stand on.
~ Ralph Ellison, 1914-1994 ~

Diversity is not an abnormality but the very reality of our planet. The human world manifests the same reality and will not seek our permission to celebrate itself in the magnificence of its endless varieties. Civility is a sensible attribute in this kind of world we have; narrowness of heart and mind is not.
~ Chinua Achebe, b. 1930 ~
Bates College Commencement Address, 1996 May 27

I have Dutch, nigger and English in me,
and either I'm nobody, or I'm a nation.
~ Derek Walcott, b. 1930 ~
"The Schooner Flight"

The plurality of existence is a given ... any cosmology that we are going to embrace from now on in the so-called twenty-first century has to take that on board.
~ Rex Nettleford, b. 1933 ~
Address, Round Table: Dialogue Among Civilizations, United Nations, New York, 2000 September 5

My work is about difference, my work is about how we learn to lie down with the different parts of ourselves, so that we can in fact learn to respect and honor the different parts of each other, so that we in fact can learn to use them moving toward something that needs being done, that has never been done before.
~ Audre Lorde, 1934-1992 ~
Radio Interview, 1988

Nobody's ordinary. Each one of us is special and it's the coming together of alla that that makes the world so fine.
~ Ntozake Shange, b. 1948 ~
Betsey Brown, 1985

We've got to conceive of new forms of community. We each have multiple identities and we're moving in and out of various communities at the same time. There is no one grand black community.
~ Cornel West, b. 1954 ~
in "Marlon Riggs' Haunting 'Black Is ... Black Ain't' to Open in New York and Boston," Standards, V5N1, 1992

We have much wisdom to gain by learning to understand other people's cultures and permitting ourselves to accept that there is more than one version of reality.
~ Malidoma Somé, b. 1956 ~

A truly multicultural society is one which is composed of multicultural individuals; people who are able to synthesize different worlds in one body and to live comfortably with these different worlds ... the society must by definition be open, fluid and confident.
~ Caryl Phillips, b. 1958 ~
"A New World Order," Selected Essays, 2001

I hope that we will learn to actually celebrate diversity, instead of painting homogeneity in different colors and calling that diversity.
~ Nalo Hopkinson, b. 1960 ~
"Filling the Sky With Islands: An Interview with Nalo Hopkinson," by Chris Aylott, Space.com

Different strokes for different folks.
~ African-American Wisdom ~

Having no diversity is a very big problem. The difference between religions and languages is not an obstacle but a wealth.
~ Youssou N'Dour, b. 1959 ~
Interview by Banning Eyre and Sean Barlow, Afropop.org, 2004 May

In terms of my growth as a human being ... I want to present a whole and complete picture – the yin, the yang; the black, the white; the boy, the girl; the sane, the insane. Because we are all Everyman – a rainbow of different roles and different people. Exploring the colors in myself and in others is my life's passion. There is no such thing as normality – each and every one of us, if we dare to be whole, is a gorgeous peacock. Whether you believe you have one life to live or hundreds, there is no reason not to spread your wings and fly!
~ RuPaul, b. 1960 ~
Lettin It All Hang Out, 1995

I am very much aware of my black heritage, but i'm also aware of the other elements of who I am. And I think sometimes it bothers people (who would prefer me to say) that I'm black and that's it ... When people ask, I say I'm black, Venezuelan, and Irish because that's who I am.
~ Mariah Carey, b. 1969 ~

I identify with all of (my ethnicities), but I understand that I am only part of some things. I am only part of some things and I don't fully belong to anything. But that's okay, you know? Being a mutt gives you access to worlds unlimited.
~ Staceyann Chin, b. 1973 ~
in Jocelyn Voo, "Staceyann Chin: More Than a Mouthful," Curve

I learned how to sing and play in Spanish ... if you're gonna make some money and make people happy, you have to do as much as you can in as many different genres as possible ... they're all equally as important.
~ Walter Beasley ~
Interview by Ben Fishner, Wers.org, 2006 April 2

We have the power to choose not to let our beautiful diversity be a source of division amongst us. We have to see ourselves as having enormous strength because of the wealth of our resources. That wealth lies in our differences.
~ Angel Kyodo Williams ~
Being Black: Zen and the Art of Living with Fearlessness and Grace, 2000

DREAMS / DREAMING

Dreaming comes prior to getting.
~ Mamprussi Wisdom ~
Wit & Wisdom of Africa: Proverbs from Africa & The Caribbean, Patrick Ibekwe, ed., 1998

Those who lose dreaming are lost.
~ Australian Aboriginal Wisdom ~

Every great dream begins with a dreamer. Always remember, you have
within you the strength, the patience, and the passion to reach for the stars
to change the world.
~ Harriet Tubman, c. 1822-1913 ~

A dream is the bearer of a new possibility, the enlarged horizon, the great
hope.
~ Howard Thurman, 1889-1981 ~
Disciplines of the Spirit, 1963

The dream is the truth.
~ Zora Neale Hurston, 1891-1960 ~

Man is what his dreams are.
~ Benjamin Mays, 1895-1984 ~
Born to Rebel, 1971

It isn't a calamity to die with dreams unfulfilled, but it is certainly a
calamity not to dream.
~ Mays ~

Hold on to your dreams for if dreams die
Life is a broken winged bird that cannot fly.
Hold fast to dreams for when dreams go
Life is a barren field frozen with snow.
~ Langston Hughes, 1902-1967 ~

It's not what the dream is, it's what the dream does.
~ John Harold Johnson, 1918-2005 ~

Don't be afraid of the space between your dreams and reality. If you can dream it, you can make it.
~ Belva Davis, b. 1932 ~

A dream doesn't become reality through magic; it takes sweat, determination and hard work.
~ Colin Powell, b. 1937 ~

The dream is real, my friends. The failure to make it work is the unreality.
~ Toni Cade Bambara, 1939-1995 ~
The Salt Eaters, 1980

When you dream, you dialogue with aspects of yourself that normally are not with you in the daytime and you discover that you know a great deal more than you thought you did.
~ Bambara ~

If you haven't dreamed that you will get there, you will not think about ever taking the steps to be there.
~ Max Robinson, 1939-1988 ~
in Brother's Keeper: Words of Inspiration for African-American Men, Roderick Terry, ed., 1996

Exercise the right to dream. You must face reality – that which is. But then dream of the reality that ought to be, that must be.
~ Jesse Jackson, b. 1941 ~

We've removed the ceiling above our dreams. There are no more impossible dreams.
~ Jackson ~

We must teach our children to dream with their eyes open.
~ Harry Edwards, Jr., b. 1942 ~

Too many of us are not living our dreams because we are living our fears.
~ Les Brown, b. 1945 ~

I am just a history of a dream ... a maker of dreams ... All my life is a dream. All my friends too.
~ Djibril Diop Mambety, 1945-1998 ~
Interview by Rachel Rawlins, Africa Film & TV Magazine, 1993

If you don't dream, you might as well be dead.
~ George Foreman, b. 1949 ~

Regardless of parentage, heritage or origin, dreams are meant to be pursued and grasped and pulled from the sky. If you work hard, educate yourself, strive, and never forget to be kind to others, your dreams can come true.
~ Michael Lee-Chin, b. 1951 ~
in "Lee Chin Crystal – Art Meets Architectural Genius," *Jamaica Daily Gleaner*, 2007 June 7

Dream the biggest dream for yourself. Hold the highest vision of life for yourself.
~ Oprah Winfrey, b. 1954 ~

Not many people listen to the echoes of their dreams in the morning. Most dreams in this world do not receive attention, they are slowly abandoned to the warpaths of this life. The poet has to come to grips, do battle with these dreams, reminding the dreamers they have a right to their own dreams. Their dreams deserve a spot on the map of the world.
~ Chenjerai Hove, b. 1956 ~
Prologue, *Shebeen Tales: Messages from Harare*, 1997

Dreams are the source of hope and possibility. They help us to see ourselves as we could be, rather than as we are. Everything ever created or achieved in the world was inspired by someone who dared to dream ... Dreams are potent forces. Regardless of our present circumstances, dreams can change our lives.
~ Roderick Terry, b. 1964 ~
"Hope Chest"

Lord knows
Dreams are hard to follow
But don't let anyone
Tear them away
Hold on
There will be tomorrow
In time
You'll find the way.
~ Mariah Carey, b. 1969 ~
"Hero," 1993

It just made me realize how important life is, how short time is, how important it is to follow your dreams and your goals. That's part of who you are and you take away from it by not doing it.
~ Queen Latifah, b. 1970 ~
Interview by Ellen Leventry, "It Was Just a Gang for God," Belief.net

ELOQUENCE / POETRY

Be a craftsman in speech that thou mayest be strong, for the strength of one is the tongue, and speech is mightier than all fighting.
~ Ptahotep, c. 2350 BCE ~
Maxims of Ptahhotep

Because a thing is eloquently expressed it should not be taken to be as necessarily true; nor because it is uttered with stammering lips should it be supposed false. Nor, again, is it necessarily true because rudely uttered, nor untrue because the language is brilliant. Wisdom and folly both are like meats that are wholesome and unwholesome, and courtly or simple words are like town-made or rustic vessels – both kinds of food may be served in either kind of dish.
~ Augustine of Hippo, 354-430 ~
Confessiones, V. 6

The new racial poetry of the Negro is the expression of something more than experimentation in a new technique. It marks the birth of a new racial consciousness and self-conception. It lacks apology, the wearying appeals to pity, and the conscious philosophy of defense. In being itself it reveals its greatest charm; and in accepting its distinctive life, invests it with a new meaning.
~ Charles S. Johnson, 1893-1956 ~
in *Songs of Wisdom: Quotations from Famous African Americans*, Jay David, ed., 2000

I was on a quest to reconquer something, my name, my country or myself. That is why my approach has in essence always been poetic. Because it seems to me that in a way that's what poetry is. The reconquest of the self by the self.
~ Aimé Césaire, b. 1913 ~
"The Liberating Power of Words," Interview by Annick Thebia Melsan in *UNESCO Courier*, 1997 May

The effective power of poetry, with its two faces, one looking nostalgically backward, the other looking prophetically forward, with the redeeming feature of its ability to redeem the self, is the power of intensifying life.
~ Césaire ~
Speech, Geneva 1978

Poetry for me is the inner knowledge of the human being. It is a call to action.
~ Césaire ~

Writing is a labor of love and also an act of defiance, a way to light a candle in a gale wind.
~ Alice Childress, 1920-1994 ~
"A Candle in a Gale Wind," in Mari Evans, *Black Women Writers*, 1984

Like how you beat a drum till it shape a tune,
words beat your brain till it language you tongue.
~ George Lamming, b. 1927 ~

Poetry is the way we help give name to the nameless so it can be thought.
~ Audre Lorde, 1934-1992 ~

Writing has made me a better man. It has put me in contact with those fleeting moments which prove the existence.
~ Ishmael Reed, b. 1938 ~
in *African-American Writers*, Valerie Smith et al., eds., 1991

Learning to sing one's own songs, to trust the particular cadences of one's own voice, is also the goal of any writer.
~ Henry Louis Gates, Jr., b. 1950 ~
in *In Our Own Words*, Elza Dinwiddie-Boyd, ed., 1996

Not only is your story worth telling, but it can be told in words so painstakingly eloquent that it becomes a song.
~ Gloria Naylor, b. 1950 ~
in *African-American Writers*, Valerie Smith et al., eds., 1991

Sometimes a word is found so right it trembles at the slightest explanation.
~ Rita Dove, b. 1952 ~
"O," *The Yellow House on the Corner*

Warm up your words before uttering them. Speak in your heart. To know how to speak is to know how to withhold the word. To speak truly is to first polish silence. True silence is one place of The Word.
~ Patrick Chamoiseau, b. 1953 ~
Texaco, Rose-Myriam Réjouis & Val Vinokurov, trs., 1992

ENGAGEMENT / INTEGRATION / INVOLVEMENT

Since you cannot do good to all, you are to pay special attention to those who, by the accidents of time, or place, or circumstances, are brought into closer connection with you.
~ Augustine of Hippo, 354-430 ~

Loving your enemy is manifest in putting your arms not around the man but around the social situation, to take power away from those who misuse it – at which point they can become human too.
~ Bayard Rustin, 1912-1987 ~
in Sally Belfrage, *Freedom Summer*, 1965

It is brave to be involved
To be not fearful to be unresolved.
~ Gwendolyn Brooks, 1917-2000 ~
"do not be afraid of no," *Annie Allen*, 1949

Life is not a spectator sport. If you're going to spend your whole life in the grandstand just watching what goes on, in my opinion you're wasting your life.
~ Jackie Robinson, 1919-1972 ~

The world is before you and you need not take it or leave it as it was when you came in.
~ James Baldwin, 1924-1987 ~
Nobody Knows My Name: More Notes of a Native Son, 1961

It is impossible to pretend that you are not heir to, and therefore, however inadequately or unwillingly, responsible to, and for, the time and place that give you life.
~ Baldwin ~

If the building of the bridge does not enrich the awareness of those who work on it, then the bridge ought not to be built.
~ Frantz Fanon, 1925-1961 ~

Stay still, and you stagnate; get concerned and active, and the prospect of change is your friend and constant guardian. And don't be sentimental about a damn thing, but at the same time never let go of compassion.
~ Andrew Salkey, 1928-1995 ~

Our lives begin to end the day we become silent about things that matter.
~ Martin Luther King, Jr., 1929-1968 ~

Pity may represent little more than the impersonal concern which prompts
the mailing of a check, but true sympathy is the personal concern which
demands the giving of one's soul.
~ King ~
The Strength to Love, 1963

Every true artist understands the tension that exists between becoming self
and having that self as agency in a wider whole. All art is, after all,
mediated by social reality and the self has to reach out as well as in, if it is
to appreciate the world we tenant.
~ Rex Nettleford, b. 1933 ~
Address, EUA Conference, 2004 June 3-5

Each one of us needs to understand that he runs the risk of denying his
own self and presence when he looks at the creations or practices produced
in his presence, in his place and time, as if he had nothing to do with them.
~ Earl Lovelace, b. 1935 ~
Salt, 1997

If you don't like the way the world is, you change it. You have an
obligation to change it. You just do it one step at a time.
~ Marion Wright Edelman, b. 1939 ~

We should be about the development of whole persons, and should begin
that wholeness with an accurate understanding and assessment of our own
involvement in our community, city, state, nation, and world.
~ Haki Madhubuti, b. 1942 ~
"Cultural Work: Planting New Trees with New Seeds," *Multi-America*, Ishmael Reed, ed., 1997

If we want to be heard, we have to engage.
~ Najat Vallaud-Belkacem, b. 1979 ~
in "New French Political Cry: Liberté, Egalité, Diversité: Minorities Run for Parliament in Record
Numbers," *Washington Post*, 2007 June 10

We each need to become even more engaged than we are. We need to
participate in the world and have our voices heard beyond our own
backyards, streets and neighborhoods ... Part of enlightened being and
living responsively is acknowledging that we are essentially in a
relationship with the rest of the world.
~ Angel Kyodo Williams ~
Being Black: Zen and the Art of Living with Fearlessness and Grace, 2000

ENJOYMENT / PLEASURE

The place of joy is better than the place one was born.
~ Tshi Wisdom ~
Wit & Wisdom of Africa: Proverbs from Africa & The Caribbean, Patrick Ibekwe, ed., 1998

Pleasure's fault is finishing.
~ Hausa Wisdom ~
Ibid.

Once we recognize what it is we are feeling, once we recognize we can feel deeply, love deeply, can feel joy, then we will demand that all parts of our lives produce that kind of joy.
~ Audre Lorde, 1934-1992 ~

You can't have this luxury of pleasure without somebody paying for it. This is nice to know. It's nice to know that when you sit down to enjoy a plate of strawberries, somebody got paid very little so that you could have your strawberries. It doesn't mean the strawberries will taste different, but it's nice to enjoy things less than we do. We enjoy things far too much, and it leads to incredible pain and suffering.
~ Jamaica Kincaid, b. 1949 ~
Interview by Marilyn Snell, *Mother Jones*, 1997 September/October

When your joy is dependent on people and conditions, it is restricted. Joy must spring forth from you before it can surround you.
~ Iyanla Vanzant, b. 1953 ~
Acts of Faith: Daily Meditations for People of Color, 1993

Enjoy life. There's plenty of time to be dead.
~ Unknown ~

Work like you don't need money,
Love like you've never been hurt,
Dance like nobody's around!!
In short, enjoy life!
~ Unknown ~

ENLIGHTENMENT / REALIZATION / TRANSCENDENCE

My mind withdrew its thoughts from experience, extracting itself from the contradictory throng of sensuous images, that it might find out what that light was wherein it was bathed ... And thus, with the flash of one hurried glance, it attained to the vision of That Which Is.
~ Augustine of Hippo, 354-430 ~

If it is true that consciousness is a process of transcendence, we have to see too that this transcendence is haunted by the problems of love and understanding. Man is a *yes* that vibrates to cosmic harmonies. Uprooted, pursued, baffled, doomed to watch the dissolution of the truths that he has worked out for himself one after another, he has to give up projecting onto the world an antinomy that coexists with him.
~ Frantz Fanon, 1925-1961 ~
Black Skin, White Masks, Charles Lam Markmann, 1967

The best way to live in this world is to live above it.
~ Sonia Sanchez, b. 1934 ~

There are times when one is struck by something – a brilliant sunset, the wonder of some small, personal discovery that comes with new love – that words or reason cannot describe; some moments that give you pause ... while you are a part of it, or witness to it, it is not yours to create or control ... when something touches a part of your insides that you *know* you cannot access wilfully; that, while felt at your very core, is outside of you ... when you *just know* that you have been touched by ... the Divine.
~ Kathleen E. Morris, b. 1962 ~
"Without Exception or Limitation," in *Spirited: Affirming the Soul and Black Gay/Lesbian Identity*, G. Winston James & Lisa C. Moore, eds., 2006

Enlightened being is not something that you can pick up and put in your purse or knapsack ... It is not tangible. You cannot hold it in your hand or pass it around. You cannot put it down. The path to it is just doing. Just being. Just starting ... When we make a commitment to enlightened being, we are at once taking on the responsibility and already fulfilling it.
~ Angel Kyodo Williams ~
Being Black: Zen and the Art of Living with Fearlessness and Grace, 2000

EQUANIMITY

Evil as well as good, both operate to advance the Great Plan.
~ Khemetic Wisdom ~
Temt Tchaas: Egyptian Proverbs, Muata Ashaya Ashby, ed., 1994

See that prosperity elate not thine heart above measure; neither adversity depress thine mind unto the depths because fortune beareth hard against you. Their smiles are not stable, therefore build not thy confidence upon them; their frowns endure not forever, therefore let hope teach you patience.
~ Ibid.

In matters that are obscure and far beyond our vision ... we should not rush in headlong and so firmly take our stand on one side that, if further progress in the search for truth undermines this position, we too fall with it.
~ Augustine of Hippo, 354-430 ~
The Literal Meaning of Genesis, John H. Taylor, tr., 1982

Fearing no insult, asking for no crown, receive with indifference both flattery and slander, and do not argue with a fool.
~ Aleksandr Pushkin, 1799-1837 ~

If white people are pleased, we are glad. If they aren't, it doesn't matter. We know we are beautiful, and ugly too ... If colored people are pleased, we are glad. If they are not, their displeasure doesn't matter either.
~ Langston Hughes, 1902-1967 ~
in *Songs of Wisdom: Quotations from Famous African Americans*, Jay David, ed., 2000

Anytime life throws you a blow you did not expect, have the grace to smile. Smiling is a simple gesture that lets the universe know we are open and receptive to the challenges of life.
~ Roderick Terry, b. 1964 ~
"Hope Chest"

ETHICS / MORALITY

There comes a time when a moral man can't obey a law which his conscience tells him is unjust ... There were those individuals in every age and generation who were willing to say, "I will be obedient to a higher law." It is important to see that there are times when a man-made law is out of harmony with the moral law of the universe.
~ Martin Luther King, Jr., 1929-1968 ~
The Words of Martin Luther King, Jr., Coretta Scott King, ed., 1983

It is easy to do right out of fear, but it is better to do right because right is right.
~ Louis Farrakhan, b. 1934 ~

The imperative is to define what is right and do it.
~ Barbara Jordan, 1936-1996 ~

The challenge of always "being good" is, obviously, daunting. Who can *always* behave morally? ... (One) need not worry about "always," because the challenge of the spiritual and moral life is simply this: to be good, truly moral and master of ourselves *for this moment only*. What time is there outside this moment that we should worry about it? This moment *here* and *now* is all that we are given or responsible for.
~ Charles Johnson, b. 1948 ~
"Reading the Eightfold Path," *Dharma, Color, and Culture,* Hilda Gutiérrez Baldoquín, ed., 2004

Rather than waiting for others to create a world that you yearn for, a world that must be in place for your so-called true self to emerge, you imbue the world with the noblest of values wrought from the depths of a dissatisfied spirit whose hunger only you can sate. Moral creativity satisfies this hunger, and in the process it provides the world with a new model, a new paradigm of existing and of dealing with your fellow human beings. In your efforts, you are in effect forging the honorable traditions of tomorrow.
~ Jason D. Hill, b. 1965 ~
Becoming a Cosmopolitan: What It Means to Be a Human Being in the New Millennium, 2000

EVIL

There is no rational creature which is not capable both of good and evil. But it does not follow, that because we say there is no nature which may not admit evil, we therefore maintain that every nature has admitted evil.
~ Origen, c. 185-255 ~
De Principiis, I.8

Without evil the All would be incomplete. For most or even all forms of evil serve the Universe … Vice itself has many useful sides.
~ Plotinus, 205-270 ~

O, it is no matter, although they say I have done wrong; but I say Unkulunkulu[2] was unable to create what is evil, and although they say it is evil, it is really good.
~ Amazulu Wisdom ~
in Henry Callaway, *The Religious System of the Amazulu*, 1873

Evil is a force, and, like the physical and chemical forces, one cannot annihilate it; we may only change its form.
~ James Weldon Johnson, 1871-1938 ~
Autobiography of an Ex-Coloured Man, 1912

You can best fight any existing evil from the inside.
~ Hattie McDaniel, 1895-1952 ~

All that good men need to do for evil to flourish is nothing.
~ Martin Luther King, Jr., 1929-1968 ~

He who passively accepts evil is as much involved in it as he who helps to perpetrate it. He who accepts evil without protesting against it is really cooperating with it.
~ King ~
Stride Toward Freedom

The purpose of evil was to survive it.
~ Toni Morrison, b. 1931 ~
Sula, 1973

---

[2] Amazulu Supreme Being

EXAMPLE

Example is the best precept.
~ Aesop, fl. c. 550 BCE ~
"The Two Crabs"

My advice is to consult the lives of other men, as one would a looking glass, and from thence fetch examples for imitation.
~ Terence, c. 190-159 BCE ~

Examples have children.
~ Tshi Wisdom ~
Wit & Wisdom of Africa: Proverbs from Africa & The Caribbean, Patrick Ibekwe, ed., 1998

You are making the first waves, and those waves reverberate. Other people come afterward and do whatever they do in the pool, but you have set the pattern.
~ Lloyd Richards, 1919-2006 ~
in Sharon Fitzgerald, "The Griot Wears a Watch," *American Visions*, 1998 August-September

Children have never been very good at listening to their elders, but they have never failed to imitate them.
~ James Baldwin, 1924-1987 ~

Each human society is a narrow world, trapped to death in paltry evils and jealousies, and for people to know that there are thoughts and generosities wider and freer than their own can be an enrichment to their lives.
~ Bessie Head, 1937-1986 ~
Epilogue: An African Story, 1972

Our freedom is precious and important but in the end what gives our movement its majesty is the example it set throughout the world for people of color and for people who were in any way oppressed and found in that example a reason to hope and strive for a different life.
~ Eleanor Holmes Norton, b. 1937 ~
in *Voices of Freedom*, Henry Hampton, ed., 1990

EXAMPLE 143

Children don't listen to what you tell them, they don't listen to the lectures. What they really respond to, what they really do, is watch how you live your life, watch how you exercise your values. If they see worth in that, if they see merit in the way you are living your life, that's what influences children.
~ Colin Powell, b. 1937 ~
"America's Premier Soldier-Statesman," Academy of Achievement Interview, 1998 May 23

Parents have become so convinced educators know what is best for children that they forget that they themselves are really the experts.
~ Marion Wright Edelman, b. 1939 ~
in *Songs of Wisdom: Quotations from Famous African Americans*, Jay David, ed., 2000

Listen and learn from people who have already been where you want to go. Benefit from their mistakes instead of repeating them.
~ Benjamin Carson, b. 1951 ~
in Anthony Robbins & Joseph McLendon III, *Unlimited Power: A Black Choice*, 1997

There is definitely a burden to carry (in creating role models), but I think that responsibility has always made blacks that choose to carry the burden stronger ... That's something to deal with, but it's almost a good thing. It makes you work harder.
~ Will Smith, b. 1968 ~

It's normal for me ... it's not a question of being a role model. Rather, I give them a mirror and a chance to recognize themselves in me.
~ Najat Vallaud-Belkacem, b. 1979 ~
in "New French Political Cry: Liberté, Egalité, Diversité: Minorities Run for Parliament in Record Numbers," *Washington Post*, 2007/6/10

EXPECTATION / HOPE

He who hopes fares better than he who wishes, and he who wishes fares better than he who despairs.
~ Moroccan Wisdom~

Hope is patience with the lamp lit.
~ Tertullian, c. 160-240 ~

Hope has two beautiful daughters. Their names are anger and courage; anger at the way things are, and courage to see that they do not remain the way they are.
~ Augustine of Hippo, 354-430 ~

Men and women are limited not by the place of their birth, not by the color of their skin, but by the size of their hope.
~ John Harold Johnson, 1918-2005 ~

We must accept finite disappointment, but we must never lose infinite hope.
~ Martin Luther King, Jr., 1929-1968 ~
The Words of Martin Luther King, Jr., Coretta Scott King, ed., 1983

Hope is delicate suffering.
~ Amiri Baraka, b. 1934 ~
Cold, Hurt, and Sorrow, 1962

We are the ones we've been waiting for.
~ June Jordan, 1936-2002 ~

Where there is hope there is life, where there is life there is possibility, and where there is possibility, change can occur.
~ Jesse Jackson, b. 1941 ~

You have to expect things of yourself before you can do them.
~ Michael Jordan, b. 1963 ~

EXPEDIENCE

It is possible for the owners of a house to warm themselves when their house is on fire.
~ Kikuyu Wisdom ~
Wit & Wisdom of Africa: Proverbs from Africa & The Caribbean, Patrick Ibekwe, ed., 1998

If you carry water in a pot and it breaks on your head, you should just wash.
~ Mamprussi Wisdom ~
Ibid.

It seems to me that it is best to lay hold of the things we can put right rather than those we can do nothing but find fault with.
~ Booker T. Washington, 1856-1915 ~
Address, Fifth Tuskegee Conference, 1896

The best time to do a thing is when it can be done.
~ William Pickens, 1881-1954 ~
Fifty Years After Emancipation, 1912

Until you can walk on water, take a boat.
~ Elma Lumsden, b. 1935 ~

I try to do the right thing at the right time. They may be just little things, but usually they make the difference between winning and losing.
~ Kareem Abdul-Jabbar, b. 1947 ~

We might seek to turn to our advantage the interdependence history has thrust upon us.
~ K. Anthony Appiah, b. 1954 ~

We have to be careful that in seeking the ideal, we do not sacrifice the possible.
~ Beverly Lopez ~

EXPERIENCE

Everything we do is sowing, and all of our experiences are harvests.
~ Khemetic Wisdom ~
Temt Tchaas: Egyptian Proverbs, Muata Ashaya Ashby, ed., 1994

A person who will not take advice gets knowledge when trouble overtakes him.
~ Xhosa Wisdom ~

Never give up what you have seen for what you have heard.
~ Swahili Wisdom ~
Wit & Wisdom of Africa: Proverbs from Africa & The Caribbean, Patrick Ibekwe, ed., 1998

A travelled child knows better than the old man who sits at home.
~ Igbo Wisdom ~
Ibid.

Those who climb with their teeth know the trees with bitter barks.
~ Nigerian Wisdom ~
Ibid.

Not until we have fallen do we know how to rearrange our burden.
~ Yoruba Wisdom ~
Ibid.

The words printed here are concepts. You must go through the experiences.
~ Augustine of Hippo, 354-430 ~

When the bird and the book disagree, always believe the bird.
~ John James Audubon, 1785-1851 ~

An ounce of application is worth a ton of abstraction.
~ Booker T. Washington, 1856-1915 ~

How far you go in life depends on you being tender with the young, compassionate with the aged, sympathetic with the striving and tolerant of the weak and the strong. Because someday in life you will have been all of these.
~ George Washington Carver, 1864-1943 ~

We learn the rope of life by untying the knots.
~ Jean Toomer, 1894-1967 ~
Essentials: Definitions and Aphorisms, LI, 1931

Most of us feel we must be mentally fortified in advance of experience. This is one of the reasons why we are buffers rather than experiencers.
~ Toomer ~

We have all had the experience of finding that our reactions and perhaps even our deeds have denied beliefs we thought were ours.
~ James Baldwin, 1924-1987 ~
in *Songs of Wisdom: Quotations from Famous African Americans*, Jay David, ed., 2000

Learning in the school of experience isn't like learning in regular school. In the school of experience you take the test first and *then* review what you've learned ... In this regard, the school of experience is a lot like regular school: If you don't get the lesson, you repeat the experience again and again.
~ Famous Amos, b. 1937 ~
Watermelon Magic, 1996

To know is to exist; to exist is to be involved, to move about, to see the world with my own eyes.
~ Alice Walker, b. 1944 ~

We are always gaining experience by working in the present for the future.
~ Salif Keita, b. 1949 ~
in *In Our Own Words*, Elza Dinwiddie-Boyd, ed., 1996

The best lessons, the best sermons are those that are lived.
~ Yolanda King, b. 1955 ~

EXPLORATION

To lose the way is to know the way.
~ Swahili Wisdom ~

No matter how far a person can go, the horizon is still way beyond you.
~ Zora Neale Hurston, 1891-1960 ~

We know the world only through accounts written by whites, travel narratives of those who colonized the world. We must get to know the world through our own narratives. It's not that we should reject the accounts written by whites, but we have to add something. There needs to be a synthesis. Thus, we need our own travel narratives ... traveling makes you feel the spirit of the system so that you can enter into the spirit of relation.
~ Édouard Glissant, b. 1928 ~
Interview by Michael Dash, *Renaissance Noire*, Hillina Seife, tr., 2006 March 22

Travellers with closed minds can tell us little except about themselves.
~ Chinua Achebe, b. 1930 ~
Hopes and Impediments: Selected Essays, 1965-1987, 1988

There is a tendency for people to find a particular niche that they feel comfortable with ... And human beings, once they find something comfortable, are not encouraged to go beyond that, because they're identified with that. As a matter of fact, they not only identify themselves with that, but others identify them with that. So everybody feels comfortable if you put everybody in a box ... But the truth of the matter is, that's just one aspect of, or one expression of, what that person is capable of doing. I think it takes more courage to say, "This is cool, but what else is out there?" and being willing to explore. And a lot of that depends on your own personality. I've always been a very curious kind of person, so it's natural for me to explore.
~ Herbie Hancock, b. 1940 ~
in J. D. Considine, "Herbie Hancock, Musical Chameleon," *Toronto Globe and Mail*, 2007 June 22

The biggest adventure you can ever take is to live the life of your dreams.
~ Oprah Winfrey, b. 1954 ~

EXPRESSION

When the heart overflows, it comes out through the mouth.
~ Ethiopian Wisdom ~

You ought to write volumes – it gives expansion to your thoughts – facility to your invention – ease to your diction – and pleases your Friend.
~ Ignatius Sancho, 1729-1780 ~
Letter II to Mr M, 1773 July 26 in *The Letters of the Late Ignatius Sancho, an African*, Vol. II, 1782

We have not however, to thank any human being, for acknowledging our right to think; as 'tis neither in their power, nor our own, to control our thoughts; neither chains, nor dungeons, nor the terrors of being burnt alive, can prevent us from thinking freely; neither ought they to prevent us from speaking freely, writing freely, and publishing freely; if we think we can benefit mankind, by exposing falsehood and error.
~ Robert Wedderburn, b. 1762 ~
Brief to court, 1820 May 9

I know why the caged bird sings ...
.. a prayer he sends from his heart's deep core.
~ Paul Laurence Dunbar, 1873-1906 ~
"Sympathy"

There is no agony like bearing an untold story inside you.
~ Zora Neale Hurston, 1891-1960 ~

To express, not suppress, the force of one's reaction, to wield reinvigorated words as a miraculous weapon against the silenced world, freeing it from gags that are often imposed from within.
~ Aimé Césaire, b. 1913 ~
"The Liberating Power of Words," Interview by Annick Thebia Melsan in *UNESCO Courier*, 1997 May

Old age reminds me these days that I don't have much time left and that I must hasten to express things I've kept to myself all my life. And hopefully express them with grace and maturity.
~ René Depestre, b. 1926 ~
"Between Utopia and Reality," Interview by Jasmine Sopova, *UNESCO Courier*, 1997 December

One of the hardest things in life is having words in your heart that you can't utter ... the human mind has not achieved anything greater than the ability to share feelings and thoughts through language.
~ James Earl Jones, b. 1931 ~
Voices and Silences, 1993

I have come to believe over and over again that what is most important to me must be spoken, made verbal and shared, even at the risk of having it bruised or misunderstood. That the speaking profits me, beyond any other effect.
~ Audre Lorde, 1934-1992 ~
"The Transformation of Silence into Language and Action," *Sister Outsider: Essays and Speeches*, 1984

It is just about impossible to make a positive contribution to the world if one cannot read, write, compute, think, and articulate one's thoughts. The major instrument for bringing out the genius of any people is the productive, creative, and stimulating use and creation of language.
~ Haki Madhubuti, b. 1942 ~

True happiness comes from genuine self-expression. Life demands that we exclude nothing of ourselves from the world. There is no shrinking back into the shadows. We are expected to show up on the world's stage every day and passionately, honestly and openly reveal who we are – to show it all, to offer ourselves in every way possible – even the pain and scars that many of us are tempted to mask.
~ Roderick Terry, b. 1964 ~
"Hope Chest"

Soul cannot be caged. Expression and the extent or manner of display is dependent on Will and Consciousness.
~ Oliver Mbamara ~

Every now and then, some thought form surfaces in us, seeking form and expression through our faculties of creativity such as poetry, speech, painting, art, writing, music, etc. At such times, perhaps the best we could do is to be the best positive channel we could be.
~ Mbamara ~

FAILURE / ERROR

Having choked you are able to chew; having fallen you are able to walk.
~ Malagasy Wisdom ~
Wit & Wisdom of Africa: Proverbs from Africa & The Caribbean, Patrick Ibekwe, ed., 1998

Where there is a purpose there is no failure.
~ Swahili Wisdom ~

The man of levity often errs – but it is the man of sense alone who can
gracefully acknowledge it.
~ Ignatius Sancho, 1729-1780 ~
Letter XIX to Mr G, 1779 February in *The Letters of the Late Ignatius Sancho, an African*, Vol. II, 1782

Ninety-nine percent of the failures come from people who have the habit
of making excuses.
~ George Washington Carver, 1864-1943 ~

Failure is a word that I simply don't accept. As long as you don't accept it,
you're not failing.
~ John Harold Johnson, 1918-2005 ~
in *Brother's Keeper: Words of Inspiration for African-American Men*, Roderick Terry, ed., 1996

It is the recovery from failure where learning exists. Learning comes about
when you fail and understood why, and understand how to get out of it,
over it, or beyond it.
~ Lloyd Richards, 1919-2006 ~
Interview by N. Graham Nesmith, *African American Review*, 2005 Fall

Do not fear mistakes. There are none.
~ Miles Davis, 1926-1991 ~

Mistakes are natural. Mistakes are how we learn. When we stop making
mistakes, we stop learning and growing. But repeating the same mistake
over and over is not continuous learning – it's not paying attention.
~ Famous Amos, b. 1937 ~
Watermelon Magic, 1996

You have to look at *why* you failed. Somewhere in that failure, there are
important lessons to be learned so that the next time ... an opportunity

presents itself, you will know what not to do. You have to do something new or something different. You can't keep planting papaya seeds if you want watermelons.
~ Ibid.

Failure to me is a catalyst to work.
~ Trevor Rhone, b. 1940 ~
Interview by Kinisha O'Neill, *Jamaica Daily Gleaner*, 2003 March 31

Mistakes are a fact of life. It is the response to the error that counts.
~ Nikki Giovanni, b. 1943 ~

Use missteps as stepping stones to deeper understanding and greater achievement.
~ Susan L. Taylor, b. 1946 ~

Taken along with our successes, failure can teach us what we are good at and what we are not, what we enjoy and what we hate. Once we know that, we can use those huge frontal lobes God gave us to better plan our lives.
~ Benjamin Carson, b. 1951 ~

It is okay to make a mistake. A mistake, an error, a poor choice, or bad decision does not equal "there is something wrong with me." It means you are on your way to being better.
~ Iyanla Vanzant, b. 1953 ~
Acts of Faith: Daily Meditations for People of Color, 1993

What appears as a failure is simply a stepping-stone to realizing success. The truth is that we can do anything we focus our mind to do. What looks like failure teaches us what not to do, what does not work. It sends us back to the drawing board. It forces us to refocus, and redo.
~ Ibid.

I will tell you that there have been no failures in my life. I don't want to sound like some metaphysical queen, but there have been no failures. There have been some tremendous lessons ... Failure is another stepping stone to greatness.
~ Oprah Winfrey, b. 1954 ~

You will be tested. You won't always succeed. But know that you have it within your power to try.
~ Barack Obama, b. 1961 ~
Commencement Address, Knox College, 2005 June 4

I can accept failure. Everyone fails at something. But I can't accept not trying.
~ Michael Jordan, b. 1963 ~
I Can't Accept Not Trying, 1994

I've missed more than 9,000 shots in my career. I've lost nearly 300 games. 26 times I've been trusted to take the game winning shot and missed. I've failed over and over again. *That* is why I succeed … The greatest inventions in the world had hundreds of failures before the answers were found.
~ Jordan ~

We're also obliged to remember that failure … is a luxury we all, taking our rightful place in the human drama, not only can, but must afford. For it is only through what we mistakenly call "failure" that we learn, graced by the humility that itself is a form of freedom, that failure is nowhere near the terrifying damnation we've so long been schooled into believing it to be. In acts of imagining and daily living, we do often fail, it's true. But in the renewed imaginings and breaths that each next moment brings us, we often succeed, also true.
~ Thomas Glave, b. 1964 ~
"Fire & Ink: Toward a Quest for Language, History, and a Moral Imagination," 2002 Conference Address

I am never daunted. If I fail once, it is not a signal that it is the end of the road: it is an opportunity to do even better on the next attempt.
~ Norman Grant, b. 1964 ~
in *Jamaica Observer*, 2006 July 3

Your purpose is to become the best person you can be. But to do this, you have to overcome your fear of failure. This doesn't mean you won't fail. It means you won't let your failures stop you from getting up and going again.
~ Keith Boykin, b. 1965 ~
Respecting the Soul: Daily Reflections for Black Lesbians and Gays, 1999

You will make mistakes. But our mistakes are even more valuable for our growth than getting it all "right." It's in the areas that are difficult for us to work with, that we make lots of mistakes in, that we gain our greatest experiences.
~ Angel Kyodo Williams ~
Being Black: Zen and the Art of Living with Fearlessness and Grace, 2000

FAITH

Faith is to believe what you do not yet see; the reward for this faith is to see what you believe.
~ Augustine of Hippo, 354-430 ~

As my faith appears to be true to me, so does another one find his own faith true; but truth is one.
~ Zara Yacob, 1599-1692 ~
The Treatise of Zara Yacob, Claude Sumner, tr., 1985

Without faith, nothing is possible. With it nothing is impossible.
~ Mary McLeod Bethune, 1875-1955 ~
in *In Our Own Words*, Elza Dinwiddie-Boyd, ed., 1996

To believe is to become what you believe.
~ June Jordan, 1936-2002 ~
Commencement Address, Dartmouth College, 1987 June 14

Suffering breeds character; character breeds faith, and in the end faith will prevail.
~ Jesse Jackson, b. 1941 ~
in *Brother's Keeper: Words of Inspiration for African-American Men*, Roderick Terry, ed., 1996

Faith has tremendous power, and it works either way. Our negative or positive faith helps shape our future. The vision you keep, the words you speak pave the way for your experiences. The mind is a prolific author. What you believe – along with the action you take – composes your life. At this moment our lives reflect where we have been in consciousness and what we have done with our time.
~ Susan L. Taylor, b. 1946 ~
Lessons in Living, 1995

Seeds of faith are always within us; sometimes it takes a crisis to nourish and encourage their growth.
~ Taylor ~

Faith is stepping out on nothing and landing on something.
~ Cornel West, b. 1954 ~

I am guided by a higher calling. It's not so much a voice as it is a feeling. If it doesn't feel right to me, I don't do it ... I am extremely spiritual. I've not gone into this before because it's personal, but faith is the core of my life.
~ Oprah Winfrey, b. 1954 ~
in *Songs of Wisdom: Quotations from Famous African Americans*, Jay David, ed., 2000

The language of faith is crucial because it affords human beings the privilege of intimacy with the ultimate.
~ Michael Eric Dyson, b. 1958 ~

Faith is believing in our personal power and trusting that we have everything we need to thrive. Faith in ourselves makes it possible for us to see ourselves, other than as we are. It removes all fear and doubt from our lives, and gives us the courage to dwell in new and unfamiliar places. With faith on our side, we are more inclined to move out of our comfort zones and risk being who we are.
~ Roderick Terry, b. 1964 ~
"Hope Chest"

What faith does is, it gives me a connection to say, "You know what? I'll understand what I can understand, and then God will give me the direction to go where I need to go from there."
~ Blair Underwood, b. 1964 ~
Interview by Michael Kress, Belief.net

And I believe in believing everyday
and for as long as we can –
I believe we should believe in something we don't
know for sure
acknowledge the range of possibilities
unlimited by what we see
move reality with imagination
we decide what our destinies will be.
~ Staceyann Chin, b. 1973 ~
" ... and these are only some of the things I believe"

When you don't see it, you don't know if it can be done. But that's what faith is for.
~ Lauryn Hill, b. 1975 ~
in Joan Morgan, "They Call Me Ms. Hill," *Essence*, 2006 January

FAULT

Men praise what they know and find fault with what they don't know.
~ Tertullian, c. 160-240 ~
Apology, 197 CE

Don't look where you fell, but look where you slipped.
~ Liberian Wisdom ~

One time mistake, two times on purpose.
~ Jamaican Wisdom ~
Wit & Wisdom of Africa: Proverbs from Africa & The Caribbean, Patrick Ibekwe, ed., 1998

A fault confessed is half redressed.
~ Zulu Wisdom ~

We have to face the uglies to admit our errors, and even if we repeat them,
we ought not to excuse them.
~ Pearl Bailey, 1918-1990 ~
Hurry Up America, and Spit, 1976

Forgive yourself for your faults and your mistakes and move on.
~ Les Brown, b. 1945 ~

The great distance between the Dream and our actual lives was not due to
any fault in the Dream: the defect was in us.
~ Marlon Riggs, 1957-1994 ~
Introduction, *Standards*, V5N1, 1992

It's better to look at the rage that exists on both sides of the fence. When
you try to sweep it under the rug and not deal with it, it shows its ugly face
later.
~ Dulé Hill, b. 1975 ~
in "The Enduring Rage of *Dutchman*," Broadway.com

The human instinct puts up a defensive attitude that tries to see how the
other person went wrong, but we usually forget to look within and figure
out if we went wrong somewhere.
~ Oliver Mbamara ~
"The Cycle of Love, Life, and Affection: Role of The Past and The Present," *Cafe Africana*, 2006 July

FEAR

Many people profit by a preliminary dose of fear or force, which makes it possible for them to be taught something, or to put into practice what had previously been only words to them.
~ Augustine of Hippo, 354-430 ~
Appeal to the Secular Arm

While the best men are well guided by love, most men need to be goaded by fear.
~ Ibid.

He who fears something gives it power over him.
~ Moorish Wisdom ~

When fear enters, truth escapes.
~ Swahili Wisdom ~
Wit & Wisdom of Africa: Proverbs from Africa & The Caribbean, Patrick Ibekwe, ed., 1998

Hatred is a form of fear. And eventually we come to love that which we fear most. For we have allowed the object of our fear to define us, to have supreme power over us; and the absence of that object would be more than we could bear. We need the fear to create us. Without this fear we are nothing. Often death itself is preferable to the excruciating process of recreating ourselves against nothing, without our ineffable totem of fear.
~ Booker T. Washington, 1856-1915 ~

There is no doubt about it that the man who is doing right is never fearful of anything.
~ Marcus Garvey, 1887-1940 ~
"The Sign by Which We Conquer," *Negro World*, 1923 September 22

He who fears is literally delivered to destruction.
~ Howard Thurman, 1889-1981 ~

To be afraid is to behave as if the truth were not true.
~ Bayard Rustin, 1912-1987 ~
"Meaning of Birmingham," *The Liberator*, 1973 June

Don't be afraid; just play the music.
~ Charlie Parker, 1920-1955 ~

To defend oneself against fear is simply to ensure that one will, one day, be conquered by it; fears must be faced.
~ James Baldwin, 1924-1987 ~
The Fire Next Time, 1962

And I began to recognize a source of power within myself that comes from the knowledge that while it is most desirable not to be afraid, learning to put fear into perspective gave me great strength.
~ Audre Lorde, 1934-1992 ~
Sister Outsider: Essays and Speeches, 1984

We have to own the fears that we have of each other, and then, in some practical way, some daily way, figure out how to see people differently than the way we were brought up to.
~ Alice Walker, b. 1944 ~

Fear does not have any special power unless you empower it by submitting to it ... When you face your fear, most of the time you will discover that it was not really such a big threat after all.
~ Les Brown, b. 1945 ~

We must have the courage to surmount our fears ... There are no limitations to the strength and intellect of a man who is able to break the chain of fear. The fearless man is able to control his destiny in life.
~ Roderick Terry, b. 1964 ~
Brother's Keeper: Words of Inspiration for African-American Men, 1996

Never being afraid isn't what fearlessness is about. What fearlessness is really about is knowing that you are afraid ... and acting anyway.
~ Angel Kyodo Williams ~
Being Black: Zen and the Art of Living with Fearlessness and Grace, 2000

FEELING / EMOTION

Feelings, emotions and passions are good servants but poor masters.
~ Khemetic Wisdom ~
Temt Tchaas: Egyptian Proverbs, Muata Ashaya Ashby, ed., 1994

You can be educated in some vision and feeling as well as in mind.
~ Marcus Garvey, 1887-1940 ~

A man is not as much as he feels he is, but as much as he feels.
~ Jean Toomer, 1894-1967 ~
Essentials: Definitions and Aphorisms, LV, 1931

Don't be afraid to feel as angry or as loving as you can, because when you
feel nothing, it's just death.
~ Lena Horne, b. 1917 ~

Our feelings are our most genuine paths to knowledge. They are chaotic,
sometimes painful, sometimes contradictory, but they come from deep
within us. And we must key into those feelings ... This is how new visions
begin.
~ Audre Lorde, 1934-1992 ~

Our society allows people to be absolutely neurotic and totally out of touch
with their feelings and everyone else's feelings, and yet be very respectable.
~ Ntozake Shange, b. 1948 ~

We must resist the temptation to take refuge in hurt feelings and raging
resentment as we grapple with how our children live, or choose to leave us,
or even how we handle our recognition of their betrayals and disaffections.
~ Michael Eric Dyson, b. 1958 ~
Is Bill Cosby Right?, 2005

The only emotion you want to consume you is love. And I don't mean that
lost love, where you are going to be depending on someone, I'm talking
about the constructive love, the love of action – that makes you want to
assist other lives ... where you try to recognize what somebody actually
wants in their life, or what they need, and try to help them fulfill that.
~ Wynton Marsalis, b. 1961 ~
"Music's Jazz Maestro," Academy of Achievement Interview, 1991 January 8

FLEXIBILITY / FLOW / FLUX

The bending tree isn't broken by the wind.
~ Sukuma Wisdom ~
Wit & Wisdom of Africa: Proverbs from Africa & The Caribbean, Patrick Ibekwe, ed., 1998

If a man doesn't bend his back, he will jam his head against the post.
~ Guyanese Wisdom ~

The Spirit freely flowing forth is restrained by no limits, is checked by no
closed barriers within certain bounded spaces; it flows perpetually, it is
exuberant in its affluence. Let our heart only be athirst, and be ready to
receive: in the degree in which we bring to it a capacious faith, in that
measure we draw from it an overflowing grace.
~ Cyprian, 200-258 ~
Epistle to Donatus

Adaptability, flexibility, ready code-switching, innovativeness and a
capacity to deal with the complexity of complexity, are all core values of
higher learning and attributes of the creative imagination which provide
yet another route to cognition other than the Cartesian rationalism we
have inherited. For if we *are* because we think, we also exist because we
feel.
~ Rex Nettleford, b. 1933 ~
Address, EUA Conference, 2004 June 3-5

It is wandering that leads to creativity. Rootedness is very bad, in the end.
It is absolutely necessary to be wandering, to be multiple, on the outside
and on the inside. A Nomad.
~ Maryse Condé, b. 1937 ~
Interview with Francoise Pfaff

Ahh that's life in the world. Sometimes you are high, you cry, you speak
louder. But other times, you speak from the heart.
~ Salif Keita, b. 1949 ~
Interview by Opiyo Oloya, *AfroDisc*, 1996 April 23

Conditions change. The truth of this moment may not be the truth of the
next. There is constant movement.
~ Angel Kyodo Williams ~
Being Black: Zen and the Art of Living with Fearlessness and Grace, 2000

FOCUS / INTENTION

If your intention is pure you can walk on the sea.
~ Swahili Wisdom ~

When we intend to do good, we do. When we intend to do harm, it happens. What each of us must come to realize is that our intent always comes through. We cannot sugarcoat the feelings in our heart of hearts. The emotion is the energy that motivates. We cannot ignore what we really want to create. We should be honest and do it the way we feel it. What we owe to ourselves and everyone around is to examine the reasons of our true intent.
~ Thurgood Marshall, 1908-1993 ~

You should concentrate on the heights which you are determined to reach, not look back into the depths to which you once fell.
~ Martin Luther King, Jr., 1929-1968 ~

Black women who define ourselves and our goals beyond the sphere of a sexual relationship can bring to any endeavor the realized focus of completed and therefore empowered individuals.
~ Audre Lorde, 1934-1992 ~
Sister Outsider: Essays and Speeches, 1984

You must see your goals clearly and specifically before you can set out for them. Hold them in your mind until they become second nature.
~ Les Brown, b.1945 ~

There's nothing mysterious about success. It's the ability to stay mentally locked in.
~ Montel Williams, b. 1956 ~

Intention is the seed we plant from which effort grows and action blossoms. If we don't plant and cultivate our intentions, they will never grow.
~ Angel Kyodo Williams ~
Being Black: Zen and the Art of Living with Fearlessness and Grace, 2000

FORGIVENESS

If you are angered by a misdeed, then lean toward a man on account of his rightness. Pass over the misdeed and don't remember it, since God was silent to you on the first day of your misdeed.
~ Khemetic Wisdom ~
Temt Tchaas: Egyptian Proverbs, Muata Ashaya Ashby, ed., 1994

One that forgives gains the victory.
~ Zulu Wisdom ~
Wit & Wisdom of Africa: Proverbs from Africa & The Caribbean, Patrick Ibekwe, ed., 1998

If you will learn to distinguish between states of consciousness and their occupant, you can forgive everyone. How? By identifying the one you would forgive with the ideal he failed to realize. The highest ideal would be to identify him with the divine image itself.
~ Neville, 1905-1972 ~
"True Forgiveness," Lecture, 1969 April 1

I don't know if I continue, even today, always liking myself. But what I learned to do many years ago was to forgive myself. It is very important for every human being to forgive herself or himself because if you live, you will make mistakes – it is inevitable. But once you do and you see the mistake, then you forgive yourself and say, "well, if I'd known better I'd have done better," that's all. So you say to people who you think you may have injured, "I'm sorry," and then you say to yourself, "I'm sorry." If we all hold on to the mistake, we can't see our own glory in the mirror because we have the mistake between our faces and the mirror; we can't see what we're capable of being. You can ask forgiveness of others, but in the end the real forgiveness is in one's own self.
~ Maya Angelou, b. 1928 ~

We must develop and maintain the capacity to forgive. He who is devoid of the power to forgive is devoid of the power to love. There is some good in the worst of us and some evil in the best of us. When we discover this, we are less prone to hate our enemies.
~ Martin Luther King, Jr., 1929-1968 ~
The Words of Martin Luther King, Jr., Coretta Scott King, ed., 1983

Forgiveness is not an occasional act; it is a permanent attitude.
~ Ibid.

People can be more forgiving than you can imagine. But you have to
forgive yourself. Let go of what's bitter and move on.
~ Bill Cosby, b. 1937 ~

A vocabulary grounded in forgiveness ... is the real foundation of love.
~ Marita Golden, b. 1950 ~
Wild Women Don't Wear No Blues, 1993

Forgiveness frees us from the pain of the past and moves us beyond our
mistakes in the future. What you give you get. When you forgive,
forgiveness is there for you if you need it.
~ Iyanla Vanzant, b. 1953 ~
Acts of Faith: Daily Meditations for People of Color, 1993

The ability to forgive heals old wounds and liberates us from past burdens.
By releasing the emotional debts of others, forgiveness clears the way for
love, peace and understanding to enter into our lives. It enables us to
transcend negative feelings of hurt and vengeance that hold us back and
prevent us from focusing on our real purpose.
~ Roderick Terry, b. 1964 ~
"Hope Chest"

If you haven't forgiven someone, it does not hurt that person. They're
sleeping at night. You're holding onto that, and all the damage is being
done to you internally. So when you learn the power of that – your being
angry with that person has no power over them, it only has power over you
– you're responsible for it, and you have to make a choice: Do I let this go,
or do I hold onto it?
~ Tyler Perry, b. 1970 ~
Interview by Michael Kress, Belief.net

Forgiveness simply remains a theory to many of us because we are yet to
summon the courage to forgive and let go our guilt, resentment, or
bitterness. We find it hard to dwell on the good times and play down the
bad times. Yet, there is little or nothing to gain by going around singing
and dwelling on bad times or planning to bring more evil times on another
... If one desires peace and love, one must forgive the falling of the cup and
rather pick it up, and hold it up to the constant flow of the blessings of life
and love which is naturally devoid of vengeance. It is never too late.
~ Oliver Mbamara ~
"The Conflict of Retaliation Versus Forgiveness," Cafe Africana, 2005 November

FRIENDSHIP

"Come see me" and "come live with me" are two different things.
~ Jamaican Wisdom ~

Real friendships are not hastily made – friendship is a plant of slow growth, and, like our English oak, spreads, is more majestically beautiful, and increases in shade, strength, and riches, as it increases in years.
~ Ignatius Sancho, 1729-1780 ~
Letter II to Mr M, 1768 August 7 in *The Letters of the Late Ignatius Sancho, an African*, Vol. I, 1782

Friendship founded upon right judgement takes the good and bad with the indulgence of blind love; – nor is it wrong – for as weakness and error is the lot of humanity – real friendship must oft kindly overlook the undesigning frailties of undisguised nature.
~ Sancho ~
Letter IX to Miss L, 1770 August 31 in *The Letters of the Late Ignatius Sancho, an African*, Vol. I, 1782

Friend! It is a common word, often lightly used. Like other good and beautiful things, it may be tarnished by careless handling.
~ Harriet Jacobs, 1813-1897 ~
Incidents in the Life of A Slave Girl, 1861

Friendship is the only cement that will hold the world together.
~ Duke Ellington, 1899-1974 ~

The most called-upon prerequisite of a friend is an accessible ear.
~ Maya Angelou, b. 1928 ~

Sometimes being a friend means mastering the art of timing. There is a time for silence. A time to let go and allow people to hurl themselves into their own destiny. And a time to prepare to pick up the pieces when it's all over.
~ Gloria Naylor, b. 1950 ~
"Etta Mae Johnson," *The Women of Brewster Place*, 1982

Lots of people want to ride with you in the limo, but what you want is someone who will take the bus with you when the limo breaks down.
~ Oprah Winfrey, b. 1954 ~

GIVING / SERVING

Sacrifice the first portions of the harvest that your strength and faith to bring about what you desire may be increased. Give the first portion to avoid danger of worldly indulgence. Give that you may receive. Fulfill the requirements of the universal law of equilibrium.
~ Khemetic Wisdom ~
Temt Tchaas: Egyptian Proverbs, Muata Ashaya Ashby, ed., 1994

Be generous as long as you live. What goes into the storehouse should come out. For bread is made to be shared ... Generosity is a memorial for those who show it, long after they have departed.
~Khemetic Wisdom ~
Selections from the Husia: Sacred Wisdom of Ancient Egypt, Maulana Karenga, tr., 1984

If thou be industrious to procure wealth, be generous in the disposal of it. Man is never so happy as when he giveth happiness unto another.
~ Akhenaton, c. 1385-c. 1355 BCE ~

Giving is storing up for yourself.
~ Ndebele Wisdom ~
Wit & Wisdom of Africa: Proverbs from Africa & The Caribbean, Patrick Ibekwe, ed., 1998

That which gives is the heart; the fingers only let go.
~ Haya Wisdom ~
Ibid.

Don't be harsh towards your fellow man; if your possessions are greater give out much; if you have only a little, share it with those who are needy and who are poorer than you.
~ Walda Heywat, 17th C. ~
The Treatise of Walda Heywat, Claude Sumner, tr. 1985

There is nothing to make you like other human beings so much as doing things for them.
~ Zora Neale Hurston, 1891-1960 ~

Everybody can be great. Because anybody can serve. You don't have to have a college degree to serve. You don't have to make your subject and verb agree to serve ... You only need a heart full of grace. A soul generated by love.
~ Martin Luther King, Jr., 1929-1968 ~
The Words of Martin Luther King, Jr., Coretta Scott King, ed., 1983

Every man must decide whether he will walk in the light of creative altruism or the darkness of destructive selfishness. This is the judgment. Life's most persistent and urgent question is, What are you doing for others?
~ Ibid.

The leader is the servant. So leadership is not having your own way. It's not for self-aggrandizement. But oddly, it is for service. It is for the sake of the led. It is a proper altruism.
~ Desmond Tutu, b. 1931 ~
"Forging Equality in South Africa," Academy of Achievement Interview, 2004 June 12

Imagine what a harmonious world it could be if every single person, both young and old, shared a little of what he is good at doing.
~ Quincy Jones, b. 1933 ~

Service is the rent we pay for living. It is the very purpose of life, and not something you do in your spare time.
~ Marion Wright Edelman, b. 1939 ~
The Measure of Our Success, 1992

True heroism is remarkably sober, very undramatic. It is not the urge to surpass all others at whatever cost, but the urge to serve others at whatever cost.
~ Arthur Ashe, 1943-1993 ~
"Points to Ponder," *Reader's Digest*, 1994 August

Giving is not always about money. All of us, regardless of the size of our incomes or bank accounts, have a wealth of inner resources we can share with others. We can give attention, smiles, prayers, love, respect, humor and hope. We can give a word of encouragement or a shoulder to lean on. Our capacity for giving is enormous.
~ Roderick Terry, b. 1964 ~
"Hope Chest"

GOAL / IDEAL / PURPOSE

Contemplate thy powers, contemplate thy wants and thy connections; so shalt thou discover the duties of life and be directed in all thy ways.
~ Khemetic Wisdom ~
Temt Tchaas: Egyptian Proverbs, Muata Ashaya Ashby, ed., 1994

We must remake the world. The task is nothing less than that. To be part of this great uniting force of our age is the crowning experience of our life.
~ Mary McLeod Bethune, 1875-1955 ~

It must be borne in mind that the tragedy in life doesn't lie in not reaching your goal. The tragedy lies in having no goal to reach. It isn't a calamity to die with dreams unfulfilled, but it is a calamity not to dream ... It is not a disgrace not to reach the stars, but it is a disgrace to have no stars to reach for. Not failure, but low aim is sin.
~ Benjamin Mays, 1895-1984 ~

Every man is born into the world to do something unique and something distinctive, and if he or she does not do it, it will never be done.
~ Mays ~

Never let the odds keep you from pursuing what you know in your heart you were meant to do.
~ Satchel Paige, 1900-1982 ~

Man cannot live without some knowledge of the purpose of life. If he can find no purpose in life, he creates one in the inevitability of death.
~ Chester Himes, 1909-1984 ~
Beyond the Angry Black, 1966

I wasn't concerned about the hardships because I always felt I was doing what I had to do, what I wanted to do, and what I was destined to do.
~ Katherine Dunham, 1910-2006 ~

The mixture of the marvelous and the terrible is a basic condition of human life ... the persistence of human ideals represents the marvelous pulling itself up out of the chaos of the universe.
~ Ralph Ellison, 1914-1994 ~

You would not exist if you did not have something to bring to the table of life.
~ Herbie Hancock, b. 1940 ~

We may run, walk, stumble, drive, or fly, but let us never lose sight of the reason for the journey, or miss a chance to see a rainbow on the way.
~ Gloria Gaither, b. 1942 ~

You've got to get to the stage in life where going for it is more important than winning or losing.
~ Arthur Ashe, 1943-1993 ~

You must take action now that will move you toward your goals. Develop a sense of urgency in your life ... People who expect to achieve their goals don't stand around talking about them.
~ Les Brown, b. 1945 ~

I shall never have the garden I have in mind, but that for me is the joy of it; certain things can never be realized and so all the more reason to attempt them.
~ Jamaica Kincaid, b. 1949 ~
My Garden (Book), 1999

Whether or not you reach your goals in life depends entirely on how well you prepare for them and how badly you want them.
~ Ronald McNair, 1950-1986 ~

Living and dying is not the big issue. The big issue is what you're going to do with your time while you're here.
~ Bill T. Jones, b. 1952 ~

The whole point of being alive is to evolve into the complete person you were intended to be.
~ Oprah Winfrey, b. 1954 ~

Purpose begins with the individual, and the sum total of all individuals' purposes creates the community's purpose. The community thus takes upon itself the responsibility of nurturing and protecting the individual, because the individual, knowing her or his purpose, will then invest energy in sustaining the community ... The community exists, in part, to

safeguard the purpose of each person within it and to awaken the memory of that purpose by recognizing the unique gifts each individual brings to the world.
~ Malidoma Somé, b. 1956 ~
The Healing Wisdom of Africa, 1999

Focusing your life solely on making a buck shows a certain poverty of ambition. It asks too little of yourself. You need to take up the challenges that we face as a nation and make them your own … primarily because you have an obligation to yourself. Because individual salvation has always depended on collective salvation. Because it's only when you hitch your wagon to something larger than yourself that you realize your true potential.
~ Barack Obama, b. 1961 ~
Commencement Address, Knox College, 2005 June 4

A well-defined sense of purpose provides a road map that guides and directs our journey through life. Life is simpler and more meaningful when we set goals for ourselves and have a particular mission in mind. Goals propel us into action and give us the driving force necessary to face life's challenges. More simply stated, goals give us a reason to get up in the morning. Even if we diverge from our path, our sense of purpose helps us to stay on a charted course.
~ Roderick Terry, b. 1964 ~
Brother's Keeper: Words of Inspiration for African-American Men, 1996

If you are going into it because you want to be a star or a celebrity and you want your picture taken, find something else to do because it is a hard journey. If you don't have the passion to do it, don't waste your time. You have to learn to face rejection. Once you know it's what you want, commit to it, the main things are power and commitment. The rewards are for those who stay the course.
~ Dulé Hill, b. 1975 ~
in Yahneake Sterling, "Dulé's Humility and Candour," Gleaner *Flair* Magazine, 2007 July 30

We're multidimensional, multifaceted beings, and there are many ways in which we express love, but each of us has a primary vision to catch or open up to, and that is the particular delivery system which enables us to serve our purpose of revealing love.
~ Michael Beckwith ~
"Visioning," Interview by Kathy Juline, *Science of Mind Magazine*, 1996 December

GOODNESS / VIRTUE

The higher the sun ariseth, the less shadow doth he cast; even so the greater is the goodness, the less doth it covet praise; yet cannot avoid its rewards in honors.
~ Akhenaton, c. 1385-c. 1355 BCE ~

Your goodness is not for yourself but for others.
~ Ewe Wisdom ~
Wit & Wisdom of Africa: Proverbs from Africa & The Caribbean, Patrick Ibekwe, ed., 1998

Return good for evil.
~ Hausa Wisdom ~
Ibid.

Ever let your actions be such as your own heart can approve – always think before you speak, and pause before you act ... To think justly – is the way to do rightly – and by that means you will ever be at peace within.
~ Ignatius Sancho, 1729-1780 ~
Letter XII to Mr B, 1772 July 18 in The Letters of the Late Ignatius Sancho, an African, Vol. I, 1782

The challenge of always "being good" is, obviously, daunting. Who can *always* behave morally? Is it not, after all, as impossible to control the mind as it would be to harness the wind? What the practitioner realizes is that he need not worry about "always," because the challenge of the spiritual and moral life is simply this: to be good, truly moral and master of ourselves *for this moment only*. What time is there outside this moment that we should worry about it? This moment *here* and *now* is all that we are given or responsible for.
~ Charles Johnson, b. 1948 ~
"Reading the Eightfold Path," Dharma, Color, and Culture, Hilda Gutiérrez Baldoquín, ed., 2004

Goodness comes naturally to all of us. It isn't something that we have to learn, but we do have to put it into practice. The more you practice, the easier it is to recall at all times that goodness is in your heart.
~ Angel Kyodo Williams ~
Being Black: Zen and the Art of Living with Fearlessness and Grace, 2000

GREED

If you want to have perfect conduct, to be free from evil, then above all guard against the vice of greed. Greed is a grievous sickness that has no cure … Greed is a compound of all the evils, a bundle of all hateful things.
~ Khemetic Wisdom ~
Temt Tchaas: Egyptian Proverbs, Muata Ashaya Ashby, ed., 1994

Do not be greedy in the division of things. Do not covet more than your share. Do not be greedy toward your relatives.
~ Ibid.

The transgressor of laws is punished, although the greedy person overlooks this. Baseness may obtain riches, yet crime never lands its wares on the shore.
~ Ptahotep, c. 2350 BCE ~
The Teachings of Ptahhotep: The Oldest Book in the World, Asa Hilliard, L. Williams and N. Damali, eds., 1987

Do not strain to seek increase,
What you have, let it suffice you.
If riches come to you by theft,
They will not stay the night with you.
They made themselves wings like geese,
And flew away to the sky.
~ Amenemope, c. 11th C. BCE ~
The Instruction of Amenemope, Ch. 7, Miriam Lichtheim, tr.

And oh, the odious blindness of perception, and the deep darkness of senseless greed! Although he might disburden himself and get rid of the load, he rather continues to brood over his vexing wealth – he goes on obstinately clinging to his tormenting hoards. From him there is no liberality to dependents, no communication to the poor. And yet such people call that their own money, which they guard with jealous labor, shut up at home as if it were another's, and from which they derive no benefit either for their friends, for their children, or, in fine, for themselves. Their possession amounts to this only, that they can keep others from possessing it; and oh, what a marvellous perversion of names! They call those things goods, which they absolutely put to none but bad uses.
~ Cyprian, 200-258 ~
Epistle to Donatus

GRIEF / SORROW

Break not your heart; sorrow will roll away like the mists at sunrise.
~ Sotho Wisdom ~

The soul-endearing soothings of cordial love have the best and strongest
effects upon the grief-torn mind … We mistake too commonly the objects
of our grief – the living demand our tears – the dead (if their lives were
virtuous) our gratulations.
~ Ignatius Sancho, 1729-1780 ~
Letter XXII to Mr WE, 1779 March 31 in *The Letters of the Late Ignatius Sancho, an African*, Vol. II,
1782

I do not think that we hot-blooded Creoles sorrow less for showing it so
impetuously; but I do think that the sharp edge of our grief wears down
sooner than theirs who preserve an outward demeanour of calmness, and
nurse their woe secretly in their hearts.
~ Mary Seacole, 1805-1881 ~
Wonderful Adventures of Mrs Seacole in Many Lands, 1857

Man needs to suffer. When he does not have real griefs he creates them.
Griefs purify and prepare him.
~ José Martí, 1853-1895 ~
"Adúltera" (Adulterous Thoughts), 1883

This is just life; it's not to be cried over, just understood.
~ Ralph Ellison, 1914-1994 ~
"And Hickman Arrives," 1960

Your eyes that sparkle teach me how to mourn
For all our deaths are certain as our births.
~ Martin Carter, 1927-1997 ~
"What We Call Wings," *Poems of Succession*, 1997

Say what you will, do what you will, life is not to be measured by the ell of
its sorrow.
~ Patrick Chamoiseau, b. 1953 ~
Texaco, Rose-Myriam Réjouis & Val Vinokurov, trs., 1992

GROWTH / EXPANSION

Everyone needs, if not a culture hero, a culturally heroic society. There is nothing stronger in a man than the need to grow.
~ Katherine Dunham, 1910-2006 ~
in *New York Times*, 2006 May 23

It takes a deep commitment to change and an even deeper commitment to grow.
~ Ralph Ellison, 1914-1994 ~

Growing is the reward of learning.
~ Malcolm X, 1925-1965 ~

Most people don't really grow up. What they do is grow old, they grow tiresome even and self-righteous maybe, for it is very hard to grow. Because it means they must give up something. Usually their ignorance.
~ Maya Angelou, b. 1928 ~
in *New York Newsday*, 1993 January 12

How I wish I could pigeon-hole myself and neatly fix a label on! But self-knowledge comes too late! By the time I've known myself I am no longer what I was.
~ Mabel Segun, b. 1930 ~

Whenever we stop growing, we start deteriorating.
~ Louis Farrakhan, b. 1934 ~

If you put yourself in a position where you have to stretch outside your comfort zone, then you are forced to expand your consciousness.
~ Les Brown, b. 1945 ~

A long and sometimes painful process of personal growth ... began with learning to tell the truth to myself, and then the truth about myself.
~ Ayaan Hirsi Ali, b. 1969 ~

You grow, we all grow, we're made to grow. You either grow or disappear.
~ Tupac Shakur, 1971-1996

GUILT

The depraved maligns the depraved, and thinks that he himself, though conscious of the guilt, has escaped, as if consciousness were not a sufficient condemnation. The same people who are accusers in public are criminals in private, condemning themselves at the same time as they condemn the culprits; they denounce abroad what they commit at home, willingly doing what, when they have done, they accuse.
~ Cyprian, 200-258 ~
Epistle to Donatus

Guilt never decays.
~ Sotho Wisdom ~
Wit & Wisdom of Africa: Proverbs from Africa & The Caribbean, Patrick Ibekwe, ed., 1998

If they are uttering insults and don't mean you, and yet you reply, you have condemned yourself.
~ Tshi Wisdom ~
Ibid.

To those who are conscious of themselves there can be no incrimination from without, it must be from within. When a man's conscience convicts him then there is no appeal.
~ Marcus Garvey, 1887-1940 ~
"Statement to Press on Release on Bail Pending Appeal," 1923 September 10

One who condones evils is just as guilty as the one who perpetrates it.
~ Martin Luther King, Jr., 1929-1968 ~

I have no creative use for guilt, yours or my own. Guilt is only another way of avoiding informed action, of buying time out of the pressing need to make clear choices, out of the approaching storm that can feed the earth as well as bend the trees.
~ Audre Lorde, 1934-1992 ~
"The Uses of Anger," 1981, *Sister Outsider: Essays and Speeches*, 1984

The best advice when called out for something that you've done or have failed to do: Swallow your pride, own up to it, take the medicine, pick up what's left and move on as best you can.
~ Colbert King, b. 1939 ~
"The Quarterback Who Won't Come Clean," *Washington Post*, 2007 August 25

HABIT

Habit is a full-grown mountain, hard to get over or to pull down.
~ Kongo Wisdom ~
Wit & Wisdom of Africa: Proverbs from Africa & The Caribbean, Patrick Ibekwe, ed., 1998

Treading on the road constantly makes it smooth.
~ Luo Wisdom ~
Ibid.

Habit is Heaven's own redress:
it takes the place of happiness.
~ Aleksandr Pushkin, 1799-1837 ~
Eugene Onegin, 1823, 2.31

(Breaking) ritual habit, ritual normality that seals our eyes and ears ... you
can advance, see things you never saw before, move out of boundaries that
have been a prison
~ Wilson Harris, b. 1921 ~
in Maya Jaggi, "Redemption Song," *The Guardian*, 2006 December 16

First forget *inspiration*. Habit is more dependable. Habit will sustain you
whether you're inspired or not ... Habit is persistence in practice.
~ Octavia Butler, 1947-2006 ~
Bloodchild and Other Stories, 1995

We are creatures of habit ... Our overall approach to life rarely changes.
Instead of being creative, and allowing ourselves to explore new ideas and
adventures, we cling to the familiar ... Our whole existence is centered
around conditioned responses and predictable outcomes. To grow and
evolve into the best persons we can be, we must have the courage and the
faith to take chances. Risk-taking is a fundamental part of living a
meaningful life. By forcing ourselves to break free of our ordinary routines,
we are able to experience the boundless.
~ Roderick Terry, b. 1964 ~
"Hope Chest"

Most of our failings are habits we have allowed ourselves to form and keep.
We will probably never be perfect, but we can be less imperfect.
~ *The Twelve Steps and Twelve Traditions of the Al-Anon Groups*, 1980 ~

HAPPINESS / CONTENTMENT

Happiness is like perfume; you can't pour it on somebody else without getting a few drops on yourself.
~ James Van Der Zee, 1886-1983 ~

Happiness shared with many creates a source of permanent affection and understanding, but private happiness is a temporary matter.
~ Haile Selassie, 1892-1975 ~

Don't wait around for other people to be happy for you. Any happiness you get you've got to make yourself.
~ Alice Walker, b. 1944 ~

I'm a slave to my heart. I don't know what's going to happen tomorrow. Happiness isn't for tomorrow. It's not hypothetical, it starts here and now.
~ Salif Keita, b. 1949 ~
GlobalVillageIdiot.net

You know that line in the Declaration of Independence, "the pursuit of happiness"? I've come to think that it has no meaning at all. You cannot pursue happiness. And to think that this bad little sentence has determined our lives.
~ Jamaica Kincaid, b. 1949 ~
Interview by Marilyn Snell, *Mother Jones*, 1997 September/October

Happiness doesn't depend nearly as much on our circumstances as it does on our relationships, our attitudes, and our beliefs. It comes not as much from what we have and acquire, but from what we accomplish in the way of attaining our goals.
~ Benjamin Carson, b. 1951 ~

The quest for happiness is something that is never resolved in any civilization. It cannot be to go to Paris or anywhere else. That would be too easy. We build happiness in different ways, and we manage when we have hope.
~ Abderrahmane Sissako, b. 1961 ~
Interview by Olivier Barlet, *Africultures*, 2003 April 18

HASTE / IMPATIENCE

Going slowly does not stop one from arriving.
~ Fulfulde Wisdom ~
in *Black Woman's Gumbo Ya-Ya*, Terri L. Jewell, ed., 1993

Running too fast does not guarantee that you reach your destination.
~ Shona Wisdom ~

He who takes his food in a hurry is also choked in a hurry.
~ Kikuyu Wisdom ~
Wit & Wisdom of Africa: Proverbs from Africa & The Caribbean, Patrick Ibekwe, ed., 1998

Hurry and well-done never go hand in hand.
~ Haitian Wisdom ~
Ibid.

So much of growing up is an unbearable waiting. A constant longing for
another time. Another season.
~ Sonia Sanchez, b. 1934 ~
"Graduation Notes," *From Under a Soprano Sky*, 1987

Trouble, turmoil, tribulation and temptation: that's the given, that's the
context. What is the response for calamity? Endurance. Don't rush, don't
panic. What are we to do in calamitous times? We are to slow down. We
are to inquire. We are to endure. Tribulation does not invite haste; it
invites contemplation, reflection, perseverance, endurance.
~ Peter J. Gomes, b. 1942 ~
Strength for the Journey: Biblical Wisdom for Daily Living, 2003

We rush from one task to the next ignoring the flashing yellow lights in our
subconscious mind, which caution us to slow down. Doing nothing or just
being overwhelms us with guilt.
~ Roderick Terry, b. 1964 ~
"Hope Chest"

One way to slow down and begin to change our perspective is to begin to
measure our lives by each breath we take, rather than by each day, month,
or year … It won't make a better you or a worse you. But it will reveal you.
~ Angel Kyodo Williams ~
Being Black: Zen and the Art of Living with Fearlessness and Grace, 2000

HATE

Men remain in ignorance as long as they hate, and they hate unjustly as long as they remain in ignorance.
~ Tertullian, c. 160-240 ~
Apology, 197

He who hates, hates himself.
~ Zulu Wisdom ~

Hate burns its preserver.
~ Swahili Wisdom ~
Wit & Wisdom of Africa: Proverbs from Africa & The Caribbean, Patrick Ibekwe, ed., 1998

Fear of something is at the root of hate for others and hate within will eventually destroy the hater.
~ George Washington Carver, 1864-1943 ~
George Washington Carver: Man of God, 1954

When our thoughts – which bring actions – are filled with hate against anyone, Negro or white, we are in a living hell. That is as real as hell will ever be.
~ Carver ~

Hate is consuming and weakening. Hateful thinking breeds negative actions. There is no sense in hate: it comes back to you; therefore make your history so laudable, magnificent, and untarnished that another generation will not seek to repay your seeds for the sins inflicted upon their fathers.
~ Marcus Garvey, 1887-1940 ~

You lose a lot of time hating people.
~ Marian Anderson, 1897-1993 ~

No one is born hating another person because of the color of his skin, or his background or his religion. People must learn to hate, and if they can learn to hate, they can be taught to love, for love comes more naturally to the human heart than its opposite.
~ Nelson Mandela, b. 1918 ~
Long Walk to Freedom, 1994

Hatred, which could destroy so much, never failed to destroy the man who hated and this is an immutable law … Remember, to hate, to be violent, is demeaning. It means you're afraid of the other side of the coin – to love and be loved.
~ James Baldwin, 1924-1987 ~

I imagine one of the reasons people cling to their hates so stubbornly is because they sense, once the hate is gone, that they will be forced to deal with pain.
~ Baldwin ~
Notes of a Native Son, 1958

Hate is too great a burden to bear. It injures the hater more than it injures the hated.
~ Coretta Scott King, 1927-2006 ~

Hatred and bitterness can never cure the disease of fear; only love can do that. Hatred paralyzes life; love releases it. Hatred confuses life; love harmonizes it. Hatred darkens life; love illuminates it.
~ Martin Luther King, Jr., 1929-1968 ~

Like an unchecked cancer, hate corrodes the personality and eats away its vital unity. Hate destroys a man's sense of values and his objectivity. It causes him to describe the beautiful as ugly and the ugly as beautiful, and to confuse the true with the false and the false with the true.
~ King ~

The price of hating other human beings is loving oneself less.
~ Eldridge Cleaver, 1935-1998 ~
"On Becoming," *Soul on Ice*, 1968

All hatred is the same in one sense; hatred always, first and foremost, diminishes the human spirit and possibility of the person who hates. It is a negative, usually destructive force. But people hate differently and for different reasons.
~ Thomas Glave, b. 1964 ~
Interview by Tanya Batson-Savage, *Jamaica Daily Gleaner*, 2006 February 12

HAVING / POSSESSING

Learn that the advantage lieth not in possessing good things but in knowing the use of them.
~ Khemetic Wisdom ~
Temt Tchaas: Egyptian Proverbs, Muata Ashaya Ashby, ed., 1994

What a person possesses is not stronger than him or herself.
~ Kanuri Wisdom ~

Whom you consider rich ... Such a one enjoys no security either in his food or in his sleep. In the midst of the banquet he sighs, although he drinks from a jewelled goblet; and when his luxurious bed has enfolded his body, languid with feasting, in its yielding bosom, he lies wakeful in the midst of the down; nor does he perceive, poor wretch, that these things are merely gilded torments, that he is held in bondage by his gold, and that he is the slave of his luxury and wealth rather than their master ... Their possession amounts to this only, that they can keep others from possessing it.
~ Cyprian, 200-258 ~
Epistle to Donatus

In an acquisitive society wealth tends to corrupt those who possess it. It tends to breed in them a desire to live more comfortably than their fellows, to dress better, and in every way to outdo them ... The visible contrast between their own comfort and the comparative discomfort of the rest of society becomes almost essential to the enjoyment of their wealth, and this sets off the spiral of personal competition – which is then anti-social.
~ Julius Nyerere, 1922-1999 ~

If you look to find meaning in owning things, you'll find that your things are never good enough and that the things end up owning you. You begin to compare your stuff with other people's stuff, and you decide your stuff isn't as good as their stuff, so you want better stuff. Then you need more money and a bigger house. That's why materialism is acid soil for the roots of your happiness.
~ Famous Amos, b. 1937 ~
Watermelon Magic, 1996

You can live without anything you weren't born with, and you can make it through on even half of that.
~ Gloria Naylor, b. 1950 ~

HEALTH / HEALING

What health is to the body, even that is honesty to the soul. Develop your spirit that it may gain strength to control the body and follow the natural laws of nutrition and hygiene.
~ Khemetic Wisdom ~
Temt Tchaas: Egyptian Proverbs, Muata Ashaya Ashby, ed., 1994

The body becomes what the foods are, as the spirit becomes what the thoughts are.
~ Ibid.

Healing without medicine is a good thing.
~ Madagascan Wisdom ~

Belief kills and belief cures.
~ Jamaican Wisdom ~

Another benefit has been conferred upon them by inclining the Creoles to practise the healing art, and inducing them to seek out the simple remedies which are available for the terrible diseases ... and which are found growing under the same circumstances which produce the ills they minister to. So true is it that beside the nettle ever grows the cure for its sting.
~ Mary Seacole, 1805-1881 ~
Wonderful Adventures of Mrs Seacole in Many Lands, 1857

If health fails, teaching, knowledge, life itself, all comes to naught. It is indispensable, so have nothing to do with alcohol and avoid all things against which conscience speaks.
~ Haile Selassie, 1892-1975 ~

Avoid fried meats, which angry up the blood. If your stomach disputes you, lie down and pacify it with cool thoughts. Keep the juices flowing by jangling around gently as you move. Go very light on the vices, such as carrying on in society – the social ramble ain't restful.
~ Satchel Paige, 1900-1982 ~
Formula for Staying Young, 1953

This is the paradox: whether healing should not be associated with seeing through the infirmities in ourselves, rather than seeking an invulnerable self ... there is a wound which ... can have healing power, provided we can understand its implications, its enormous implications, its subtle implications, so that you move into timelessness through a wound.
~ Wilson Harris, b. 1921 ~
"Theatre of the Arts," 2001

As soon as healing takes place, go out and heal somebody else.
~ Maya Angelou, b. 1928 ~

Whatever we can do to facilitate learning on the one hand and loving on the other is important, because those are the most healing forces we have available to us.
~ Na'im Akbar, b. 1944 ~
Interview by Jill Nelson, *Essence*, 1989 February

Sunlight and good food ... can cure spiritual cancer.
~ Bill Strickland, b. 1947 ~
Sierra Club "Spirit in Nature" Address, 2004

Methods of healing must take into account the energetic or spiritual condition that is in turmoil, thereby affecting the physical condition. If you focus only on the physical translation of the underlying energetic disorder, then you are ignoring the source of the physical illness ... If you instead address the energy of the mind and Spirit, whose status is affecting the physical body, then you are likely to heal truly.
~ Malidoma Somé, b. 1956 ~
The Healing Wisdom of Africa, 1999

Healing comes when the individual remembers his or her identity – the purpose chosen in the world of ancestral wisdom – and reconnects with that world of Spirit.
~ Ibid.

You can't help anyone else if you haven't helped yourself first ... Many of us try to save the world without first saving ourselves from destruction, addiction, negative relationships, or even financial ruin ... it's much easier to tell others how to solve their problems than to solve your own. But we are more effective and more persuasive as healers of others when we are healing ourselves as well.
~ Keith Boykin, b. 1965 ~
Respecting the Soul: Daily Reflections for Black Lesbians and Gays, 1999

HUMILITY / MODESTY

Humility is a greater virtue than defying death; it triumphs over vanity and conceit; conquer them in yourself first.
~ Khemetic Wisdom ~
Temt Tchaas: Egyptian Proverbs, Muata Ashaya Ashby, ed., 1994

Be not arrogant because of your knowledge, but confer with the ignorant man as with the learned.
~ Ptahotep, c. 2350 BCE ~

Humility is the foundation of all the other virtues hence, in the soul in which this virtue does not exist there cannot be any other virtue except in mere appearance.
~ Augustine of Hippo, 354-430 ~

It was pride that changed angels into devils; it is humility that makes men as angels.
~ Augustine ~

You need to recognise your own mortality and should recognise that whatever talents you have were given to you, and it is for you to use them carefully and not to be arrogant with them or to believe that you are some "almighty."
~ Trevor Rhone, b. 1940 ~
Interview by Kinisha O'Neill, *Jamaica Daily Gleaner*, 2003 March 31

Humility is the fruit of inner security and wise maturity.
~ Cornel West, b. 1954 ~

Our egos ... jump ahead of us and prejudicially judge the situation from the surface. We dwell on the frivolities and we think it is insulting or degrading for us to do that which is only an expression of our humble divine nature. We refuse to budge from our positions of pride and authority and we refuse to compromise even when such a little concession would make all the difference in the world. And by so doing we unconsciously extend the difficult situation not knowing that our momentary ego-triumph is only a postponement of that which we think we are running from.
~ Oliver Mbamara ~
"A Little Smile (A Harmless Reminder)," *Cafe Africana*, 2006 September

HUMOR / LAUGHTER

Take bad things make jokes.
~ Jamaican Wisdom ~

Like a welcome summer rain, humor may suddenly cleanse and cool the earth, the air and you.
~ Langston Hughes, 1902-1967 ~

Thank God you've got a sense of humor or you'd be in trouble.
~ Eartha Kitt, b. 1927 ~
Interview by Blase DiStefano, "Eartha Kitt *Purr*-severes: The Feline Feminist Talks About Her Two Lives as the Child and the Woman," *OutSmart*

You repossess your life when you laugh at the things that try to destroy you.
~ Toni Morrison, b. 1931 ~
in *Washington Post*, 1993 October 10

You can turn painful situations around through laughter. If you can find humor in anything – even poverty – you can survive it.
~ Bill Cosby, b. 1937 ~

We laugh from relief, from grief, from fear and from anxiety. We laugh the laugh perfected by Africans and people of African descent everywhere over the last 500 years. The kind we do to stop ourselves from crying.
~ Ama Ata Aidoo, b. 1942 ~
"And All the Jokes Are Cruel," *New Internationalist*, No. 333, 2001 April

A good source of humor is the ability to laugh at oneself. When we are able to laugh at our own shortcomings and imperfections, we more readily empathize with the shortcomings and imperfections of others. Laughter helps us to bridge the gap between ourselves and the outside world. By taking attention away from our own problems and concerns, laughter allows us to be absorbed in something other than ourselves; it allows us to look at life in a more delightful way.
~ Roderick Terry, b. 1964 ~
"Hope Chest"

IDEA / OPINION

When an idea exclusively occupies the mind, it is transformed into an actual physical state.
~ Khemetic Wisdom ~
Temt Tchaas: Egyptian Proverbs, Muata Ashaya Ashby, ed., 1994

Two fixed ideas can no more exist together in the moral world than two bodies can occupy one and the same place in the physical world.
~ Aleksandr Pushkin, 1799-1837 ~
The Queen of Spades, 1890

Let's trace the birth of an idea. It's born as rampant radicalism, then it becomes progressivism, then liberalism, then it becomes moderate, conservative, outmoded, and gone.
~ Adam Clayton Powell, Jr., 1908-1972 ~

Individual ideas, like breaths, are waiting to be drawn from unlimited supply.
~ Margaret Danner, 1915-1984 ~

I'll tell you this, I may be dead but my ideas will not die.
~ Ken Saro-Wiwa, 1941-1995 ~

Someone's opinion of you does not have to become your reality.
~ Les Brown, b. 1945 ~

What other people may have to say about you is simply their opinion. It's not who you are. Their opinion about you is not reality. Reality is what is inside you.
~ RuPaul, b. 1960 ~
Lettin It All Hang Out, 1995

When people try to force their definitions and perspectives on others ... independence of thought becomes threatened and perhaps gradually eroded. Inevitably, opinions are formed based on wrong impressions and as many begin to buy into such flawed impressions, it becomes the generally acceptable truth for many believers. It becomes the norm and the one who disagrees ... is cast aside as the unbeliever or the unorthodox one.
~ Oliver Mbamara ~
"Who is A Wealthy Person? (Impressions, Beliefs, and Definitions)," Part 1, ExpressionsofSoul.com, 2007 May

IDENTITY

It is not what I call you, it's what you answer to: but if you don't know who you are, anyone can name you. If anybody can name you, you will answer to anything.
~ African Wisdom ~

We ain't what we wanna be, and we ain't what we gonna be. But thank God, we ain't what we was.
~ Afican-American Wisdom ~

God made us in his own image, and he had some purpose when he thus created us; then why should we seek to destroy our identity?
~ Marcus Garvey, 1887-1940 ~

Identity would seem to be the garment with which one covers the nakedness of the self, in which case, it is best that the garment be loose, a little like the robes of the desert, through which one's nakedness can always be felt, and, sometimes, discerned.
~ James Baldwin, 1924-1987 ~

An identity would seem to be arrived at by the way in which the person faces and uses his experience.
~ Baldwin ~

Through many experiences, I have instilled in myself diverse cultures, without losing my Haitian roots. My roots are very diverse ... people believe they can reveal the identity of a person through only one of its roots. It is a lure. More and more, the identity of the whole humanity is becoming very diverse.
~ René Depestre, b. 1926 ~

We must dispense with the notion of a fixed identity. But this is difficult because, for example, blacks, who are suffering, cannot renounce the idea of a fixed identity because a fixed identity is like a weapon. It is a means to do battle, to defend oneself. But in my opinion the more that we employ this method, the more we defer the moment of true relation.
~ Édouard Glissant, b. 1928 ~
Interview by Michael Dash, *Renaissance Noire*, Hillina Seife, tr., 2006 March 22

We should also get accustomed to the idea that our identity is going to change profoundly on contact with the Other as his will on contact with us, without either of them losing their essential nature or being diluted in a multicultural magma.
~ Glissant ~
Interview by Tirthankar Chanda, *Label France*, 2000 January, No. 38

And she had nothing to fall back on; not maleness, not whiteness, not ladyhood, not anything. And out of profound desolation of her reality she may very well have invented herself.
~ Toni Morrison, b. 1931 ~

We need to update the vision of who we really are. We need to recognize that wherever we have come from and whatever we have brought from different regions, even in awkward circumstances – all of it – is really our heritage.
~ Earl Lovelace, b. 1935 ~
Speech, University of the West Indies, St. Augustine, Trinidad, 2002 November 1

Many people have trouble separating what they do and what happens to them from who they are. They think they are their behavior. You are not your behavior. You are separate from and more than your behavior. Who you are is much more important than how you behave. When you begin to appreciate the fantastic being that you are, you will also begin to see a change in your behavior.
~ Famous Amos, b. 1937 ~
Watermelon Magic, 1996

Once you know who you are, you don't have to worry any more ... She knows who she is because she knows who she isn't.
~ Nikki Giovanni, b. 1943 ~

Whatever is a source of shame – if you are not responsible for it, such as the color of your skin or your sexuality – you should just wear it as a badge.
~ Jamaica Kincaid, b. 1949 ~
Interview by Dwight Garner, *Salon*

I rebel at the notion that I can't be part of other groups, that I can't construct identities through elective affinity, that race must be the most important thing about me ... I want to be black, to know black, to luxuriate in whatever I might be calling blackness at any particular time – but to do so in order to come out the other side, to experience a humanity

that is neither colorless nor reducible to color.
~ Henry Louis Gates, Jr., b. 1950 ~
Colored People: A Memoir, 1994

I wanted freedom to invent and reinvent myself. You have to tell the world, "I define myself. I will not be defined."
~ Bill T. Jones, b. 1952 ~
in *Metro Weekly*, 2002 February 7

The Medusa Syndrome: It's really about freezing people in their identities by looking at them. Real identities have a kind of historical flexibility. A lot of cultural preservationists who purport to be respecting people in their identities are really just insisting that they stay the way they were.
~ K. Anthony Appiah, b. 1954 ~
Interview by Drake Bennett, *Boston Globe*, 2005 February 6

We can't rely on anyone but ourselves to define our existence, to shape the image of ourselves.
~ Spike Lee, b. 1957 ~

Labels are very important to me. They're a way of finding community and a way of community finding you … For me, identity is kind of a mailbox.
~ Nalo Hopkinson, b. 1960 ~
Interview by Kellie Magnus, *Caribbean Review of Books*, Issue 73

You're born naked. The rest is drag.
~ RuPaul, b. 1960 ~
"On Being Almost Seven Feet Tall Without Shoes," *New York Times*, 1993 July 11

Many of us are confused about what to call ourselves … As important as they are … (no) words can encompass your whole identity. Don't allow anyone to box you into a category that doesn't satisfy you and, just as importantly, do not allow anyone to remove a part of your identity as a price for their acceptance of you.
~ Keith Boykin, b. 1965 ~
Respecting the Soul: Daily Reflections for Black Lesbians and Gays, 1999

My identity shifts; it's a constant issue for Africans. I'm here in the U.S. now, so I'm "African" or "black." If I went to another African country, I'd be Nigerian. When I'm back in Nigeria, I would primarily be seen as Igbo. And for me, really, it depends on where I am.
~ Chimamanda Ngozi Adichie, b. 1977 ~
Interview by Rita Palter, *Mother Jones*, 2006 October 24

IMAGINATION

Distant fire-wood is good fire-wood.
~ Ewe Wisdom ~
Wit & Wisdom of Africa: Proverbs from Africa & The Caribbean, Patrick Ibekwe, ed., 1998

If you have no eye, the mind takes you there.
~Jabo Wisdom ~
Ibid.

Imagination! Who can sing thy force?
Or who describe the swiftness of thy course? ...
We on thy pinions can surpass the wind
And leave the rolling universe behind.
~ Phillis Wheatley, 1753-1784 ~
"On Imagination"

Your imagination is the instrument, the means, whereby your redemption from slavery, sickness, and poverty is effected. If you refuse to assume the responsibility of the incarnation of a new and higher concept of yourself, then you *reject the means, the only means, whereby your redemption – that is, the attainment of your ideal – can be effected.* Imagination is the only redemptive power in the universe.
~ Neville, 1905-1972 ~
The Power of Awareness, 1952

A lot of living is done in the imagination.
~ Ralph Ellison, 1914-1994 ~

If one is lucky, a solitary fantasy can totally transform one million realities.
~ Maya Angelou, b. 1928 ~

The creative imagination lies beyond the reach of the vilest oppressor.
~ Rex Nettleford, b. 1933 ~
Dance Jamaica: Cultural Definition and Artistic Discovery, 1985

Dream big dreams! Others may deprive you of your material wealth and cheat you in a thousand ways, but no man can deprive you of the control and use of your imagination.
~ Jesse Jackson, b. 1941 ~
in *Brother's Keeper: Words of Inspiration for African-American Men*, Roderick Terry, ed., 1996

Although the human imagination is boundless, it can only ride on the realities of our individual lives. We dream out of who we are and something of our tangible lives is bound to be part of our writing.
~ Ama Ata Aidoo, b. 1942 ~

A man who has no imagination has no wings.
~ Muhammad Ali, b. 1942 ~

Operate out of your imagination, not your memory.
~ Les Brown, b. 1945 ~

I began to learn how to use my imagination more, because it doesn't really require a lot of imagination to watch television, but it does to read. You've got to take those letters and make them into words, and those words into sentences, and those sentences into concepts, and the more you do that, the more vivid your imagination becomes.
~ Benjamin Carson, b. 1951 ~
"Gifted Hands That Heal," Academy of Achievement Interview, 2002 June 7

Without imagination we can go nowhere. And imagination is not something that's just restricted to the arts. Every scientist that I have met who has been a success has had to imagine. You have to imagine it possible before you can see something, sometimes. You can have the evidence right in front of you, but if you can't imagine something that has never existed before, it's impossible.
~ Rita Dove, b. 1952 ~
"The Possibility Poet," Academy of Achievement Interview, 1994 June 18

The human capacity to imagine is an example of our connection with remote fields of energy. If human consciousness is able to capture, and thereby understand, these realities, then imagination and visionary consciousness are linking us to other types of realties, directly or otherwise.
~ Malidoma Somé, b. 1956 ~
The Healing Wisdom of Africa, 1999

Imagination is the bridge between
the things we know for sure
and the things we need to believe
when our world becomes unbearable.
~ Staceyann Chin, b. 1973 ~

IMPERMANENCE

Come in peace, enjoy life on earth but do not become attached to it; it is transitory.
~ Khemetic Wisdom ~
from the Stele of Abu, in *Temt Tchaas: Egyptian Proverbs*, Muata Ashaya Ashby, ed., 1994

Life is a shadow and a mist; it passes quickly by, and is no more.
~ Madagascan Wisdom ~

No plant comes to flower but to wither.
~ South African Wisdom ~
Wit & Wisdom of Africa: Proverbs from Africa & The Caribbean, Patrick Ibekwe, ed., 1998

What happened to the old winnowing tray will happen to the new one.
~ Swahili Wisdom ~
Ibid.

Sad that our finest aspiration
Our freshest dreams and meditations,
In swift succession should decay,
Like Autumn leaves that rot away.
~ Aleksandr Pushkin, 1799-1837 ~
Eugene Onegin, 1823, 8.10

The changes which take place in the affairs of this world show the instability of sublunary things. Empires rise and fall, flourish and decay. Knowledge follows revolutions and travels over the globe.
~ John B. Russwurm, 1799-1851 ~
"The Condition and Prospects of Haiti," Commencement Address, Bowdoin College, 1826 September 6

Every artist wants his work to be permanent. But what is? The Aswan Dam covered some of the greatest art in the world. Venice is sinking. Great books and pictures were lost in the Florence floods. In the meantime we still enjoy butterflies.
~ Romare Bearden, 1914-1988 ~

It is a fact of the human condition that each shall, like a meteor, a mere brief passing moment in time, flit across the human stage and pass out of existence.
~ Nelson Mandela, b. 1918 ~
Address to US Congress, 1990 January 26

the man spiritual is above all
the man thinkin is "me"
thinkin on the care of my body
of my worldly possessions
never stoppin to know
that all worldly
things
must
go
~ Mutabaruka, b. 1952 ~
The First Poems, 1983

If it was not here before, it's not permanent, it belongs to the changeful. It will go. Let it come and go, this is natural and this is freedom itself.
~ Mooji, b. 1954 ~

So many things became transient, and more valuable. It was not that these things had value, it was that the ephemeral quality hanging over me, over life, gave value to them.
~ Chimamanda Ngozi Adichie, b. 1977 ~
Half of A Yellow Sun, 2006

Mindful attention helped me see that what I experienced as being solid, this very body, my feelings, my thoughts, my sensations – are impermanent. They come and go, and if I am able to just be present with them in the movement of coming and going without holding on to them or identifying with them, I don't suffer. What a discovery!
~ Hilda Gutiérrez Baldoquín ~
"Don't Waste Time," Dharma, Color, and Culture, Hilda Gutiérrez Baldoquín, ed., 2004

Conditions change. The truth of this moment may not be the truth of the next. There is constant movement. Still, we have to honor this moment, because we do not know what the next one holds. And the truth of the past is, well, in the past.
~ Angel Kyodo Williams ~
Being Black: Zen and the Art of Living with Fearlessness and Grace, 2000

INACTION

If you do not gather firewood you cannot keep warm.
~ Ovambo Wisdom ~
Wit & Wisdom of Africa: Proverbs from Africa & The Caribbean, Patrick Ibekwe, ed., 1998

If you send no one to the market, the market will send no one to you.
~ Yoruba Wisdom ~
Ibid.

Leaning against a full granary will not help a hungry man.
~ Fulfulde Wisdom ~
Ibid.

Talking 'bout a fire doesn't boil the pot.
~ African-American Wisdom ~
Ibid.

An untouched drum does not speak.
~ Jabo Wisdom ~
Ibid.

Freedom was something internal. The outside signs were just signs and symbols of the man inside. All you could do was to give the opportunity for freedom and the man himself must make his own emancipation.
~ Zora Neale Hurston, 1891-1960 ~
in *Songs of Wisdom: Quotations from Famous African Americans*, Jay David, ed., 2000

Throughout history it has been the inaction of those who could have acted, the indifference of those who should have known better, the silence of the voice of justice when it mattered most, that has made it possible for evil to triumph.
~ Haile Selassie, 1892-1975 ~

We can go on talking about racism and who treated whom badly, but what are you going to do about it? Are you going to wallow in that or are you going to create your own agenda?
~ Judith Jamison, b. 1943 ~
in *Songs of Wisdom: Quotations from Famous African Americans*, Jay David, ed., 2000

INDIVIDUALITY

Everybody to his or her own calling and none to any other.
~ Bakongo Wisdom ~

The earth is a beehive; we all enter by the same door but live in different cells.
~ Bantu Wisdom ~

Nobody walks with another man's gait.
~ Kikuyu Wisdom ~

If a man is not faithful to his own individuality, he cannot be loyal to anything.
~ Claude McKay, 1889-1948 ~

Every man's spice box seasons his own food.
~ Zora Neale Hurston, 1891-1960 ~

Every person is born into the world to do something unique and something distinctive, and if he or she does not do it, it will never be done.
~ Benjamin Mays, 1895-1984 ~

Like snowflakes, the human pattern is never cast twice. We are uncommonly and marvelously intricate in thought and action, our problems are most complex and, too often, silently borne.
~ Alice Childress, 1920-1994 ~
"A Candle in a Gale Wind," in Mari Evans, *Black Women Writers*, 1984

I gotta be me.
~ Sammy Davis, Jr., 1925-1990 ~

If you understood everything I said, you'd be me.
~ Miles Davis, 1926-1991 ~

When we are individuals and we want to have our own style of living, it is nobody's business but ours. And what we do in private is our private business. And just because you are different does not mean that you have

to be rejected ... We are different, but I'll tell you a phrase we have in French. *Je suis comme je suis.* "I am as I am" – I was born this way, but it's nothing for me to explain. As long as we are not trying to change somebody else to be like me, or like you, or like him, or like her, what's your problem?
~ Eartha Kitt, b. 1927 ~
Interview by Blase DiStefano, "Eartha Kitt *Purr*-severes: The Feline Feminist Talks About Her Two Lives as the Child and the Woman," *OutSmart*

Being your own man does not mean taking advantage of anyone else.
~ Flip Wilson, 1933-1998 ~

Each of us is unique and special. No two sets of fingerprints are the same. Although twins appear alike, they too are different. Out of all the billions of people since the beginning of time, there will never be another you. So enjoy and appreciate your uniqueness.
~ Famous Amos, b. 1937 ~
Watermelon Magic, 1996

You can't be nobody but who you are ... that shadow wasn't nothing but you growing into yourself. You either got to grow into it or cut it down to fit you. But that's all you got to make life with. That's all you got to measure yourself against the world out there.
~ August Wilson, 1945-2005 ~

Life and Jah are one and the same. Jah is the gift of existence. I am in some way eternal, I will never be duplicated. The singularity of every man and woman is Jah's gift. What we struggle to make of it is our sole gift to Jah. The process of what that struggle becomes, in time, the Truth.
~ Bob Marley, 1946-1981 ~

Our identities are a product of our interactions from our earliest years with others. We have a dependence on relationships with others — without them, we couldn't become free selves, or selves at all. Individuality presupposes sociality.
~ K. Anthony Appiah, b. 1954 ~
Interview by Neir Eschel, *Daily Princetonian*, 2003 December 11

There is something about democratic individuality which is very different from rugged, ragged, rapacious individualism.
~ Cornel West, b. 1954 ~

Individuality, not individualism, is the cornerstone of community. Individuality is synonymous with uniqueness. This means that a person and his or her unique gifts are irreplaceable. The community loves to see all of its members flourish and function at optimum potential. In fact, a community can flourish and survive only when each member flourishes, living in the full potential of his or her purpose.
~ Malidoma Somé, b. 1956 ~
The Healing Wisdom of Africa, 1999

I've never understood why people find it so hard to recognize the real person inside of me.
~ RuPaul, b. 1960 ~

Make your purpose "to be yourself" as genuinely and authentically as only you can. No matter how much pressure you face to conform, try to resist the temptation to change those things about you that make you happy, healthy, and unique.
~ Keith Boykin, b. 1965 ~
Respecting the Soul: Daily Reflections for Black Lesbians and Gays, 1999

Our singularity terrifies us. It is not the same as individuality, which we often conflate with the type of music we like, the values and principles we self-righteously cling to, or our deepest sense of self-image. Singularity is the embodiment of our entire being – down to the smallest cellular and microscopic aspect of our corporeal bodies – as well as the non-substantive immaterial spirit that is both contained in and outside our bodies ... Our singularity terrifies us because we know that there is no other like it. To live a life faithful to its architectural spirit, to live in accordance with the demands of its identity (which is singularly our own but has a share in a greater singularity – The One – from which our indubitable version derives its imprint) is to live a life alone in the midst of others.
~ Jason D. Hill, b. 1965 ~
"Moral Hierarchy: The Key to Evolving Consciousness," *What Is Enlightenment? Magazine*, Issue 31

People are afraid to embrace the world as themselves, of walking in this world as themselves. Society, which makes us emulate each other, has created this dynamic where we are all A's and B's, and not the whole of the alphabet, from A to Z. We need to embrace our individuality again, because it's like generational abortion.
~ Lauryn Hill, b. 1975 ~
in Claude Grunitzky, "The Prophet," *Trace*

INDULGENCE / TEMPTATION

If thou wouldst preserve understanding and health to old age, avoid the allurements of Voluptuousness, and fly from her temptations ... The joy which she promiseth changeth to madness, and her enjoyments lead on to disease and death.
~ Akhenaton, c. 1385-c. 1355 BCE ~

We do not pray not to be tempted, but not to be conquered when we are tempted.
~ Origen, c. 185-255 ~
De Principiis, Book 3

Give me chastity and continence – but not yet.
~ Augustine of Hippo, 354-430 ~
Confessions, VIII, 7

There comes the testing of long cherished desires, the thirst for forbidden fruit – and disillusionment, partial or complete, almost inevitably.
~ Charles S. Johnson, 1893-1956 ~
"The New Frontage on American Life," *The New Negro*, 1925

Somebody once said we never know what is enough until we know what's more than enough.
~ Billie Holiday, 1915-1959 ~
Lady Sings the Blues, 1956

Resist no temptation: a guilty conscience is more honorable than regret.
~ Unknown ~

We are free to be tempted.
~ Abderrahmane Sissako, b. 1961 ~
Interview by Olivier Barlet, *Africultures*, 2003April 18

Craving is our habitual thirst, our addictions, our obsessive-compulsiveness in looking for happiness and fulfilment in the wrong ways, as if equanimity could be found from using objects, substances and people ... That is not the way out of suffering.
~ Ralph M. Steele ~
"A Teaching on the Second Noble Truth," *Dharma, Color, and Culture*, Hilda Gutiérrez Baldoquín, ed., 2004

INFLUENCE / EFFECT

One cannot force another to grow beyond their capacity.
~ Khemetic Wisdom ~
Temt Tchaas: Egyptian Proverbs, Muata Ashaya Ashby, ed., 1994

There is no power on earth that can neutralize the influence of a high, simple and useful life.
~ Booker T. Washington, 1856-1915 ~

The course of history can be changed but not halted.
~ Paul Robeson, 1898-1976 ~

A life is not important, except in the impact it has on other lives.
~ Jackie Robinson, 1919-1972 ~

In a way reading is like eating, whatever goes into the body has some influence on the metabolism. You are absorbing things.
~ George Lamming, b. 1927 ~

Everybody is influenced by somebody or something. If there is an original who is the original?
~ Ernestine Anderson, b. 1928 ~

While I was sleeping in my bed there, things were happening in this world that directly concerned me – nobody asked me, consulted me – they just went out and did things – and changed my life.
~ Lorraine Hansberry, 1930-1965 ~
Raisin in the Sun, 1959

You have to be someone who affirms others, someone who is ready to see the good that is in others, and perhaps help to coax it from them.
~ Desmond Tutu, b. 1931 ~
"Forging Equality in South Africa," Academy of Achievement Interview, 2004 June 12

I am who I am, doing what I came to do, acting upon you like a drug or chisel to remind you of your me-ness as I discover you in myself.
~ Audre Lorde, 1934-1992 ~
"Eye to Eye," *Sister Outsider: Essays and Speeches*, 1984

The truly liberated mind is never aggressive about his or her system of beliefs. Because it is founded on such total self confidence, such acceptance of others, that there is no need to march out and propagate one's cause ... The person who needs to convert others is a creature of total insecurity.
~ Wole Soyinka, b. 1934 ~
Interview by Ulli Beier in *Isokan Yoruba Magazine*, Vol. III, No. 3, Summer 1997

Most of our earliest programming comes from our parents. Whether we like it or realize it, we absorb their habits and beliefs at an age when we are under their control and unable to do much about it. Their concerns and values act on us for the better part of our lives, and unless we redefine ourselves and form our own beliefs, we continue to run our parents' programs in our thoughts and actions.
~ Famous Amos, b. 1937 ~
Watermelon Magic, 1996

this the confederacy that i wish: those
who in some way keep the light
from going out. In them
is the small miracle, the tenderness of a desire
that has no reason, that stops us falling
weightless into the dark, that offers us
a difficult and joyful fire.
~ Dennis Scott, 1939-1991 ~
"Companysong"

I don't deal with hope, I deal with work. I consider myself a sower of seeds. One of my golden points is not to turn back to see what is happening, to see what's happening with the seeds; let's keep going sowing. It is a feeling I've been developing for a long, long time. I have the feeling that I came to sow things. You have to know what you can do best.
~ Gilberto Gil, b. 1942 ~
in "Minister of Cool," *Observer* (UK), 2003 October 19

Align yourself with powerful people. Align yourself with people that you can learn from, people who want more out of life, people who are stretching and searching and seeking some higher ground in life.
~ Les Brown, b. 1945 ~
in *Brother's Keeper: Words of Inspiration for African-American Men*, Roderick Terry, ed., 1996

Many a revolution started with the actions of a few. Only 56 men signed the Declaration of Independence. A few hanging together can lead a nation to change.
~ Wynton Marsalis, b. 1961 ~

If you try to cleanse others, like soap you will waste away in the process.
~ Madagascan Wisdom ~

If we think about emotion this way – as outside-in, not inside out – it is possible to understand how some people can have an enormous amount of influence over others. Some of us, after all, are very good at expressiing emotions and feelings, which means that we are far more emotionally contagious than the rest of us.
~ Malcolm Gladwell, b. 1963 ~
The Tipping Point: How Little Things Can Make a Big Difference, 2000

You have power at your disposal that you can use for the benefit of others. To share yourself means to open yourself to other people or to share your talents and resources and experiences with other people. You can start now by thinking of at least one step you can take today to make a difference.
~ Keith Boykin, b. 1965 ~
Respecting the Soul: Daily Reflections for Black Lesbians and Gays, 1999

One must dare to consciously craft a new type of self and reject the old culturally determined self. To change the self is also to change the world. Despite the fact that there might be no political, legislative, and procedural mechanism to sanction such a change, one self that dares to effect such a change leaves the world, in the deepest existential sense, radically altered. It is not the same. A solitary effrontery does leave the world changed.
~ Jason D. Hill, b. 1965 ~
"Moral Hierarchy: The Key to Evolving Consciousness," *What Is Enlightenment? Magazine*, Issue 27

When even one individual is true to his or her vision, it assists in liberating everyone. When even one individual neutralizes or requalifies the thought forms of separation and lack and limitation that run rampant in human experience, he or she creates a spiritual vortex that allows others to be pulled into that same vibration … Whoever touches that spiritual realm has a tendency to lift everyone else up. Whoever has the ability and the willingness to become very still and catch a vision will create an opening for others.
~ Michael Beckwith ~
"Visioning," Interview by Kathy Juline, *Science of Mind Magazine*, 1996 December

It remains certain that the pressure of society is one thing while the consciousness and perspective of parents/guardians remains different but very significant in molding the child's preferences and perspectives.
~ Oliver Mbamara ~
"Who is A Wealthy Person? (Impressions, Beliefs, and Definitions)," Part 2, ExpressionsofSoul.com, 2007 May

INGENUITY

Rice is one, but there are many ways of cooking.
~ Swahili Wisdom ~
Wit & Wisdom of Africa: Proverbs from Africa & The Caribbean, Patrick Ibekwe, ed., 1998

Making do when *don't* prevails is, quite simply, a kind of genius.
~ Johnnetta Cole, b. 1936 ~
"Sturdy Black Bridges," *Being Black in America*, 1993

You start with the perception that the world is an unlimited opportunity.
Then the question becomes, "How are we going to rebuild the planet?"
~ Bill Strickland, b. 1947 ~
in Sara Terry, "Genius at Work," *Fast Company*, No. 17, 1998 August

Can't nothing be wrong in bringing on life, knowing how to get under,
around, and beside nature to give it a slight push. Most folks just don't
know what can be done with a little will and their own hands.
~ Gloria Naylor, b. 1950 ~
Mama Day, 1988

There's that kind of resistance and affirmation ... a way to separate and
deliberately distinguish yourself. You need somehow to affirm those
gestures which the dominant culture looks down upon and considers
inferior or reflecting a flawed personality or a flawed culture. We take that
and reverse it in a way, so that it becomes a virtue rather than a vice or
flaw.
~ Marlon Riggs, 1957-1994 ~
in Chuck Kleinhans & Julia Lesage, "Listening to the Heartbeat: Interview with Marlon Riggs," *Jump Cut: A Review of Contemporary Media*, No.36, 1991

If you run into a wall, don't turn around and give up. Figure out how to
climb it, go through it, or work around it.
~ Michael Jordan, b. 1963 ~
I Can't Accept Not Trying, 1994

Good ideas need landing gear as well as wings.
~ C. D. Jackson ~

INITIATIVE

If initiative is the ability to do the right thing, then efficiency is the ability to do the thing right.
~ Kelly Miller, 1863-1939 ~
Out of the House of Bondage, 1914

I got myself a start by giving myself a start.
~ Madame C. J. Walker, 1867-1919 ~

The man who simply sets and waits
Fur good to come along,
Ain't worth the breath that one would take
To tell him he is wrong.
Fur good ain't flowin' round this world
For every fool to sup;
You've got to put your see-ers on,
An' go an' hunt it up.
~ Paul Laurence Dunbar, 1873-1906 ~
in *Brother's Keeper: Words of Inspiration for African-American Men*, Roderick Terry, ed., 1996

Lift up yourselves. Take yourselves out of the mire and hitch your hopes to the stars.
~ Marcus Garvey, 1887-1940 ~

The first thing is to believe that we can change. It's so easy to sit down and say, I don't like this, I don't like that, and I don't like the other. The central question is, what are you prepared to do about it?
~ Johnnetta Cole, b. 1936 ~
"Spelman's First Female President," Academy of Achievement Interview, 1996 June 28

You can't just sit there and wait for people to give you that golden dream, you've got to get out there and make it happen for yourself.
~ Diana Ross, b. 1944 ~

Nothing is going to be handed to you. You have to make things happen.
~ Florence Griffith Joyner, b. 1959 ~

INNOCENCE

The composure of the one who does no wrong is not disturbed.
~ Mamprussi Wisdom ~
Wit & Wisdom of Africa: Proverbs from Africa & The Caribbean, Patrick Ibekwe, ed., 1998

As there is guilt in innocence, there is innocence in guilt.
~ Yoruba Wisdom ~
Ibid.

If you keep the way of innocence, the way of righteousness, if you walk
with a firm and steady step, if, depending on God with your whole strength
and with your whole heart, you only be what you have begun to be, liberty
and power to do is given you in proportion to the increase of your spiritual
grace. For there is not, as is the case with earthly benefits, any measure or
stint in the dispensing of the heavenly gift.
~ Cyprian, 200-258 ~
Epistle to Donatus

Part of what makes my life so exciting is the innocence I put on myself.
There are some things I don't know and other things I don't want to know.
I'm not carrying any extra baggage with me, so it clears a path and I can do
what I have to do.
~ Judith Jamison, b. 1943 ~
Dancing Spirit: An Autobiography, 1993

Any literal return to childhood is really a revision of childhood experiences
– a reinvention of it since the past is unrecoverable ... It's a wonderful
chance to look at history and all the big ideas through the simplifying lens
of a child's eyes ... There would have to be interruptions or there'd be a
pretense of a unified childhood and then there'd be a showing of how it's
destroyed. After Blake not even innocence can be presumed.
~ Fred D'Aguiar, b. 1960 ~
Interview by Joanne Hyppolite, Fall 1997, *Anthurium: A Caribbean Studies Journal*, II.1, Spring 2004

Giving clear, nonjudgmental attention to everything, true equality
becomes evident.
~ Merle Kodo Boyd ~
"A Child of the South in Long Black Robes," *Dharma, Color, and Culture*, Hilda Gutiérrez Baldoquín,
ed., 2004

INSANITY

Insanity can be treated but not foolishness.
~ Sukuma Wisdom ~
Wit & Wisdom of Africa: Proverbs from Africa & The Caribbean, Patrick Ibekwe, ed., 1998

What is sensible today may be madness tomorrow.
~ Yoruba Wisdom ~
Ibid.

Insanity is a matter of degree.
~ Joaquim Machado de Assis, 1839-1908 ~
Epitaph of a Small Winner, William L. Grossman, tr., 1952

Sometimes it's to your advantage for people to think you're crazy.
~ Thelonious Monk, 1917-1982 ~

When a man asks himself what is meant by action he proves that he isn't a man of action. Action is a lack of balance. In order to act you must be somewhat insane. A reasonably sensible man is satisfied with thinking.
~ James Baldwin, 1924-1987 ~

In Africa, madmen are tolerated because madness is sacred ... A madman no longer decides, no longer distinguishes between good and bad. So we can't judge him. He is untouchable. The origin of madness is a mystery and we don't meddle with it.
~ Assane Kouyaté, b. 1954 ~
Interview by Olivier Barlet, *Africultures*, 2002 July 23

Ideas flow naturally from my original dream, from conception to finish ... It's the way I dream. To do that, one must have a mad belief that everything is possible – you have to be mad to the point of being irresponsible.
~ Djibril Diop Mambety, 1945-1998 ~
in N. Frank Ukadike, "The Hyena's Last Laugh: A Conversation with Djibril Diop Mambety," *Transition 78*, Vol. 8, No. 2, 1999

When the madness of an entire nation disturbs a solitary mind, it is not enough to say the man is mad.
~ Francis Imbuga, b. 1947 ~
Betrayal in the City, 1987

INSECURITY / RISK

Think you that even those are secure – that those at least are safe with some stable permanence among the chaplets of honor and vast wealth, whom, in the glitter of royal palaces, the safeguard of watchful arms surrounds? They have greater fear than others. A man is constrained to dread no less than he is dreaded. Exaltation exacts its penalties equally from the more powerful, although he may be hedged in with bands of satellites, and may guard his person with the enclosure and protection of a numerous retinue. Even as he does not allow his inferiors to feel security, it is inevitable that he himself should want the sense of security.
~ Cyprian, 200-258 ~
Epistle to Donatus

It's very important for members of a minority group to develop inner security. For in that way we become fearless and very decent human beings.
~ Bayard Rustin, 1912-1987 ~
"Black and Gay in The Civil Rights Movement: An Interview with Open Hands," *Time on Two Crosses: The Collected Writings of Bayard Rustin*, Devon W. Carbado & Donald Weise, eds., 2003

If you aspire at all, you are taking a risk. If you aspire as a young black person to something where there is not a beaten path, you are taking a risk. So risk is nothing new in your life. But then, some risks cost more than others, and I guess those are the ones that you recognize as risks. But life is a risk. You try and achieve whatever you as an individual human being can achieve. To make that attempt is a risk.
~ Lloyd Richards, 1919-2006 ~
"Broadway's Groundbreaking Director," Academy of Achievement Interview, 1991 February 15

Most of us, no matter what we say, are walking in the dark, whistling in the dark. Nobody knows what is going to happen to him from one moment to the next, or how one will bear it. This is irreducible. And it's true of everybody. Now, it is true that the nature of society is to create, among its citizens, an illusion of safety; but it is also absolutely true that the safety is always necessarily an illusion.
~ James Baldwin, 1924-1987 ~
"An interview with James Baldwin" by Studs Terkel, 1961
in *Conversations With James Baldwin*, 1989

The unprotected town has never had enemies.
~ Namibian Wisdom ~
Wit & Wisdom of Africa: Proverbs from Africa & The Caribbean, Patrick Ibekwe, ed., 1998

The soft-minded man always fears change. He feels security in the status quo, and he has an almost morbid fear of the new. For him, the greatest pain is the pain of a new idea.
~ Martin Luther King, Jr., 1929-1968 ~

The security of every one of us is linked to that of everyone else ... We all share responsibility for each other's security, and only by working to make each other secure can we hope to achieve lasting security for ourselves.
~ Kofi Annan, b. 1938 ~
Address atTruman Presidential Museum & Library, 2006 December 11

Cliques are all about people trying to find security in groups ... People aren't really together in cliques, and the sense of security they feel is just an illusion. Eventually, all cliques disintegrate. That's why I've always felt secure in my insecurity.
~ RuPaul, b. 1960 ~
Lettin It All Hang Out, 1995

What would happen if you reprogrammed yourself to find security in unfamiliarity? ... By consistently pushing yourself beyond your comfort zone, you'll notice your comfort zone expanding and your fear zone diminishing.
~ Keith Boykin, b. 1965 ~
Respecting the Soul: Daily Reflections for Black Lesbians and Gays, 1999

You have to go through the fear. You do have to do something with the insecurity, ghosts and demons that have been programmed in us for centuries. You have to master the voices, all the insecure and inadequate men who put garbage in a woman's mind, soul, spirit and psyche just so they can use her. You've got to break free of that crap.
~ Lauryn Hill, b. 1975 ~
in Joan Morgan, "They Call Me Ms. Hill," *Essence*, 2006 January

The walls we build around ourselves both mentally and physically give us the false illusion that we are safe, but there's no such thing as a wall that cannot be torn down. When we invest in the idea that we have erected this wall of protection, we naturally make enemies of anything on the other side of the wall.
~ Angel Kyodo Williams ~
Being Black: Zen and the Art of Living with Fearlessness and Grace, 2000

INSIGHT / INSTINCT / INTUITION

Strive to see with the inner eye, the heart. It sees the reality not subject to emotional or personal error; it sees the essence. Intuition then is the most important quality to develop.
~ Khemetic Wisdom ~
Temt Tchaas: Egyptian Proverbs, Muata Ashaya Ashby, ed., 1994

There is something in every one of you that waits and listens for the sound of the genuine in yourself. It is the only true guide you will ever have. And if you cannot hear it, you will all of your life spend your days on the ends of strings that somebody else pulls.
~ Howard Thurman, 1889-1981 ~

One of my little rules is, you get all the facts you can. You get all of the analysis you can. You grind it up in your mental computer and then, when you have all the facts available to you, go with your instinct. I go with my instinct a great deal, but it is not just snap-go. You have to learn the technique of informing your instinct, of educating that little place down in your stomach where instinct resides, so that it is not blind instinct, but informed instinct. Built into each of us is a little calculator that can make judgments that will never appear on a piece of paper. And sometimes you just know something's right – you can't prove it to anybody – or you know something's wrong. Little ethical circuit breakers you carry around inside of you, or little right and wrong circuit breakers ... So, I go with my instinct a great deal.
~ Colin Powell, b. 1937 ~
"America's Premier Soldier-Statesman," Academy of Achievement Interview, 1998 May 23

When you sit silently and pensively, reflecting in moments of introspection in your mind, you are capable or receiving information, like telegrams from the soul of the past.
~ Haile Gerima, b. 1946 ~
in *Atlanta Tribune*, 1994 September 15

Think about it: ain't nobody really talking to you … Uh huh, listen. Really listen this time: the only voice is your own.
~ Gloria Naylor, b. 1950 ~
Mama Day, 1988

The next time you want to know who you are, what you are or if something is the right thing to do, don't ask a neighbour – ask the power within … and pay attention to the response.
~ Iyanla Vanzant, b. 1953 ~
Acts of Faith: Daily Meditations for People of Color, 1993

Follow your instincts. That's where true wisdom manifests itself.
~ Oprah Winfrey, b. 1954 ~

You have to be still. I don't work with a technique – I'm instinctual. I don't try to over-think. I get out of the way.
~ Laurence Fishburne, b. 1961 ~
Interview by Nell Minow, Belief.net

Making sense of ourselves and our behavior requires that we acknowledge there can be as much value in the blink of an eye as in months of rational analysis.
~ Malcolm Gladwell, b. 1963 ~
Blink: The Power of Thinking Without Thinking, 2005

The more diversely you see something, the more you have to grapple with the fact that it's not just the one thing you might have been conditioned to think it was.
~ Thomas Glave, b. 1964 ~
in *Advocate*, 2001 August 14

Rarely does our inner voice speak to us through words. It usually comes to us in the form of images, urges, hunches or intuition. It is a gut feeling that something is right or wrong, the same feeling of knowing one gets before making an important decision. Although we are not always attuned to our innermost perceptions, our inner voice is always there to lead and guide us.
~ Roderick Terry, b. 1964 ~
"Hope Chest"

You can only study but so much. You really have to (look) inward and speak to your soul, and open up your soul and try to connect to that higher being.
~ Blair Underwood, b. 1964 ~
Interview by Michael Kress, Belief.net

INSPIRATION

Just don't give up trying to do what you really want to do. Where there's love and inspiration, I don't think you can go wrong.
~ Ella Fitzgerald, 1917-1996 ~

I don't feel that I am a creator or a performer. I feel that the music of the universe passes through me.
~ Joseph Jarman, b. 1937 ~
Interview by Kurt Gottschalk, *All About Jazz*, 2003 November 8

I'm looking less to musical sources for inspiration and broadening my scope beyond the entertainment field and looking more into life itself. Life today.
~ Herbie Hancock, b. 1940 ~

Helped are those who create anything at all, for they shall relive the thrill of their own conception and realize a partnership in the creation of the Universe that keeps them responsible and cheerful.
~ Alice Walker, b. 1944 ~
in *Songs of Wisdom: Quotations from Famous African Americans*, Jay David, ed., 2000

When I'm working ... I maintain focus until the next burst of activity. It is an intense and sometimes furious activity. To find yourself there at that moment, in a way that you will never be again, is full of what I call "tremor and trust."
~ August Wilson, 1945-2005 ~
Interview by Bonnie Lyons & George Plimpton, *Paris Review*, No. 153, Winter 1999

It is not a question of sitting down under a tree and having inspiration come down. If you wait for inspiration, inspiration's going to go away and look for more fertile ground to work with. There's a lot of work involved in it too. There's a lot of feeling that you're almost there, but you don't even know how to get to that point ... you just simply keep working.
~ Rita Dove, b. 1952 ~
"The Possibility Poet," Academy of Achievement Interview, 1994 June 18

The greatest inspiration is often born of desperation.
~ Comer J. Cotrell, Jr. ~

INTEGRITY

It nothing profits to show virtue in words and destroy truth in deeds.
~ Cyprian, 200-258 ~
On Morality

The remedy for "don't let it be heard" is "don't let it be done."
~ Hausa Wisdom ~
Wit & Wisdom of Africa: Proverbs from Africa & The Caribbean, Patrick Ibekwe, ed., 1998

I prefer to be true to myself, even at the hazard of incurring the ridicule of
others, rather than to be false, and incur my own abhorrence.
~ Frederick Douglass, 1817-1895 ~
Narrative of the Life of Frederick Douglass, An American Slave, Ch.5, 1845

Just be honest. You may only become rich in reputation, but they will
record you as a success.
~ Isaac Murphy, 1856-1896 ~

If a man is not faithful to his own individuality, he cannot be loyal to
anything.
~ Claude McKay, 1889-1948 ~
A Long Way From Home, 1937

If a man can reach the latter days of his life with his soul intact, he has
mastered life.
~ Gordon Parks, 1912-2006 ~

One of the truest tests of integrity is its blunt refusal to be compromised.
~ Chinua Achebe, b. 1930 ~

When we live outside ourselves, and by that I mean on external directives
only rather than from our internal knowledge and needs, when we move
away from those erotic guides within ourselves, then our lives are limited
by external and alien forms, and we conform to the needs of a structure
that is not based on human need, let alone an individual's. When we begin
to live from within *outward*, in touch with the power of the erotic within
ourselves, and allowing the power to inform and illuminate our actions
upon the world around us, then we begin to be responsible to ourselves in
the deepest sense. For as we begin to realize our deepest feelings, we begin

to give up, of necessity, being satisfied with suffering and self-negation, and with the numbness which so often seems like their only alternative in our society. Our acts against oppression become integral with self, motivated and empowered from within.
~ Audre Lorde, 1934-1992 ~

It is impossible for someone to succeed in anything if that person lacks integrity ... without a moral core, without a center, without a set of beliefs about what is right and what is not right ... we can live in this world together with different values, but you've got to have some and you've got to call them your own. And you've got to be true to them.
~ Johnnetta Cole, b. 1936 ~
"Spelman's First Female President," Academy of Achievement Interview, 1996 June 28

I'm the one that has to die when it's time for me to die, so let me live my life, the way I want to.
~ Jimi Hendrix, 1942-1970 ~
"If 6 Was 9," The Jimi Hendrix Experience, *Axis: Bold As Love*, 1967

Being true to yourself really means being true to all the complexities of the human spirit. And as much as ... we want to be perfect, well-rounded individuals – all of us have our quirks. We all know we've had our foibles. And we've got these embarrassing moments in our lives, and things that we're ultimately ashamed of ... Let us see again and experience again, all the ambiguities that make up – and the contradictions that make up – a human being: the good and the bad and how they can exist in one person and make a complex individual. And to do that, that means being very honest. Being honest all the time.
~ Rita Dove, b. 1952 ~
"The Possibility Poet," Academy of Achievement Interview, 1994 June 18

Don't let what other people think decide who you are.
~ Dennis Rodman, b. 1961 ~

I'm coming out 100% real. I ain't compromising anything.
~ Tupac Shakur, 1971-1996 ~

What I want to now, is to manifest the truth, unapologetically; to remain clear; to maintain integrity; to never take advantage of people, even though there may be enticement to do so.
~ Lauryn Hill, b. 1975 ~
in Claude Grunitzky, "The Prophet," *Trace*

INTROSPECTION / SELF-KNOWLEDGE

Make yourself the object of intense study and you will discover God.
~ Khemetic Wisdom ~
Temt Tchaas: Egyptian Proverbs, Muata Ashaya Ashby, ed., 1994

To the possession of the self the way is inward.
~ Plotinus, 205-270 ~

Lack of self- knowledge makes one a slave.
~Ewe Wisdom ~
Wit & Wisdom of Africa: Proverbs from Africa & The Caribbean, Patrick Ibekwe, ed., 1998

Look into yourself.
~ Ovambo Wisdom ~
Ibid.

If you adopt the rule of writing every evening your remarks of the past day, it will be a kind of friendly *tête à tête* between you and yourself, wherein you may sometimes happily become your own Monitor; – and hereafter those little notes will afford you a rich fund, whenever you shall be inclined to retrace past times and places.
~ Ignatius Sancho, 1729-1780 ~
Letter I to Mr JWE, 1768 February 14 in *The Letters of the Late Ignatius Sancho, an African*, Vol. I, 1782

People must be taught the knowledge of self. Then and only then will they be able to understand others and that which surrounds them. Anyone who does not have a knowledge of self is considered a victim of either amnesia or unconsciousness and is not very competent. The lack of knowledge of self is a prevailing condition ... Knowledge of self makes you take on the great virtue of learning.
~ Elijah Muhammad, 1897-1975 ~

When face to face with one's self ... there is no cop-out.
~ Duke Ellington, 1899-1974 ~
Music Is My Mistress, 1973

When I discover who I am, I'll be free.
~ Ralph Ellison, 1914-1994 ~
Invisible Man, 1952

You never find yourself until you face the truth.
~ Pearl Bailey, 1918-1990 ~
The Raw Pearl, 1968

There's a period of life when we swallow a knowledge of ourselves and it becomes either good or sour inside.
~ Bailey ~

The questions which one asks oneself begin, at last, to illuminate the world, and become one's key to the experience of others.
~ James Baldwin, 1924-1987 ~
Nobody Knows My Name: More Notes of a Native Son, 1961

An individual is in part a dream, in part a freedom to be, in part a way of accommodating at the same time to the things one expects, which are perhaps made up of tradition, and then a large part of innovation, of newness. But it is very hard work to arrive at knowing who one is.
~ Maryse Condé, b. 1937 ~

Open your eyes, and look within
Are you satisfied with the life you're living?
~ Bob Marley, 1946-1981 ~

Life is a journey in self-discovery. If we're not growing, we're not living fully. Growth requires self-examination. It requires that we slow the pace, step back from our lives and assess where we are and where we want to go, that we create and live the plan that will take us there.
~ Susan L. Taylor, b. 1946 ~
in *Essence*, 1992 October

In search of self, I listen to the beat of my heart.
~ Marlon Riggs, 1957-1994 ~
Tongues Untied, 1988

Most people are afraid of what lurks deep inside of themselves. They spend a lifetime running away from it or smothering it with food, sex, drugs, or alcohol. One of life's biggest challenges is to look in the mirror, because there's really nothing to be afraid of.
~ RuPaul, b. 1960 ~
Lettin It All Hang Out, 1995

My spirituality is coming alive as I walk, talk and become my path. This is the result of my "coming in" process, my going inside to understand and be with the question "Who am I?" The answer must come from within. Who I am is about discovering, accepting and appreciating all of me.
~ Anthony Farmer, b. 1960 ~
"Shamanism: My Path to Self-Discovery," in *Spirited: Affirming the Soul and Black Gay/Lesbian Identity*, G. Winston James & Lisa C. Moore, eds., 2006

Only through deliberate and serious introspection are we able to develop a positive self-concept. Self-esteem is raised when we acknowledge and take pride in our achievements, make accurate and honest assessments of our strengths and weaknesses, and learn to recognize and appreciate our own attributes and talents.
~ Roderick Terry, b. 1964 ~
Brother's Keeper: Words of Inspiration for African-American Men, 1996

If you look inside your heart
You don't have to be afraid
Of what you are
There's an answer
If you reach into your soul
And the sorrow that you know
Will melt away.
~ Mariah Carey, b. 1969 ~
"Hero," 1993

(My past) very clearly and very brutally affects who I am. In a very good way. It's made me ask myself very hard questions, and it's made me be comfortable with who I am on a level that maybe people aren't.
~ Staceyann Chin, b. 1973 ~
in Jocelyn Voo, "Staceyann Chin: More Than a Mouthful," *Curve*

It is always constructive to reflect on life and evaluate oneself on how far one has made it in this journey of life. No one is a better judge of oneself than one's own self. One can lie to others, display false impressions, or pretend to be what one is not, but one cannot hide from oneself no matter how one tries.
~ Oliver Mbamara ~
"Will You Keep Your New Year Resolution?" *Cafe Africana*, 2003

JEALOUSY / ENVY

Attribute not the good actions of another to bad causes: thou canst not know his heart; but the world will know by this that thine is full of envy.
~ Akhenaton, c. 1385-c. 1355 BCE ~

The heart of the envious is gall and bitterness; his tongue spitteth venom; the success of his neighbor breaketh his rest. He sitteth in his cell repining; and the good that happeneth to another, is to him an evil. Hatred and malice feed upon his heart, and there is no rest in him.
~ Akhenaton ~

What a gnawing worm of the soul is it, what a plague-spot of our thoughts, what a rust of the heart, to be jealous of another, either in respect of his virtue or of his happiness.
~ Cyprian, 200-258 ~
Treatise X: On Jealousy and Envy, 250

An envious heart makes a treacherous ear.
~ Zora Neale Hurston, 1891-1960 ~

Underneath what is sometimes glibly labeled racism or sexism or caste-ism, there lurks covetousness, envy, and greed. All human states that can, through practice, be worked with and transformed.
~ Alice Walker, b. 1944 ~
"This Was Not an Area of Large Plantations," in *Dharma, Color, and Culture*, Hilda Gutiérrez Baldoquín, ed., 2004

Jealousy is the surest way to get rid of the very person you are afraid of losing. When you say I love you, it means "I want the very best for you whether or not I am included" … When jealousy comes up, stop and recognize that it is actually fear raising its ugly head. Fear of losing someone or something, fear that there is not enough. If you allow yourself to be jealous, you cannot love.
~ Iyanla Vanzant, b. 1953 ~
Acts of Faith: Daily Meditations for People of Color, 1993

JOURNEY / PATH

On the journey to the truth, one must stay on the path of love and enlightenment; the heart filled with greed and lust will be overcome by its selfishness.
~ Khemetic Wisdom ~
Temt Tchaas: Egyptian Proverbs, Muata Ashaya Ashby, ed., 1994

Go forth on your path, as it exists only through your walking.
~ Augustine of Hippo, 354-430 ~

To lose your way is one way of finding it.
~ Swahili Wisdom ~
Wit & Wisdom of Africa: Proverbs from Africa & The Caribbean, Patrick Ibekwe, ed., 1998

To miss the trail is to know the trail.
~ Sukuma Wisdom ~
Ibid.

I journey alone because I have resolved to go in search of that which most people do not understand; besides, I was caused to leave by the things which most people love.
~ Thomas Mofolo, 1876-1948 ~
Moeti oa Bochabela (East-Bound Traveler), 1907

You have still far to go. Along the tortuous paths that now lie ahead, you will be exposed to the rigorous teachings of life itself. There you will find no reference books, no study guides. There, there is no going back.
~ Haile Selassie, 1892-1975 ~
Important Utterances of H.I.M. Emperor Haile Selassie I, Jah Rastafari, Volume 1, 1963-1972, 1994

The river is constantly turning and bending and you never know where it's going to go and where you'll wind up. Following the bend in the river and staying on your own path means that you are on the right track. Don't let anyone deter you from that.
~ Eartha Kitt, b. 1927 ~
Interview by Blase DiStefano, "Eartha Kitt *Purr*-severes: The Feline Feminist Talks About Her Two Lives as the Child and the Woman," *OutSmart*

The idea of travel, the thought of wandering, of errancy – which isn't to err, which isn't about getting lost, we are not lost when we wander – is that

we move, we are not fixed in one place, we don't follow one line. If we do, we are thinking systematically. Non-systematic thinking is nurtured and reinforced by errancy and our travels in the world. And this is why I believe in a certain type of nomadism in the world ... Everyone is subject to this.
~ Édouard Glissant, b. 1928 ~
Interview by Michael Dash, *Renaissance Noire*, Hillina Seife, tr., 2006 March 22

Salvation is being on the right road, not having reached a destination.
~ Martin Luther King, Jr., 1929-1968 ~

Instead of asking what are people's roots, we ought to think about what are their *routes*, the different points by which they have come to be now; they are, in a sense, the sum of those differences ... These routes hold us in places, but what they don't do is hold us in the same place. We need to try to make sense of the connections with where we think we were *then* as compared to where we are *now*.
~ Stuart Hall, b. 1932 ~
Seminar, Program in the Comparative Study of Social Transformations (CSST), 1999 April 15

My experiences have shown me that life is truly a journey, and the less baggage we carry the easier the ride.
~ Famous Amos, b. 1937 ~
Watermelon Magic, 1996

My journey is a journey to learn who I am, how to be me, how to love myself and share this love with others. To love myself is to learn to understand me from the inside out and not from the words and beliefs of others. To love myself is to detach from the labels, categories and limited understandings of society, and to redefine myself as I live, think and feel. To love myself is to have the courage to be who I am even when that goes against my cultural norms and I am standing alone.
~ Anthony Farmer, b. 1960 ~
"Shamanism: My Path to Self-Discovery," in *Spirited: Affirming the Soul and Black Gay/Lesbian Identity*, G. Winston James & Lisa C. Moore, eds., 2006

If we hold on to an idea about what the right way to be spiritual is, we may never see ourselves as ready or worthy enough to step out onto a path.
~ Angel Kyodo Williams ~
Being Black: Zen and the Art of Living with Fearlessness and Grace, 2000

The path that you follow is not about going somewhere, but about coming back to you. Over and over again. Only this time, you are awake to who that is and the life you are living.
~ Ibid.

LAZINESS

The slothful man is a burden to himself, his hours hang heavy on his head;
he loitereth about, and knoweth not what he would do.
~ Akhenaton, c. 1385-c. 1355 BCE ~

He who sleeps until the sun is overhead
He who relies on that which is possessed through inheritance
exposes himself to suffering
If we do not toil and sweat profusely today
We cannot become wealthy tomorrow
He who possesses strong limbs but refuses to work
He who chooses to be idle in the morning
He is only resting for suffering in the evening
~ *Eji Ogbe* ~

If you sleep, your business sleeps too.
~ Swahili Wisdom ~
Wit & Wisdom of Africa: Proverbs from Africa & The Caribbean, Patrick Ibekwe, ed., 1998

The idler eats his laziness.
~ Ndebele Wisdom ~
Ibid.

Taking time isn't laziness.
~ Barbadian Wisdom ~
Ibid.

He who lives on the works of another man while he has himself the
capacity to work is a thief and a plunderer.
~ Walda Heywat, 17th C. ~
The Treatise of Walda Heywat, Claude Sumner, tr. 1985

Life is short. Work only pleases those who will never understand it.
Idleness cannot degrade anybody. It differs greatly from laziness.
~ René Maran, 1887-1960 ~
Batouala, 1972

LEARNING

When the student is ready the master will appear.
~ Khemetic Wisdom ~
Temt Tchaas: Egyptian Proverbs, Muata Ashaya Ashby, ed., 1994

Wealth, if you use it, comes to an end; learning, if you use it, increases.
~ Swahili Wisdom ~

Don't become disheartened with having to go on learning and don't give it up during all your life. Even if you learn the teachings of all men, there are many things you don't know.
~ Walda Heywat, 17th C. ~
The Treatise of Walda Heywat, Claude Sumner, tr. 1985

One's work may be finished someday but one's education, never.
~ Alexandre Dumas, père, 1802-1870 ~

A little learning, indeed, may be a dangerous thing, but the want of learning is a calamity to any people.
~ Frederick Douglass, 1817-1895 ~
Commencement Address, The Colored High School, Baltimore, Maryland, 1894 June 22

Customs that are more important than information: To be educated, not to meddle in other folks' problems, speak softly, be respectful, be religious, be a hard worker ... All of that the African taught me.
~ Esteban Montejo, 1856-1965 ~
in Miguel Barnet, *Biography of a Runaway Slave*, W. Nick Hill, tr., 1994

A system of education is not one thing, not does it have a single definite object, nor is it a mere matter of schools. Education is that whole system of human training within and without the schoolhouse walls, which molds and develops men.
~ W. E. B. Du Bois, 1868-1963 ~
in *Songs of Wisdom: Quotations from Famous African Americans*, Jay David, ed., 2000

Let there be light, two kinds of light: to light the outside world, to light the world within the soul. Each generation with its own lamp gave out the lamp of learning, education.
~ Mary McLeod Bethune, 1875-1955 ~

An honest and persistent quest for truth is essential to the attainment of higher learning ... Education and the quest for knowledge stops only at the grave.
~ Haile Selassie, 1892-1975 ~

Education is the most powerful weapon which you can use to change the world.
~ Nelson Mandela, b. 1918 ~

Education is your passport to the future, for tomorrow belongs to the people who prepare for it today.
~ Malcolm X, 1925-1965 ~
in *Brother's Keeper: Words of Inspiration for African-American Men*, Roderick Terry, ed., 1996

There is no age for learning. You can learn at any age. You simply must do it.
~ Ousmane Sembène, 1923-2007 ~
"Woman Is the Future of Man: Ousmane Sembène on *Moolaadé*," Interview by Ray Pride, CinemaScope.com

I am learning all the time. The tombstone will be my diploma.
~ Eartha Kitt, b. 1927 ~

It is only an education that liberates. Education helps one cease being intimidated by strange situations. Once you have it in your mind, you can go anywhere.
~ Maya Angelou, b. 1928 ~

The learning process is something you can incite, literally incite, like a riot.
~ Audre Lorde, 1934-1992 ~
in *African-American Writers*, Valerie Smith et al., eds., 1991

Just remember the world is not a playground but a schoolroom. Life is not a holiday but an education. One eternal lesson for us all: to teach us how better we should love.
~ Barbara Jordan, 1936-1996 ~

We cannot afford to settle for being just average; we must learn as much as we can to be the best that we can. The key word is *education* – that's knowledge – education with maximum effort.
~ Bill Cosby, b. 1937 ~
in *Brother's Keeper: Words of Inspiration for African-American Men*, Roderick Terry, ed., 1996

I try to learn as much as I can because I know nothing compared with what I need to know.
~ Muhammad Ali, b. 1942 ~

Get yourself educated and you can emancipate yourself from any kind of slavery. Education is freedom. You have to keep making mistakes and being aware that one day – ... Whilst you are doing that, you are learning. And listening to what other people are saying.
~ Buchi Emecheta, b. 1944 ~
Interview by Zhana, 1966

Now I'm daring much more. Before, I did all what I did in order to learn. When I started my career, I knew nothing about music. I was not a griot, I didn't go to school to learn music. So I went away to meet jazzman and other musicians all over the world ... I learnt a lot and now I feel stronger and therefore freer. I know a little bit more than before.
~ Salif Keita, b. 1949 ~
GlobalVillageIdiot.net

You come here for one thing and one thing only, and that is to learn. I used to spend a lot of my life waiting for the day I could quit school, but then I came to realize that so long as we are alive we never leave school. Life is a series of high schools, one after the other. And if you don't study, do your homework, and learn enough in one lifetime, you just get sent back and have to do it all over again.
~ RuPaul, b. 1960 ~
Lettin It All Hang Out, 1995

We should always be involved in the quest for knowledge. Education liberates our minds and widens our horizons, and gives us the ability to make informed choices ... We live in an ever-changing world which requires us constantly to be prepared to adapt to new ideas, different cultures, and conflicting views.
~ Roderick Terry, b. 1964 ~
Brother's Keeper: Words of Inspiration for African-American Men, 1996

Real education doesn't just take place in school; it takes place every day of our lives. Each day we can learn something new about ourselves and our world, if we're open to it.
~ Keith Boykin, b. 1965 ~
Respecting the Soul: Daily Reflections for Black Lesbians and Gays, 1999

LEGACY

Follow in the footsteps of your ancestors, for the mind is trained through knowledge. Behold their words endure in books. Open them and follow their wise counsel.
~ *Book of Kheti* ~
in *Kemet and the African Worldview*, Maulana Karenga and Jacob Carruthers, eds., 1986

One who knows no proverbs knows not their ancestors.
~ Nigerian Wisdom ~
Wit & Wisdom of Africa: Proverbs from Africa & The Caribbean, Patrick Ibekwe, ed., 1998

If we stand tall it is because we stand on the backs of those who came before us.
~ Yoruba Wisdom ~

A people without the knowledge of their past history, origin and culture is like a tree without roots.
~ Marcus Garvey, 1887-1940 ~

History is a clock that people use to tell their time of day. It is a compass they use to find themselves on the map of human geography. It tells them where they are and what they are.
~ John Henrik Clarke, 1915-1998 ~

I acknowledge immense debt to the griots of Africa – where today it is rightly said that when a griot dies, it is as if a library has burned to the ground.
~ Alex Haley, 1921-1992 ~
Roots, 1976

Unless one has the past in the present, one can't understand oneself.
~ Wilson Harris, b. 1921 ~
in Maya Jaggi, "Redemption Song," *The Guardian*, 2006 December 16

I am a direct descendant of Prospero worshipping in the same temple of endeavor, using his legacy of language – not to curse our meeting – but to push it further, reminding the descendants of both sides that what's done is done, and can only be seen as a soil from which other gifts, or the same gift

endowed with different meanings, may grow towards a future which is colonised by our acts in this moment, but which must always remain open.
~ George Lamming, b. 1927 ~
The Pleasures of Exile, 1960

All men are interdependent. Every nation is an heir of a vast treasury of ideas and labor to which both the living and the dead of all nations have contributed. Whether we realize it or not, each of us lives eternally "in the red." We are everlasting debtors to known and unknown men and women.
~ Martin Luther King, Jr., 1929-1968 ~
The Words of Martin Luther King, Jr., Coretta Scott King, ed., 1983

You cannot change your past, but you can accept it, learn from it, use it to make your future different, and move on with your life. The quicker you can process it, the happier and more magical and peaceful your life becomes.
~ Famous Amos, b. 1937 ~
Watermelon Magic, 1996

One of the joys of reading is the ability to plug into the shared wisdom of mankind.
~ Ishmael Reed, b. 1938 ~

If you as parents cut corners, your children will too. If you lie, they will too. If you spend all your money on yourselves and tithe no portion of it for charities, colleges, churches, synagogues, and civic causes, your children won't either. And if parents snicker at racial and gender jokes, another generation will pass on the poison adults still have not had the courage to snuff out.
~ Marion Wright Edelman, b. 1939 ~

We have no sense of balance – because we have removed a sense of asthetics from our lives ... When you remove that, people's spirit shrinks into the mundane, into narrow places, into fear of the unknown, fear of other places, other people. Instead of recognising that it all belongs to us – that the world in a sense is part of our heritage – we retreat into holes.
~ Horace Ové, b. 1939 ~
Interview by Ira Mathur, 2002 September 29

Every generation needs the instruction and insights of past generations in order to forge its own vision.
~ Jesse Jackson, b. 1941 ~

If you are carrying strong feelings about something that happened in your past, they may hinder your ability to live in the present.
~ Les Brown, b. 1945 ~

We are made up physically and spiritually of the billions who have passed before us. They gave us life, they gave us our culture, they gave us the world on which we have built our present world. Our values and traditions, our habits of thought are in large measure the wisdom of their experience passed down through the ages. Our breath, the very air we breathe, was once their breath.
~ Susan L. Taylor, b. 1946 ~
Lessons in Living, 1995

Every decision made is not entirely one's own to make ... Do what you have to, but just understand what effect it will have, what legacy you will leave.
~ Rita Dove, b. 1952 ~
Interview by M. Wynn Thomas, *The Swansea Review*, 1995 August 12

We must stand tall knowing the power, strength and wisdom of the ancestors is as close as breath. All that we ever need to be, to do, to know, to have is available. All we need do is take a stand.
~ Iyanla Vanzant, b. 1953 ~
Acts of Faith: Daily Meditations for People of Color, 1993

Our decisions, feelings and experiences are determined by our wishes, legends and the past. I believe ... that people themselves are bits of imagination. We are invented. We are invented by other people. Others have dreamed about us, we ourselves are a dream, a shadow of the past. Long ago my ancestor dreamed of me. In that way they took care of the continuity of existence.
~ Chenjerai Hove, b. 1956 ~
Prologue, *Shebeen Tales: Messages from Harare*, 1997

We do not just risk repeating history if we sweep it under the carpet, we also risk being myopic about our present.
~ Chimamanda Ngozi Adichie, b. 1977 ~
in Ike Anya, "In the Footsteps of Achebe: Enter Chimamanda Ngozi Adichie, Nigeria's Newest Literary Voice," 2003 October 10

LIBERATION / LIBERTY / FREEDOM

You cannot parcel out freedom in pieces because freedom is all or nothing.
~ Tertullian, c. 160-240 ~

The price of liberty is eternal vigilance.
~ Frederick Douglass, 1817-1895 ~

Home is where freedom is. The house can be ever so nice, with a soft bed, fine food, and fire in the fireplace, but it ain't home if it ain't where freedom is. I live where the fire is out, where the bed is hard and the bread is scarce, and maybe you work and maybe you eat and maybe you don't ... but freedom is there.
~ Harriet Tubman, c. 1822-1913 ~

The cost of liberty is less than the price of repression.
~ W. E. B. Du Bois, 1868-1963 ~
"The Legacy of John Brown," *John Brown: A Biography*, 1909

Freedom is a state of mind: a spiritual unchoking of the wells of human power and superhuman love.
~ Du Bois ~

The mind of the Negro seems suddenly to have slipped from under the tyranny of social intimidation and to be shaking off the psychology of imitation and implied inferiority. By shedding the old chrysalis of the Negro problem we are achieving something like a spiritual emancipation. Until recently, lacking self-understanding, we have been almost as much of a problem to ourselves as we still are to others.
~ Alain Locke, 1886-1954 ~
The New Negro, 1925

We must emancipate ourselves from mental slavery, because while others might free the body, none but ourselves can free the mind.
~ Marcus Garvey, 1887-1940 ~
Philosophy and Opinions of Marcus Garvey, Vol. I, Amy Jacques Garvey, ed., 1923

The most rewarding freedom is freedom of the mind.
~ Amy Jacques Garvey, 1896-1973 ~

Freedom is an internal achievement rather than an external adjustment.
~ Adam Clayton Powell, Jr., 1908-1972 ~
"Man's Debt to God," *Keep the Faith, Baby*, 1967

When people made up their minds that they wanted to be free and took action, then there was a change. But they cannot rest on just that change. It has to continue.
~ Rosa Parks, 1913-2005 ~

To be free is not to cast off one's chains, but to live in a way that respects and enhances the freedom of others.
~ Nelson Mandela, b. 1918 ~

Human freedom is a complex, difficult – and private – thing. If we can liken life, for a moment, to a furnace, the freedom is a fire which burns away illusion.
~ James Baldwin, 1924-1987 ~

Freedom is not something that anybody can be given. Freedom is something that people take, and people are as free as they want to be.
~ Baldwin ~
Nobody Knows My Name: More Notes of a Native Son, 1961

Nobody can give you freedom. Nobody can give you equality or justice or anything. If you're a man, you take it.
~ Malcolm X, 1925-1965 ~
Malcolm X Speaks, 1965

Freedom, in the larger and higher sense, every man must gain for himself.
~ Martin Luther King, Jr., 1929-1968 ~

Freedom is indivisible or it is nothing at all besides sloganeering and temporary, short-sighted, and short-lived advancement for a few.
~ June Jordan, 1936-2002 ~

In the act of resistance, the rudiments of freedom are already present.
~ Angela Davis, b. 1944 ~

Our liberation begins when the truth of our own experiences is admitted to ourselves ... In the end, freedom is a personal and lonely battle and one faces down fears of today so that those of tomorrow might be engaged.
~ Alice Walker, b. 1944 ~

Emancipate yourselves from mental slavery; none but ourselves can free our minds.
~ Bob Marley, 1946-1981 ~
"Redemption Song," *Uprising*, 1980

You are your own master. Moment by moment, whatever suffering, joy, or peace we experience is always the direct result of our past and present decisions. If we wish to be free, we must liberate ourselves. No one can do this for us. No one can lead us. Or place insurmountable obstacles in our way.
~ Charles Johnson, b. 1948 ~
"Reading the Eightfold Path," *Dharma, Color, and Culture*, Hilda Gutiérrez Baldoquín, ed., 2004

Freedom is not given, must not be given. Liberty awarded does not liberate your soul.
~ Patrick Chamoiseau, b. 1953 ~
Texaco, Rose-Myriam Réjouis & Val Vinokurov, trs., 1992

The only thing that can free you is the belief that you can be free.
~ Oprah Winfrey, b. 1954 ~

Sexism is an issue that affects all women and men, of all races. The same is true of racism or homophobia; all of us suffer when the lives of other humans are devalued. It's time for us to learn that liberation is not only for the oppressed, but for the oppressor as well. Liberation means opening your mind to the world beyond your own borders.
~ Keith Boykin, b. 1965 ~
Respecting the Soul: Daily Reflections for Black Lesbians and Gays, 1999

Awareness gives me the clarity that as soon as I am present in this moment, my suffering lessens. This clarity helps me to see I am responsible for my feelings, for my choices, and for my liberation. This, my friends, is true freedom.
~ Hilda Gutiérrez Baldoquín ~
"Don't Waste Time," *Dharma, Color, and Culture*, Hilda Gutiérrez Baldoquín, ed., 2004

But it's the day that you lift a finger to help, open your ears to hear, and raise your voice to advocate truth that you have taken a step toward freedom.
~ Angel Kyodo Williams ~
Being Black: Zen and the Art of Living with Fearlessness and Grace, 2000

LIFE / LIVING

Life is exquisitely a time-thing, like music.
~ E. E. Just, 1883-1941 ~

You have to go the way your blood beats. If you don't live the only life you
have, you won't live some other life, you won't live any life at all.
~ James Baldwin, 1924-1987 ~

I think part of life is to proceed as if you are charmed, held in the spell of a
beautiful image. For me, that is the pleasure of life ... I don't think there is
anything more beautiful than life. But you have to be able to share life.
~ Ousmane Sembène, 1923-2007 ~
"Woman Is the Future of Man: Ousmane Sembène on *Moolaadé*," Ray Pride Interview, CinemaScope

Life is a school and we're not on holiday.
~ Elma Lumsden, b. 1935 ~

Life is a marvelous, transitory adventure.
~ Nikki Giovanni, b. 1943 ~

Words can be webs, making us think in terms of essences; language is all
concept, but things in the world are devoid of essence, changing as we
chase them. Life must always be greater than our ideas about life.
~ Charles Johnson, b. 1948 ~
"Reading the Eightfold Path," *Dharma, Color, and Culture*, Hilda Gutiérrez Baldoquín, ed., 2004

I don't believe that life is supposed to make you feel good, or to make you
feel miserable either. Life is just supposed to make you feel.
~ Gloria Naylor, b. 1950 ~

Life is ultimately a challenge and a discipline.
~ Cornel West, b. 1954 ~

How amazing life seems when it stands around death ... I must live, not
dream about living.
~ Binyavanga Wainaina, b. 1971 ~
"Discovering Home," *G21*, 1995

We can't plan life. All we can do is be available for it.
~ Lauryn Hill, b. 1975 ~

LILA / LEISURE

There are toys for every age.
~ Haitian Wisdom ~
Wit & Wisdom of Africa: Proverbs from Africa & The Caribbean, Patrick Ibekwe, ed., 1998

"Social exclusion" from regular work and income has been a long-term and dire experience. Yet social exclusion ... with its enforced leisure, produced forms of cultural creativity which engendered marvels of reality.
~ John La Rose, 1927-2006 ~
"Unemployment, Leisure and the Birth of Creativity," *The Black Scholar*, Volume 26, No.2

The ultimate of being successful is the luxury of giving yourself the time to do what you want to do.
~ Leontyne Price, b. 1927 ~

The concept of contentment was what you were after, not to keep up with the Joneses, not to be driven ... And I'm not saying the virtue of laziness, but the virtue of being easy on yourself. The virtue of finding an ambition that carried with it lack of anxiety.
~ James Earl Jones, b. 1931 ~
"The Voice of Triumph," Academy of Achievement Interview, 1996 June 29

There is no reason why we can't work less hours and enjoy our lives more. But if we do get more time, we have to organize ourselves to get some benefit from it. What is life if we cannot get some pleasure from friends and family, from relaxation and contemplation? Most people do not have an idea of what their human potential is, we are so used to not having time.
~ Linton Kwesi Johnson, b. 1952 ~
SpikeMagazine.com, 1998 December

All the money in the world doesn't mean a thing if you don't have time to enjoy it.
~ Oprah Winfrey, b. 1954 ~

If it's what you want to do with your whole heart and soul, come on. Go everywhere, learn everything ... Write things for yourself. Come on, it's a great way to spend time. It's a great way to learn history. It's a great way to learn all kinds of things. But only come if you're coming to play. If you're not coming to play, you should get another gig.
~ Whoopi Goldberg, b. 1955 ~
"The One-Woman Show," Academy of Achievement Interview, 1994 June 17

LIMITATION

The world is a book, and those who do not travel, read only a page.
~ Augustine of Hippo, 354-430 ~

Don't hang your clothes on one nail.
~ Barbadian Wisdom ~

No man can put a chain about the ankle of his fellow man, without at least finding the other end of it about his own neck.
~ Frederick Douglass, 1817-1895 ~
Speech at Civil Rights Mass Meeting, Washington, D.C., 1883 October 22

Let the sky and God be our limit, and Eternity our measurement. There is no height to which we cannot climb by using the active intelligence of our own minds.
~ Marcus Garvey, 1887-1940 ~
"African Fundamentalism," *Negro World*, 1925 June 6

People mistake their limitations for high standards.
~ Jean Toomer, 1894-1967 ~
Essentials: Definitions and Aphorisms, XL, 1931

The slave master is no longer hindering us; we're hindering ourselves.
~ Elijah Muhammad, 1897-1975 ~
in "The Messenger Passes," *Time Magazine*, 1975 March 10

As long as you keep a person down, some part of you has to be down there to hold him down, so it means you cannot soar as you otherwise might.
~ Marian Anderson, 1902-1993 ~

What and how much had I lost by trying to do only what was expected of me instead of what I myself had wished to do? What a waste, what a senseless waste.
~ Ralph Ellison, 1914-1994 ~
Invisible Man, 1952

We have been believers believing in our burdens and our demigods too long. Now the needy no longer weep and pray; the long-suffering arise, and our fists bleed against the bars with a strange insistency.
~ Margaret Walker, 1915-1998 ~
"We Have Been Believers"

The pigeon with only one source of food is likely to die of hunger.
~ Kikuyu Wisdom ~

I have never been contained except that I made the prison.
~ Mari Evans, b. 1923 ~

Everything in life depends on how that life accepts its limits.
~ James Baldwin, 1924-1987 ~

We spend most of our days preventing the heart from beating out its
greatness. The things we would rather encourage lie choking among the
weeds of our restrictions. And before we know it time has eluded us. There
is not much time allotted us, and half of that we sleep. While we are awake
we should allow our hearts to bear the shame of being seen living.
~ Efua Sutherland, 1924-1996 ~

An individual has not started living until he can rise above the narrow
confines of his individualistic concerns to the broader concerns of all
humanity.
~ Martin Luther King, Jr., 1929-1968 ~
The Words of Martin Luther King, Jr., Coretta Scott King, ed., 1983

There is nothing more tragic than to find an individual bogged down in the
length of life, devoid of breadth.
~ King ~

He who gives you the diameter of your knowledge, prescribes the
circumference of your activities.
~ Louis Farrakhan, b. 1934 ~
in Roderick Terry, One Million Strong: A Photographic Tribute of the Million Man March, 1996

Life is too large to hang out a sign: "For Men Only."
~ Barbara Jordan, 1936-1996 ~

People harass us West Indians a lot. People are always saying to us:
"Choose! Are you African? Are you European? Are you this? Are you
that?" The time will come one day when we won't have to choose
anymore. We will simply be able to say I am what I am, with a lot of
shortcomings, voids, which we haven't filled, but which we have
nevertheless managed to identify.
~ Maryse Condé, b. 1937 ~
"One Day, People Are Going to Manage Simply to Say : I Am What I am," Interview by Catherine
Dana, Africultures, 2002 October 21

All my limitations are self-imposed, and my liberation can only come from
true self-love.
~ Max Robinson, 1939-1988 ~

Life is not about finding our limitations, it's about finding our infinity.
~ Herbie Hancock, b. 1940 ~

Life has no limitations, except the ones you make ... The only limits to the
possibilities in your life tomorrow are the buts you use today.
~ Les Brown, b. 1945 ~

While there is a place for racial identities in a world shaped by racism ... if
we are to move beyond racism we shall have, in the end, to move beyond
current racial identities.
~ K. Anthony Appiah, b. 1954 ~

A person wrapped up in himself makes a very small package.
~ Denzel Washington, b. 1954 ~

Many of us would rather hide behind the labels by which we live ... To step
outside of these confines would make us more vulnerable than many of us
care to become publicly or privately. So we hide behind the singularity that
is our own deep isolation.
~ Conrad Pegues, b. 1964 ~
"Reflections Upon the Bambara Creation Myth," in *Spirited: Affirming the Soul and Black Gay/Lesbian
Identity*, G. Winston James & Lisa C. Moore, eds., 2006

The insistence of binding an individual to specific forms of identity, and
the environment in which such an identity is affirmed, validated, and
allowed expression, is irrational. Whether it is the family that tries to bind
its offspring to the image of parental hopes and aspirations, or the ethnic or
racial community that demands that one's identity and thinking align
themselves with the schemata of the group, such bondage retards the
individual's capacity to evolve and become. It hinges on the premise that
he or she is embalmed, static, and nonevolving.
~ Jason D. Hill, b. 1965 ~
Becoming a Cosmopolitan: What It Means to Be a Human Being in the New Millennium, 2000

The reality I construct is limited and what I think, believe, and hold fast to
about the world completely obscures the true reality.
~ Hilda Gutiérrez Baldoquín ~
"Don't Waste Time," *Dharma, Color, and Culture*, Hilda Gutiérrez Baldoquín, ed., 2004

LISTENING

Give your ears, hear the sayings,
Give your heart to understand them;
It profits to put them in your heart.
~ Amenemope, c. 11th C. BCE ~
The Instruction of Amenemope, Ch. 1, Miriam Lichtheim, tr.

The fault in every kind of character is not listening.
~ Khemetic Wisdom ~
Wit & Wisdom of Africa: Proverbs from Africa & The Caribbean, Patrick Ibekwe, ed., 1998

A good listener makes a single trip; a bad listener makes fifty.
~ Haitian Wisdom ~
Ibid.

The beginning of wisdom is silence. The second step is listening.
~ Unknown ~

Listen more often
To things than to beings;
The fire's voice is heard,
Hear the voice of the water.
Hear in the wind
The bush's sob:
It is the ancestors' breath.
~ Birago Diop, 1906-1989 ~
"Breaths," *African Heritage: Intimate Views of the Black Africans from Life, Love, Literature*, Jacob
Drachler, ed., 1963

You don't know what the hell they are talking about, so the best thing to
do is be like a sponge and listen and absorb.
~ Eartha Kitt, b. 1927 ~
Interview by Blase DiStefano, "Eartha Kitt *Purr*-severes: The Feline Feminist Talks About Her Two
Lives as the Child and the Woman," *OutSmart*

You have to listen to not only what is being said, but what is not said –
which is often more important than what they say.
~ Kofi Annan, b. 1938 ~
"Kofi Annan: Center of the Storm," PBS, 2002

Learn to be quiet enough to hear the sound of the genuine within yourself so that you can hear it in other people.
~ Marion Wright Edelman, b. 1939 ~

My first task is to listen inside myself and listen outside.
~ Gilberto Gil, b. 1942 ~
BBC News, 2002 December 19

I know you believe you understand what you think I said, but I am not sure you realize that what you heard is not what I meant.
~ Unknown ~

I'm glad I understand that while language is a gift, listening is a responsibility.
~ Nikki Giovanni, b. 1943 ~
"Griots," Racism 101

Once a person gives you the benefit of listening to you, you owe them to listen back to their feedback.
~ Haile Gerima, b. 1946 ~
Interview by Lee Thornton, University of Maryland

The problem of life is, to a great degree, the problem of attention. Of listening, which is one of the attributes of love.
~ Charles Johnson, b. 1948 ~
"Reading the Eightfold Path," Dharma, Color, and Culture, Hilda Gutiérrez Baldoquín, ed., 2004

No real benefit can derive from having made up one's mind before a dialogue even begins, though I recognize how much easier this is "said than done." We usually listen only to hear our own opinions echoed. Not hearing that, we don't hear anything at all.
~ Jan Willis, b. 1948 ~
"We Must ... Become as Empty Vessels," janwillis.net

Just stay open, allowing what is being said to simply be heard in the consciousness without taking hold of any particular thought or idea such as what to do with what's being heard; let the listening just "happen," as it were. You are there behind the listening mind.
~ Mooji, b. 1954 ~

LITTLE

Little by little does the trick.
~ Aesop, fl. c. 550 BCE ~
"The Crow and the Pitcher"

You aspire to great things? Begin with little ones.
~ Augustine of Hippo, 354-430 ~

Small showers fill the stream.
~ Hausa Wisdom ~
Wit & Wisdom of Africa: Proverbs from Africa & The Caribbean, Patrick Ibekwe, ed., 1998

A little is better than nothing.
~ Guyanese Wisdom ~

Little by little the bird makes its nest.
~ Haitian Wisdom ~

A little lantern can do what the great sun can never do – it can shine in
the night.
~ Unknown ~

An insignificant right becomes important when it is assailed.
~ William Pickens, 1881-1954 ~
"The Ultimate Effects of Segregation and Discrimination," 1915

We must not, in trying to think about how we can make a big difference,
ignore the small daily differences we can make which, over time, add up to
big differences that we often cannot foresee.
~ Marion Wright Edelman, b. 1939 ~

A key criterion for success is how you use your pennies, not just how you
manage your dollars.
~ Haki Madhubuti, b. 1942 ~

There is more going on beneath the surface than we think, and more going
on in little, finite moments of time than we would guess.
~ Malcolm Gladwell, b. 1963 ~
in Dave Welch, "A Few Thin Slices of Malcolm Gladwell," Powells.com, 2005

LOGOS

If Mind and Divine Speech are used as meant, you will not differ from the immortals in any way.
~ Khemetic Wisdom ~
Temt Tchaas: Egyptian Proverbs, Muata Ashaya Ashby, ed., 1994

The tongue of a man is his sword and effective speech is stronger than all fighting.
~Khemetic Wisdom ~
Selections from the Husia: Sacred Wisdom of Ancient Egypt, Maulana Karenga, tr., 1984

All change, all production and generation are effected through the word.
~ Léopold Senghor, 1906-2001 ~

I have always taken care to put an idea or emotion behind my words. I have made it a habit to be suspicious of the mere music of words.
~ Senghor ~

Words are your business, boy. Not just *the* Word. Words are everything. The key to the Rock, the answer to the Question.
~ Ralph Ellison, 1914-1994 ~
"And Hickman Arrives," 1960

If we have the Word let us say it
If we have the Word let us be it
If we have the Word let us DO.
~ Mari Evans, b. 1923 ~
"Nightstar"

Every legend contains its residuum of truth, and the root function of language is to control the universe by describing it.
~ James Baldwin, 1924-1987 ~
Notes of a Native Son, 1963

The words were living things to her. She sensed them bestriding the air and charging the room with strong colors.
~ Paule Marshall, b. 1929 ~
Brown Girl, Brownstones, 1959

To change your language you must change your life.
~ Derek Walcott, b. 1930 ~

We die. That may be the meaning of life. But we do language. That may be
the measure of our lives.
~ Toni Morrison, b. 1931 ~
Nobel Prize Address, 1993 December 7

The very language we use to describe the so-called facts interferes in this
process of finally deciding what is true and what is false.
~ Stuart Hall, b. 1932 ~
"The West and the Rest: Discourse and Power," *Modernity: An Introduction to Modern Societies*, S. Hall,
D. Held, D. Hubert, and K. Thompson, eds., 1996

Words set things in motion. I've seen them doing it. Words set up
atmospheres, electrical fields, charges.
~ Toni Cade Bambara, 1939-1995 ~

Language used correctly … expands the brain, increases one's knowledge
bank, enlarges the world, and challenges the vision of those who may not
have a vision.
~ Haki Madhubuti, b. 1942 ~

Oral tradition is a tradition of images. What is said is stronger than what is
written; the word addresses itself to the imagination, not the ear.
Imagination creates the image and the image creates.
~ Djibril Diop Mambety, 1945-1998 ~
in N. Frank Ukadike, "The Hyena's Last Laugh: A Conversation with Djibril Diop Mambety,"
Transition 78, Vol. 8, No. 2, 1999

There's a sense of liberation in being able to reconstruct one's own
language, that's connected up certainly to reconstructing history, and also
reconstructing experience.
~ Michelle Cliff, b. 1946 ~
"Re-visioning Our History," Interview by Jim Clawson, *Nidus*, 2002

We daily abuse the power of language, diminish and trivialize it when we
use talk as merely another form of entertainment, or a way to amuse
ourselves and others; to pass the time, or fill the silence that envelops us
and is the ground and precondition for speech.
~ Charles Johnson, b. 1948 ~
"Reading the Eightfold Path," *Dharma, Color, and Culture*, Hilda Gutiérrez Baldoquín, ed., 2004

I found a way to make peace with the recent past by turning it into WORD.
~ Johnson ~
Middle Passage, 1990

We can translate *ase* in many ways, but the *ase* used to create the universe I translate as "logos," the word as understanding, the word as the audible, and later the visible, sign of reason. *Ase* is more weighty, forceful, and action-packed than the ordinary word. It is the word with irrevocability, reinforced with double assuredness and undaunted authenticity.
~ Henry Louis Gates, Jr., b. 1950 ~
The Signifying Monkey: A Theory of African American Literary Criticism, 1988

What is *The Word*? If it carries you, it's *The Word*. Only if it carries you and without any illusion. Anyone who holds words-that-carry holds *The Word*. He can do everything. It's more than the Power ... But *The Word* is not words. *The Word* is more a silence than the noise of a tongue, and more like an emptiness than just silence.
~ Patrick Chamoiseau, b. 1953 ~
Texaco, Rose-Myriam Réjouis & Val Vinokurov, trs., 1992

You relate to and experience the world through language ... existence is seen and dreamed from the point of view of this language. For me languages are schools of life.
~ Chenjerai Hove, b. 1956 ~
Prologue, *Shebeen Tales: Messages from Harare*, 1997

Language is power. He who names things has the power. If we call something a cow, we can milk it, we can rob it, because we called it a cow. But if we had called it a gentleman, we wouldn't milk it. He who has the power to name things has also the power to control language.
~ Hove ~
Interview by Taina Ternoven, *Africultures*, 2003 March

We are all bearers of an ever living and evolving word constantly creating itself anew in our everyday existence in the world. We are each, literally and figuratively, the Word of God. With this perpetually creative and communal consciousness must come responsibility and accountability.
~ Conrad Pegues, b. 1964 ~
"Reflections Upon the Bambara Creation Myth," in *Spirited: Affirming the Soul and Black Gay/Lesbian Identity*, G. Winston James & Lisa C. Moore, eds., 2006

The word can be a bullet or a hole to plant a seed.
~ Malachi Smith ~

LONELINESS

Eat on your own is dying on your own.
~ Mamprussi Wisdom ~
Wit & Wisdom of Africa: Proverbs from Africa & The Caribbean, Patrick Ibekwe, ed., 1998

Through a marvelous law of natural compensation, he who gives of himself grows, and he who turns inward and lives from small pleasures, is afraid to share them with others, and only thinks avariciously of cultivating his appetites loses his humanity and becomes loneliness itself. He carries in his breast all the dreariness of winter.
~ José Martí, 1853-1895 ~
Martí Pensamientos, Carlos Ripoll, ed.

The thing that makes you exceptional, if you are at all, is inevitably that which must also make you lonely.
~ Lorraine Hansberry, 1930-1965 ~

The gift of loneliness is sometimes a radical vision of society or one's people that has not previously been taken into account.
~ Alice Walker, b. 1944 ~
in *Interviews With Black Writers*, John O'Brien, ed., 1973

The moment we allow the self to believe it can do without other people we create the kind of loneliness, depression and disconnection that makes life not worth living.
~ Iyanla Vanzant, b. 1953 ~
Acts of Faith: Daily Meditations for People of Color, 1993

Loneliness is never easy but is fairly inevitable – for, as you learned long ago ... "everyone" does not finally find "someone." Solitude often is simply the way things *are*, not necessarily as one would wish them to be.
~ Thomas Glave, b. 1964 ~
"Panic, Despair: When the Words Do Not Come," *Words to Our Now: Imagination and Dissent*, 2005

I see myself craving control by having to know it all and being able to provide all the answers. This, in turn, feeds into the delusion of separateness. I justify my craving for control by telling myself that I am alone.
~ Hilda Gutiérrez Baldoquín ~
"Don't Waste Time," *Dharma, Color, and Culture*, Hilda Gutiérrez Baldoquín, ed., 2004

LOQUACITY

Put a bridle on thy tongue; set a guard before thy lips, lest the words of thine own mouth destroy thy peace ... On much speaking cometh repentance, but in silence is safety ... It is better to be silent or to say things of more value than silence. Sooner throw a pearl than hazard an idle or useless word; and do not say a little in many words, but a great deal in few.
~ Khemetic Wisdom ~
Temt Tchaas: Egyptian Proverbs, Muata Ashaya Ashby, ed., 1994

He who talks incessantly, talks nonsense.
~ Ivory Coast Wisdom ~

Nothing is more unseemly than to give very long legs to very brief ideas.
~ Joaquim Machado de Assis, 1839-1908 ~
Dom Casmurro, 1924

There are rare instances when truth is best served by silence.
~ Gordon Parks, 1912-2006 ~

You don't always have to have something to say.
~ Sammy Davis, Jr., 1925-1990 ~

Every time we open our mouths we release a powerful energy. If we could learn to hold on to that energy, it could be used to nurture our dreams, heal our bodies and fuel our minds. But we always have so much to say. Talking can take us off the track, knock us off our center and kill off our dreams when we speak mindlessly. Talking is something we must learn to use, not something we must always do.
~ Iyanla Vanzant, b. 1953 ~
Acts of Faith: Daily Meditations for People of Color, 1993

LOVE - AGAPE

Once for all, then, a short precept is given thee: Love, and do what thou wilt: whether thou hold thy peace, through love hold thy peace; whether thou cry out, through love cry out; whether thou correct, through love correct; whether thou spare, through love do thou spare: let the root of love be within, of this root can nothing spring but what is good.
~ Augustine of Hippo, 354-430 ~
In epistulam Ioannis ad Parthos, VII, 8

Love has no awareness of merit or demerit; it has no scale by which its portion may be weighed or measured. It does not seek to balance giving and receiving. Love loves; this is its nature.
~ Howard Thurman, 1889-1981 ~

Love is indescribable and unconditional. I could tell you a thousand things that it is not, but not one that it is.
~ Duke Ellington, 1899-1974 ~
Music Is My Mistress, 1973

Unconditional love not only means that I am with you, but also that I am for you, all the way, right or wrong.
~ Ellington ~

Love stretches your heart and makes you big inside.
~ Margaret Walker, 1915-1998 ~
Jubilee, 1966

Love is the only force capable of transforming an enemy into a friend.
~ Martin Luther King, Jr., 1929-1968 ~
The Words of Martin Luther King, Jr., Coretta Scott King, ed., 1983

The most revolutionary statement in history is "Love thine enemy."
~ Eldridge Cleaver, 1935-1998 ~

In real love, real union, or communion there are no rules.
~ bell hooks, b. 1952 ~
in *Tricycle: The Buddhist Review*, 1992 Fall

LOVE - EROS

Love, you know, is strangely whimsical, containing affronts, jars, parleys, wars, then peace again. For you to ask advice to love by, is all one as if you ask advice to run mad by.
~ Terence, c. 190-159 BCE ~
The Eunuch, Act I

Better to have loved and lost, than to have never loved at all.
~ Augustine of Hippo, 354-430 ~

The cricket match yield(s) no amusement – all sport is dull, books unentertaining – Wisdom's self but folly – to a mind under Cupidical influence.
~ Ignatius Sancho, 1729-1780 ~
Letter VIII to Mr K, 1770 July 16 in The Letters of the Late Ignatius Sancho, an African, Vol. I, 1782

To love is to make of one's heart a swinging door.
~ Howard Thurman, 1889-1981 ~
Recapture the Spirit, 1963

Love, I find, is like singing. Everybody can do enough to satisfy themselves, though it may not impress the neighbors as being very much.
~ Zora Neale Hurston, 1891-1960 ~
Dust Tracks on a Road: An Autobiography, 1942

In real love you want the other person's good. In romantic love you want the other person.
~ Margaret Anderson, 1891-1973 ~

We love because it's the only true adventure … Most of us love from our need to love, not because we find someone deserving.
~ Nikki Giovanni, b. 1943 ~

Love means exposing yourself to the pains of being hurt, deeply hurt by someone you trust.
~ Renita Weems, b. 1954 ~

MANIFESTATION

When the tongue announces
what the heart conceives, only then
does anything take a step
from non-existence into being.
~ Hymn to Ptah ~
3rd Millennium BCE, Khemetic Sacred Text
in *Desert Wisdom: Sacred Middle Eastern Writings from the Goddess Through the Sufis*, Neil Douglas-Klotz,
tr., 1995

It is the mind that makes the body.
~ Sojourner Truth, 1797-1883 ~

There is a definite connection between what is outer and what is inner in
man, and it is ever our inner states that attract our outer life. Therefore,
the individual must always start with himself. It is one's self that must be
changed.
~ Neville, 1905-1972 ~
"Fundamentals," *New Thought*, Summer 1953

The tongue can create. The intent of the mind creates a force for the
tongue. The power of this force will materialize as a physical condition or
an emotional state for the owner. The tongue knows, even when the owner
forgets, what you say is what you get – whether you want it or not.
~ Iyanla Vanzant, b. 1953 ~
Acts of Faith: Daily Meditations for People of Color, 1993

To imagine something, to closely focus one's thoughts upon it, has the
potential to bring that "something" into being. Thus, people who take a
tragic view of life and are always expecting the worst, usually manifest that
reality. Those who expect that things will work together for the good,
usually experience just that. In the realm of the sacred, this concept is
taken even further, for what is magic but the ability to focus thought and
energy to get results on the human plane.
~ Malidoma Somé, b. 1956 ~

MEANING

It takes a strong disciple to rule over the mountainous thoughts and constantly go to the essence of the meaning; as mental complexity increases, thus will the depth of your decadence and challenge both be revealed.
~ Khemetic Wisdom ~
Temt Tchaas: Egyptian Proverbs, Muata Ashaya Ashby, ed., 1994

As long as one has a dream in his heart, he cannot lose the significance of living.
~ Howard Thurman, 1889-1981 ~

There is no agony like learning an untold story inside you.
~ Zora Neale Hurston, 1891-1960 ~

I do not deal in happiness. I deal in meaning.
~ Richard Wright, 1908-1960 ~

We search for the meaning of life in the realities of our experiences, in the realities of our dreams, our hopes, our memories.
~ Chester Himes, 1909-1984 ~

It can't be any new note. When you look at the keyboard, all the notes are there already. But if you mean a note enough, it will sound different. You got to pick the notes you really mean!
~ Thelonious Monk, 1917-1982 ~

For, while the tale of how we suffer, and how we are delighted, and how we may triumph is never new, it always must be heard. There isn't any other tale to tell, it's the only light we've got in all this darkness.
~ James Baldwin, 1924-1987 ~

The story is our escort; without it we are blind. Does the blind man own his escort? No, neither do we the story; rather it is the thing that owns us and directs us. It is the thing that makes us different from cattle; it is the mark on the face that sets one people apart from their neighbors.
~ Chinua Achebe, b. 1930 ~
Anthills of the Savannah, 1987

What biography or the unfolding sense of the self or the stories we tell ourselves or the autobiographies we write are meant to do, (is) to convince ourselves that these are not a series of leaps in the dark that we took, but they did have some logic, though it's not the logic of time or cause or sequence. But there is a logic of connected meaning.
~ Stuart Hall, b. 1932 ~
Seminar, Program in the Comparative Study of Social Transformations (CSST), 1999 April 15

Life takes on meaning when you become motivated, set goals and charge after them in an unstoppable manner.
~ Les Brown, b. 1945 ~

We're free to find significance, intended or no, where we uncover it.
~ Henry Louis Gates, Jr., b. 1950 ~
"Mister Jefferson and The Trials of Phillis Wheatley," 2002 Jefferson Lecture in the Humanities

What he sees in his mind is what is in man. There is no other concept outside of man. Is man make God. If there was no man, there wouldn't be any concept of God. So you have to look within man to find the reality of life and what life really mean. So when man is him good, him say is God, and when man is him bad, him say is the devil, but is really man still. So all concepts of good and bad is coming from man is emanate from man.
~ Mutabaruka, b. 1952 ~
Interview by Carter Van Pelt, 1998

It matters to people that their lives have a certain narrative unity; they want to be able to tell a story of their lives that makes sense. The story – my story – should cohere in the way appropriate by the standards made available in my culture to a person of my identity. In telling that story, how I fit into the wider story of various collectivities is, for most of us, important. It is not just gender identities that give shape (through, for example, rites of passage into woman- or manhood) to one's life: ethnic and national identities too fit each individual story into a larger narrative.
~ K. Anthony Appiah, b. 1954 ~
Color Conscious: The Political Morality of Race, 1996

We are always deciding what things are and applying labels to them and then believing those labels just because we put them there. We forget that they come from us. We forget that the fact that we applied them doesn't make the labels true.
~ Angel Kyodo Williams ~
Being Black: Zen and the Art of Living with Fearlessness and Grace, 2000

MEANS

It is a small thing which is taken to measure a big thing.
~ Tshi Wisdom ~
Wit & Wisdom of Africa: Proverbs from Africa & The Caribbean, Patrick Ibekwe, ed., 1998

A thorn which has pierced you in the wild, take another thorn to get it out.
~ Ganda Wisdom ~
Ibid.

The same hammer that drives the nail will take it out.
~ Guyanese Wisdom ~
Ibid.

I have often observed – there is more of value in the manner of doing the thing – than in the thing itself.
~ Ignatius Sancho, 1729-1780 ~
Letter XXXVI to Mr M, 1776 August 12 in *The Letters of the Late Ignatius Sancho, an African*, Vol. I, 1782

I have discovered in life that there are ways of getting almost anywhere you want to go, if you really want to go.
~ Langston Hughes, 1902-1967 ~

We will never have peace in the world until men everywhere recognize that ends are not cut off from means, because means represent the ideal in the making, and the end in process, and ultimately you can't reach good ends through evil means, because the means represent the seed and the end represents the tree.
~ Martin Luther King, Jr., 1929-1968 ~
The Trumpet of Conscience, 1967

There is really nothing more to say – except why. But since why is difficult to handle, one must take refuge in how.
~ Toni Morrison, b. 1931 ~
The Bluest Eye, 1969

MEDITATION

Now, make thy body still. Meditate that you may know truth.
~ Khemetic Wisdom ~
Temt Tchaas: Egyptian Proverbs, Muata Ashaya Ashby, ed., 1994

When my daughter was five or so, she saw me sitting, and referred to my practice as "medicating," and in a sense she was right; each meditation is both medicinal and the opportunity to hold a funeral for the ego.
~ Charles Johnson, b. 1948 ~
"Reading the Eightfold Path," *Dharma, Color, and Culture*, Hilda Gutiérrez Baldoquín, ed., 2004

In order to live a more serene and peaceful life, we have to reduce both external and internal noise levels. All of us need quiet time to reflect and meditate. Silence allows us to explore the deepest dimensions of our being, enabling us to hear who we really are ... Through silent meditation, we are able to transcend the material world and gain access to our inner source.
~ Roderick Terry, b. 1964 ~
"Hope Chest"

Meditation is training the mind. This is where the hard insights come.
~ Ralph M. Steele ~
"A Teaching on the Second Noble Truth," *Dharma, Color, and Culture*, Hilda Gutiérrez Baldoquín, ed., 2004

There is nothing to attain or achieve, a rather difficult concept for the western mind to understand. One lets go of any solemnity and even of the idea that one is meditating. One lets the body remain as it is and breath as one finds it naturally. As for the mind, the point is not to suppress thoughts or trail them, but just let them be, without being seduced or distracted by them. One does not try to manipulate the thought process. If one doesn't add fuel, thoughts will just play themselves out. Gradually the body and mind will settle and fall into a place of just being.
~ Steele ~
An Introduction to Vipassana Meditation, 1995

Meditation reveals that the obvious place to begin is not in some other place, it's right here.
~ Angel Kyodo Williams ~
Being Black: Zen and the Art of Living with Fearlessness and Grace, 2000

MEMORY

I must have sweets to remember by,
Some blossom saved from the mire,
Some death-rebellious ember
I can fan into a fire.
~ Countée Cullen, 1903-1946 ~
"Youth Sings a Song of Rosebuds"

Take down the love letters from the bookshelf,
the photographs, the desperate notes,
peel your own image from the mirror.
Sit. Feast on your life.
~ Derek Walcott, b. 1930 ~
"Love after Love," *Collected Poems 1948-1984*, 1986

Negritude was a necessary tool of combat for its time for the recovery of
the authentic nature of the African and also for memory. Memory is a
crucial part of the development of negritude and negritude underlined the
importance of memory ... The totality of memory is very important. One
must not cripple oneself by carrying memory on the head like a burden,
you know. But memory should serve as a background.
~ Wole Soyinka, b. 1934 ~
Interview by Boniface Mongo-Boussa, with Tanella Boni, *Africultures*, Allyson McKay & Alexandre
Mensah, trs.

To be without documentation is to be without a legitimate history. In the
culture of forgetfulness, memory alone has no meaning.
~ bell hooks, b. 1952 ~

We are products of our past, the environment of our childhood. For those
of us who had painful childhoods, we are determined to get away from our
memories. We cannot. Our past is a part of our today. We carry it in our
hearts ... We must relive the memories before we can erase them.
~ Iyanla Vanzant, b. 1953 ~
Acts of Faith: Daily Meditations for People of Color, 1993

Man's memory is often limited to the present, and even when he decides to
remember, he often applies the false relief of selective remembrance.
~ Oliver Mbamara ~
"What Is Your Attitude of The Present?" *Why Are We Here?*, 2003

MIND

The All is Mind. The universe is mental.
~ Hermes Trismegistus ~
in *The Kybalion: A Study of the Hermetic Philosophy of Ancient Egypt and Greece*, 1908

How great is this empire of the mind, and what a power it has, not alone that itself is withdrawn from the mischievous associations of the world, as one who is purged and pure can suffer no stain of a hostile irruption, but that it becomes still greater and stronger in its might, so that it can rule over all the imperious host of the attacking adversary with its sway!
~ Cyprian, 200-258 ~
Epistle to Donatus

The mind is the standard of the man.
~ Paul Laurence Dunbar, 1873-1906 ~
in *Brother's Keeper: Words of Inspiration for African-American Men*, Roderick Terry, ed., 1996

There is no height to which we cannot climb by using the active intelligence of our own minds. Mind creates, and as much as we desire in Nature we can have through the creation of our own minds.
~ Marcus Garvey, 1887-1940 ~
"African Fundamentalism," *Negro World*, 1925 June 6

The mind is and always will be our primary business.
~ Benjamin Mays, 1895-1984 ~

A mind is a terrible thing to waste.
~ United Negro College Fund Slogan ~

The mind is like the body. If you don't work actively to protect its health, you can lose it, especially if you're black ... and wondering ... if you were born into the wrong world.
~ Nathan McCall, b. 1955 ~
Makes Me Wanna Holler: A Young Black Man in America, 1994

Our minds require exercise just like our bodies. If you take a moment each morning and clean your mind, meditate, or relax, it will function much more efficiently as you face the challenges of the day.
~ Keith Boykin, b. 1965 ~
Respecting the Soul: Daily Reflections for Black Lesbians and Gays, 1999

MODERATION

Neither let prosperity put out the eyes of circumspection, nor abundance cut off the hands of frugality. They that too much indulge in the superfluities of life shall live to lament the want of its necessities.
~ Khemetic Wisdom ~
Temt Tchaas: Egyptian Proverbs, Muata Ashaya Ashby, ed., 1994

Moderation is a tree with roots of contentment, and fruits of tranquility and peace.
~ Khemetic Wisdom ~

If one overeats, one must overwork.
~ Igbo Wisdom ~
Wit & Wisdom of Africa: Proverbs from Africa & The Caribbean, Patrick Ibekwe, ed., 1998

To do too much to obtain a thing makes one miss it.
~ Fulfulde Wisdom ~
Ibid.

To be hard does not mean to be hard as stone, and to be soft does not mean to be soft as water.
~ Kikuyu Wisdom ~
Ibid.

My view is that the golden rule in life is never to have too much of anything.
~ Terence, c. 190-159 BCE ~
Andria, 166 BCE

Use common sense ... Everything should be done with moderation and using common sense.
~ Eartha Kitt, b. 1927 ~
Interview by Blase DiStefano, "Eartha Kitt *Purr*-severes: The Feline Feminist Talks About Her Two Lives as the Child and the Woman," *OutSmart*

When you are right you cannot be too radical; when you are wrong, you cannot be too conservative.
~ Martin Luther King, Jr., 1929-1968 ~

MUSIC

Music is the healing force of the universe.
~ Sun Ra, 1914-1993 ~

Music is your own experience, your thoughts, your wisdom. If you don't live it, it won't come out of your horn. They teach you there's a boundary line to music. But, man, there's no boundary line to art.
~ Charlie Parker, 1920-1955 ~
"Coda," *Hear Me Talkin' to Ya*, Nat Shapiro & Nat Hentoff, eds., 1955

The possibilities of music. First
that it does exist. And that we do,
in that scripture of rhythms. The earth,
I mean the soil, as melody. The fit you need,
the throes. To pick it up and cut
away what does not singularly express.
~ Amiri Baraka, b. 1934 ~
"Leadbelly Gives an Autograph," *Black Magic Poetry 1961-1967*, 1969

Music is the greatest communication in the world. Even if people don't understand the language you're singing in, they still know good music when they hear it.
~ Lou Rawls, 1937-2006 ~

Music is one of the closest link-ups with God that we can probably experience. I think it's a common vibrating tone of the musical notes that holds all life together.
~ Marvin Gaye, 1939-1984 ~
in Sharon Davis, *I Heard It Through the Grapevine*, 1991

If you wanna call everybody, one thing you have to do is to call them with music. To tell you the truth, music is everybody's name ... If it comes from your heart, people will love it because everyone has a heart too. It's from one heart to another heart.
~ Salif Keita, b. 1949 ~
Interview by Opiyo Oloya, *AfroDisc*, 1996 April 23

Music is about movement, the rhythm of life.
~ Cornel West, b. 1954 ~

ONENESS / UNITY / WHOLENESS

As is the inner, so is the outer; as is the great, so is the small; as it is above, so it is below; there is but One Life and Law: and he that worketh it is ONE. Nothing is inner, nothing is outer; nothing is great, nothing is small; nothing is high, nothing is low, in the Divine Economy.
~ Hermes Trismegistus ~

Man is one name belonging to every nation upon earth. In them all is one soul though many tongues. Every country has its own language, yet the subjects of which the untutored soul speaks are the same everywhere.
~ Tertullian, c. 160-240 ~
De Testimonio Animae (The Testimony of the Soul), 6.3

For as long as this body endures, it must needs have a common lot with others, and its bodily condition must be common. Nor is it given to any of the human race to be separated one from another, except by withdrawal from this present life. In the meantime, we are all, good and evil, contained in one household. Whatever happens within the house, we suffer with equal fate.
~ Cyprian, 200-258 ~
Treatise V: Address to Demetrianus

Each being contains in itself the whole intelligible world. Therefore All is everywhere. Each is there All, and All is each. Man as he now is has ceased to be the All. But when he ceases to be an individual, he raises himself again and penetrates the whole world.
~ Plotinus, 205-270 ~

In our realm all is part rising from part and nothing can be more than partial; but There each being is an eternal product of a whole and is at once a whole and an individual manifesting as part but, to the keen vision There, known for the whole it is.
~ Plotinus ~
The Enneads, S. McKenna, tr., 1956

For the whole universe is interconnected; if something is distorted, the other things connected with it suffer.
~ Walda Heywat, 17th C. ~
The Treatise of Walda Heywat, Claude Sumner, tr. 1985

To all of humankind benignant heaven
(Since nought forbids) one common soul has given.
~ Francis Williams, c. 1700-c. 1774 ~
"Ode"

There can be no racial hate because there are no races.
~ José Martí, 1853-1895 ~

Nature is everything. Even what you can't see.
~ Esteban Montejo, 1856-1965 ~
in Miguel Barnet, *Biography of a Runaway Slave*, W. Nick Hill, tr., 1994

More and more we must learn to think not in terms of race or color or
language or religion or of political boundaries, but in terms of humanity.
Above all races and political boundaries there is humanity.
~ Booker T. Washington, 1856-1915 ~

We are all one, and if we don't know it, we will learn it the hard way.
~ Bayard Rustin, 1912-1987 ~

To be *whole* – politically, psychically, spiritually, culturally, intellectually,
aesthetically, physically, and economically – is of profound significance. It
is significant because there is a correlative to this. There is a responsibility
to self and to history that is developed once you are "whole," once you
acknowledge your powers.
~ Toni Cade Bambara, 1939-1995 ~

One love. One heart. Let's get together and feel alright.
~ Bob Marley, 1946-1981 ~

A truly moral imagination that by its very nature and outlook is imbued
with a profound respect for other people's lives ... demands that we assume
the challenge – and challenge it is – of envisioning, as compassionately and
with as much depth and breadth as possible, others beyond ourselves –
others who, in our truly seeing and feeling them through a creative act that
is itself, in the greatest sense of the word, holy, will no longer be, to us, the
"other."
~ Thomas Glave, b. 1964 ~
"Fire & Ink: Toward a Quest for Language, History, and a Moral Imagination," 2002 Conference
Address

OPENNESS / RECEPTIVITY

Disregarding the absurd or unorthodox may mean a lost chance to understand the universal laws.
~ Khemetic Wisdom ~
Temt Tchaas: Egyptian Proverbs, Muata Ashaya Ashby, ed., 1994

Consult with the ignorant and wise. Truth may be found among maids at the grindstones.
~ Ibid.

Many people – often people who consider themselves to be quite "religious" – believe that they have a monopoly on truth. Such a belief, however, can clearly be seen to limit one's flexibility and ability to learn. It greatly hampers even the possibility for one to listen deeply to what is being said. Without such listening capability, no genuine dialogue can be had or progress made. A closed mind cannot open to hear another opinion.
~ Jan Willis, b. 1948~

Always understand that you have to constantly work to develop your intellect, and just increase your curiosity.
~ Wynton Marsalis, b. 1961 ~
"Music's Jazz Maestro," Academy of Achievement Interview, 1991 January 8

I don't really have high expectations about much. It's a good psychological position to be in, because that means I'm usually delighted by what happens in my life.
~ Malcolm Gladwell, b. 1963 ~
in Danielle Sacks, "The Accidental Guru," FastCompany.com, No. 90, 2005 January

I open myself as a canvas on which you may inscribe your wisdom, teachings, and generosity and share your enlightenment – or whatever seeds of it you may have discovered in your own soul. The openness of the submissive is an act of enlightened humility. Enlightened because one knows that one is unable to acquire even an infinitesimal amount of evolutionary consciousness entirely on one's own.
~ Jason D. Hill, b. 1965 ~
"Moral Hierarchy: The Key to Evolving Consciousness," *What Is Enlightenment? Magazine*, Issue 31

OPPORTUNITY

When fortune knocks at the door, you have to open the door yourself.
~ Swahili Wisdom ~
Wit & Wisdom of Africa: Proverbs from Africa & The Caribbean, Patrick Ibekwe, ed., 1998

We should not permit our grievances to overshadow our opportunities.
~ Booker T. Washington, 1856-1915 ~

In these strenuous times, we are likely to become morbid and look
constantly on the dark side of life, and spend entirely too much time
considering and brooding over what we can't do, rather than what we can
do, and instead of growing morose and despondent over opportunities that
are shut from us, let us rejoice at the many unexplored fields in which
there is unlimited fame and fortune to the successful explorer.
~ George Washington Carver, 1864-1943 ~

I had to make my own living and my own opportunity ... Don't sit down
and wait for opportunities to come; you have to get up and make them.
~ Madame C. J. Walker, 1867-1919 ~

Take advantage of every opportunity; where there is none, make it for
yourself.
~ Marcus Garvey, 1887-1940 ~

One chance is all you need.
~ Jesse Owens, 1913-1980 ~
Blackthink, 1970

Successful people know how to seize opportunity – not tomorrow, not later
on today, but right now!
~ Les Brown, b. 1945 ~

If fate closes the door, climb in through the window.
~ Unknown ~

OPPRESSION

When emotions are society's objective, tyranny will govern regardless of the ruling class.
~ Khemetic Wisdom ~
Temt Tchaas: Egyptian Proverbs, Muata Ashaya Ashby, ed., 1994

Who oppresses the weak is a reproach to his maker.
~ Igbo Wisdom ~
Wit & Wisdom of Africa: Proverbs from Africa & The Caribbean, Patrick Ibekwe, ed., 1998

You can't hold a man down without staying down with him.
~ Booker T. Washington, 1856-1915 ~
Speeches of Booker T. Washington, 1932

One has to fight for justice for all. If I do not fight bigotry wherever it is, bigotry is thereby strengthened. And to the degree that it is strengthened, it will thereby have the power to turn on me.
~ Bayard Rustin, 1912-1987 ~

I knew as well as I knew anything that the oppressor must be liberated just as surely as the oppressed. A man who takes away another man's freedom is a prisoner of hatred; he is locked behind bars of prejudice and narrow-mindedness. I am not truly free if I am taking away someone else's freedom, just as surely as I am not free when my freedom is taken from me. The oppressed and the oppressor alike are robbed of freedom.
~ Nelson Mandela, b. 1918 ~

A culture that has suffered grave disadvantages tends to build on its humiliation as the everlasting model of experience.
~ Wilson Harris, b. 1921 ~
"The Fabric of the Imagination," 1989

Injustice anywhere is a threat to justice everywhere. We are caught in an inescapable network of mutuality, tied in a single garment of destiny. Whatever affects one directly affects all indirectly.
~ Martin Luther King, Jr., 1929-1968 ~
Letter from a Birmingham Jail, 1963 April 16

Freedom is never voluntarily given by the oppressor; it must be demanded by the oppressed.
~ King ~
Letter from Birmingham Jail, 1963 April 16

We must learn that passively to accept an unjust system is to co-operate with that system, and thereby to become a participant in its evil.
~ King ~
The Strength to Love, 1963

If you live in an oppressive society, you've got to be resilient. You can't let each little thing crush you. You have to take every encounter and make yourself larger, rather than allow yourself to be diminished by it.
~ James Earl Jones, b. 1931 ~
in Roderick Terry, One Million Strong: A PhotographicTribute of the Million Man March, 1996

If you are going to hold someone down, you're going to have to hold on to the other end of the chain. You are confined by your own system of oppression.
~ Toni Morrison, b. 1931 ~

As we begin to recognize our deepest feeling, we begin to give up, of necessity, being satisfied with suffering and self-negation, and with the numbness which so often seems like their only alternative in our society. Our acts against oppression become integral with self, motivated and empowered from within.
~ Audre Lorde, 1934-1992 ~
Sister Outsider: Essays and Speeches, 1984

The most potent weapon in the hands of the oppressor is the mind of the oppressed.
~ Steve Biko, 1946-1977 ~
"White Racism and Black Consciousness," in I Write What I Like, 1978

Sometimes the identity of the "outsider" may have changed, but the social, religious, economic, and cultural raison d'etre for exclusion is employed with the same degree of self-righteous vigor.
~ Caryl Phillips, b. 1958 ~
"They Are Us," Interview by Adrian Grima

Systems of oppression necessitate notions of identity, and consequently, our habitual attachment to this notion perpetuates oppression.
~ Hilda Gutiérrez Baldoquín ~
"Don't Waste Time," Dharma, Color, and Culture, Hilda Gutiérrez Baldoquín, ed., 2004

OPTIMISM / POSITIVISM

Optimism is making the most of all that comes and the least of all that goes.
~ Unknown ~

Grey skies are just clouds passing over.
~ Duke Ellington, 1899-1974 ~

I am fundamentally an optimist. Whether that comes from nature or nurture, I cannot say. Part of being optimistic is keeping one's head pointed toward the sun, one's feet moving forward. There were many dark moments when my faith in humanity was sorely tested, but I would not and could not give up to despair. That way lay defeat and death.
~ Nelson Mandela, b. 1918 ~
Long Walk to Freedom, 1994

Perpetual optimism is a force multiplier.
~ Colin Powell, b. 1937 ~

We've got a story to tell that isn't just against something but is for something.
~ Barack Obama, b. 1961 ~
Speech, Take Back America Conference, 2006 June 14

The key to personal transformation is being able to see the positive in every situation. Being positive means that, rather than complaining about a situation, we learn from it. Being positive means that we accept others as they are, instead of finding fault in them or passing judgment on them. Being positive means taking risks and embracing the unfamiliar. Being positive means being able to view ourselves in the most favorable light.
~ Roderick Terry, b. 1964 ~
"Hope Chest"

To become a champion, a leader, or a success, you have to think of yourself as one before you become one. After all, success doesn't lead to a positive attitude; a positive attitude leads to success.
~ Keith Boykin, b. 1965 ~
Respecting the Soul: Daily Reflections for Black Lesbians and Gays, 1999

PARADOX

Do you wish to rise? Begin by descending. You plan a tower that will pierce the clouds? Lay first the foundation of humility.
~ Augustine of Hippo, 354-430 ~

Out of crooked things develop straight things.
~ Ganda Wisdom ~
Wit & Wisdom of Africa: Proverbs from Africa & The Caribbean, Patrick Ibekwe, ed., 1998

As there is guilt in innocence, there is innocence in guilt.
~ Yoruba Wisdom ~
Ibid.

What makes you happy is what will make you sad.
~ Haitian Wisdom ~
Ibid.

We're attracted to the European thing, what I call the European Binary Syndrome of being either this or that. But you know the truth of the matter is that among ordinary people, life is not cut and dry. In the midst of iniquity people can be most saintly; and a church pillar may blaspheme.
~ Rex Nettleford, b. 1933 ~
"Nurturing the Yeast that Makes the Dough Rise: Caribbean Theatre and Dance in a Cultural Context," Interview by David Edgecombe, 1996

You can't win unless you learn how to lose.
~ Kareem Abdul-Jabbar, b. 1947 ~

And why is it that joy, encountered unexpectedly and fully, will have at its core a replication of your own sorrow, will in the very near distance cause you to feel disemboweled, lost, as if your own self was somewhere else, while at the same time you can see yourself in front of you, you are far away and you are right there nearby and how lost, how lost you are and you go searching for that joy, that original joy, but your joy is your sorrow, your joy has not turned to sorrow, your joy was always sorrow, a form of sorrow, just sorrow.
~ Jamaica Kincaid, b. 1949 ~
Mr. Potter, 2002

PARTNERSHIP / MARRIAGE

Marriage is not a fast knot, but a slip knot.
~ Madagascan Wisdom ~

There is no secret to a long marriage – it's hard work … It's serious
business, and certainly not for cowards.
~ Ossie B. Davis, 1917-2005 ~

You cannot belong to anyone else until you belong to yourself.
~ Pearl Bailey, 1918-1990 ~

I will bring you a whole person
and you will bring me a whole person
and we will have us twice as much
of love and everything.
~ Mari Evans, b. 1923 ~
"Celebration"

A woman who stands behind her man will not be able to see where *she* is
going. But when one person stands alongside another, there is an increased
strength and $1+1=11$!
~ Johnnetta Cole, b. 1936 ~

Race, in fact, is not the essential factor. What is important is culture …
the color of one's skin does not matter. I found that a white man was closer
to me than my first husband, even closer to me than the majority of the
people I knew. It is a matter of understanding: in a word, love. Marriage
should not be viewed as part of a political agenda. It concerns the feelings
and personal choices of two people.
~ Maryse Condé, b. 1937 ~
Interview by Elizabeth Nunez

Real marriage is the sacrificing of your ego, not for the other person, but for
the relationship.
~ Oprah Winfrey, b. 1954 ~

PASSION

Mastery of the passions allows divine thought and action.
~ Khemetic Wisdom ~
Temt Tchaas: Egyptian Proverbs, Muata Ashaya Ashby, ed., 1994

It is with our passions as it is with fire and water;
they are good servants, but bad masters.
~ Aesop, fl. c. 550 BCE ~

Fire begets ashes.
~ Tsonga Wisdom ~
Wit & Wisdom of Africa: Proverbs from Africa & The Caribbean, Patrick Ibekwe, ed., 1998

Our boasted civilization is but a veneer which cracks and scrubs off at the
first impact of primal passions.
~ Charles Chestnutt, 1858-1932 ~
The Marrow of Tradition, 1901

Don't ask what the world needs. Ask what makes you come alive, and go
do it. Because what the world needs is people who have come alive.
~ Howard Thurman, 1889-1981 ~

I had a way of life inside me and I wanted it with a want that was twisting
me.
~ Zora Neale Hurston, 1891-1960 ~

Fervor is the weapon of choice of the impotent.
~ Frantz Fanon, 1925-1961 ~
Black Skins, White Masks, 1967

Passion often leads to new worlds that you possibly never imagined.
~ Trevor Rhone, b. 1940 ~
Interview by Kinisha O'Neill, *Jamaica Daily Gleaner*, 2003 March 31

Wanting something is not enough. You must hunger for it. Your
motivation must be absolutely compelling in order to overcome the
obstacles that will invariably come your way.
~ Les Brown, b. 1945 ~

PATIENCE

Patience is the companion of wisdom.
~ Augustine of Hippo, 354-430 ~
On Patience

Patience is the best of dispositions: one who possesses patience, possesses all things.
~ Yoruba Wisdom ~
Wit & Wisdom of Africa: Proverbs from Africa & The Caribbean, Patrick Ibekwe, ed., 1998

One who is patient has more value than one who is powerful and a Wiseman is preferable to an angry man. In all difficulties make use of patience, because although patience is bitter when it is exercised, it turns out later to be more pleasant than honey and sugar.
~ Walda Heywat, 17th C. ~
The Treatise of Walda Heywat, Claude Sumner, tr. 1985

You have to be very patient and lay strong foundations so that when hurricanes come and blow everything away, you can rebuild.
~ Rex Nettleford, b. 1933 ~
"Nurturing the Yeast that Makes the Dough Rise: Caribbean Theatre and Dance in a Cultural Context," Interview by David Edgecombe, 1996

Many people have walked out of life because they stopped seeing it. Many have fallen into the abyss because they were looking for solid ground, for certainties. Happy are those who are still, and to whom things come.
~ Ben Okri, b. 1959 ~
The Famished Road, 1991

Patience is understanding and accepting the fact that things must unfold in their own time. The practice of patience can reduce agitation and anxiety. To be patient is to be aware of each moment, and to act with understanding. Patience is not a passive but an active skill.
~ Ralph M. Steele ~
An Introduction to Vipassana Meditation, 1995

PERSPECTIVE

A matter which in one place causes laughter, at another place causes tears.
~ Tshi Wisdom ~
Wit & Wisdom of Africa: Proverbs from Africa & The Caribbean, Patrick Ibekwe, ed., 1998

It is playing for the children and an emergency for the butterfly.
~ Oromo Wisdom ~
Ibid.

When an old thing belonging to one person gets into another person's
hands it is a new thing to her.
~ Tshi Wisdom ~
Ibid.

Nothing that God ever made is the same thing to more than one person.
That is natural. There is no single face in nature, because every eye that
looks upon it, sees it from its own angle. So every man's spice box seasons
his own food.
~ Zora Neale Hurston, 1891-1960 ~

How something is seen I suppose depends on whose eyes are looking at it.
~ Langston Hughes, 1902-1967 ~

An artist deals with aspects of reality different from those which a scientist
sees.
~ Richard Wright, 1908-1960 ~

The world changes according to the way people see it, and if you alter,
even by a millimeter, the way ... people look at reality, then you can
change it.
~ James Baldwin, 1924-1987 ~

If you view all the things that happen to you, both good and bad, as
opportunities, then you operate out of a higher level of consciousness.
~ Les Brown, b. 1945 ~

Some of us want to tie the world down into spaces that we own. You can
map a place, and write observations, but that's strictly a reflection of your
own point of view. If that point of view is rigid enough, that's all you see. A

map should be a larger place – a place filled with the endlessness of living, the hugeness of the imagination.
~ Dionne Brand, b. 1953 ~
"She's A Wanderer," Interview by Suzanne Methot, *Quill & Quire*, 1999 April

Normal is in the eyes of the beholder.
~ Whoopi Goldberg, b. 1955 ~

We perceive the world based on our expectations, which are heavily determined by our context. If your background or culture has convinced you that what is real is only what is palpable and physical and that seeing is believing, then you will begin to subscribe to … the narrowest horizon of vision. What you see will be based on an internal programming that expects the things of the world to present themselves in ways that you expect so as not to disrupt your entire belief system.
~ Malidoma Somé, b. 1956 ~
The Healing Wisdom of Africa, 1999

I tell the kids all the time who are angry, you should never lose your anger. You should stay mad. But you have to always realize that everything is a balance. And that your perspective is one perspective in the world. And it's a needed perspective, but it's one perspective. That's all. There are other perspectives that are equally as valid, they exist, and they are fueled by something too. So what you do is, figure out what your role is, and fulfill that role as successfully as you can.
~ Wynton Marsalis, b. 1961 ~
"Music's Jazz Maestro," Academy of Achievement Interview, 1991 January 8

It is a great gift to realize that whether one is wealthy or poor is mostly dependent on one's perspective and level of contentment. Such an understanding is priceless.
~ Oliver Mbamara ~
"Who is A Wealthy Person? (Impressions, Beliefs, and Definitions)," Part 2, ExpressionsofSoul.com, 2007 May

Whether you see a staircase as heading up or down depends on where you are standing … You classify the staircase the way you do because you see it only from your perspective. The fact that you see it as either up or down is because you haven't practiced becoming open enough to see from all perspectives. When you do see from all sides you will not see either one any more … No up and no down. Just the staircase as it is.
~ Angel Kyodo Williams ~
Being Black: Zen and the Art of Living with Fearlessness and Grace, 2000

POLARITY / CONTRAST

Everything is dual; everything has poles; everything has its pair of opposites; like and unlike are the same; opposites are identical in nature, but different in degree; extremes meet; all truths are but half-truths; all paradoxes may be reconciled.
~ Hermes Trismegistus ~
in *The Kybalion: A Study of the Hermetic Philosophy of Ancient Egypt and Greece*, 1908

As joy is not without its alloy of pain, so neither is sorrow without its portion of pleasure.
~ Khemetic Wisdom ~
from the Stele of Tefuti-Nefer, in *Temt Tchaas: Egyptian Proverbs*, Muata Ashaya Ashby, ed., 1994

The workings of the human heart are the profoundest mystery of the universe. One moment they make us despair of our kind, and the next we see in them the reflection of the divine image.
~ Charles Chestnutt, 1858-1932 ~
The Marrow of Tradition, 1901

We, the creators of the new generation, want to give expression to our *black personality* without shame or fear ... We know we are handsome. Ugly as well. The drums weep and the drums laugh.
~ Langston Hughes, 1902-1967 ~

Each of the identifiable life forces of the universe – from the grain of sand to the ancestor – is, itself and in its turn, a network of life forces – as modern physical chemistry confirms: a network of elements that are contradictory in appearance but really *complementary*. Thus, for the African, man is composed, of course, of matter and spirit, of body and soul; but at the same time he is also composed of a virile and a feminine element: indeed of several "souls." Man is therefore a composition of mobile life forces which interlock.
~ Léopold Senghor, 1906-2001 ~
Négritude: a Humanism of the Twentieth Century, 1970

Perhaps she was both ... child and woman, darkness and light, past and present, life and death – all the opposites contained and reconciled in her.
~ Paule Marshall, b. 1929 ~
"To Da-duh in Memoriam," 1966

One thing about catastrophe, for me, is that it always seems to lead to a kind of magical realism. That moment of utter disaster, the very moment when it seems almost hopeless, too difficult to proceed, you begin to glimpse a kind of radiance on the other end of the maelstrom.
~ Kamau Brathwaite, b. 1930 ~
Interview by Joyelle McSweeney, "Poetics, Revelations, and Catastrophes," *Raintaxi Review of Books*, Fall 2005

I have come to realize the extraordinary capacity for evil that all of us have ... there have been revelations of horrendous atrocities that people have committed. Any and every one of us could have perpetrated those atrocities. The people who were perpetrators of the most gruesome things didn't have horns, didn't have tails. They were ordinary human beings like you and me. That's the one thing. Devastating! But the other, more exhilarating than anything that I have ever experienced – and something I hadn't expected – to discover that we have an extraordinary capacity for good. People who suffered untold misery, people who should have been riddled with bitterness, resentment and anger ... exhibit an extraordinary magnanimity and nobility of spirit in their willingness to forgive.
~ Desmond Tutu, b. 1931 ~
"Forging Equality in South Africa," Academy of Achievement Interview, 2004 June 12

What we constitute as a whole within the subject is fundamentally constituted by that which is not itself, by its constitutive outside. Put in another way, every self or every identity is constituted by that which it lacks, which is the Other.
~ Stuart Hall, b. 1932 ~
Seminar, Program in the Comparative Study of Social Transformations (CSST), 1999 April 15

Who needs "up" if there is no "down"? They are so linked together that they are the same thing; different perspectives on the very same thing.
~ Angel Kyodo Williams ~
Being Black: Zen and the Art of Living with Fearlessness and Grace, 2000

POSSIBILITY / POTENTIAL

What is tried may become true.
~ Ovambo Wisdom ~
Wit & Wisdom of Africa: Proverbs from Africa & The Caribbean, Patrick Ibekwe, ed., 1998

Impossibilities are merely things of which we have not learned, or which we do not wish to happen.
~ Charles Chestnutt, 1858-1932 ~
The Marrow of Tradition, 1901

Man is a promise that he must never break.
~ Richard Wright, 1908-1960 ~

A person never knows what he can do until he does it.
~ Gordon Parks, 1912-2006 ~

Know whence you came. If you know whence you came, there is really no limit to where you can go.
~ James Baldwin, 1924-1987 ~
The Fire Next Time, 1962

A woman who is willing to be herself and pursue her own potential runs not so much the risk of loneliness as the challenge of exposure to more interesting men – and people in general.
~ Lorraine Hansberry, 1930-1965 ~

You aim at the impossible to get the unusual.
~ Floyd Patterson, b. 1935 ~

All my growth and development led me to believe that if you really do the right thing, and if you play by the rules, and if you've got good enough, solid judgment and common sense, that you're going to be able to do whatever you want to do with your life.
~ Barbara Jordan, 1936-1996 ~

Never underestimate the power of dreams and the influence of the human spirit. We are all the same in this notion: The potential for greatness lives within each of us.
~ Wilma Rudolph, 1940-1994 ~

We have these immense possibilites of making something of ourselves, but we get sidetracked, by being a man, by being a woman, or being black, being white. All the dichotomies that western thinking pushes us into.
~ John Edgar Wideman, b. 1941 ~
Interview by Laura Miller, *Salon*

I think everything is possible, especially for the next generation. Just look at what we've overcome.
~ Nikki Giovanni, b. 1943 ~

The limitations you have and the negative things you internalize are given to you by the world. The things that empower you – the possibilities – *come from within*.
~ Les Brown, b. 1945 ~

Everybody is special if they believe they're special, because there's so much potential in each human being. When you look at the human brain and how little of it we actually use, how little of our potential we actually use, if you can convince somebody that they've got a lot of potential and get them moving in that direction, then obviously they are going to be persons of accomplishment.
~ Benjamin Carson, b. 1951 ~
"Gifted Hands That Heal," Academy of Achievement Interview, 2002 June 7

Failure to recognize possibilities is the most dangerous and common mistake one can make.
~ Mae Jemison, b. 1956 ~

The most authentic thing about us is our capacity to create, to overcome, to endure, to transform, to love and to be greater than our suffering.
~ Ben Okri, b. 1959 ~

The word "retire" means you can do anything you want. I'm not going to close the door on it … I will never say never. I don't close the door to any possibilities.
~ Michael Jordan, b. 1963 ~
Press Conference, 1993 October 6

Our potential is limitless. Many of us have hidden talents and abilities that we have yet to discover. The measure of our success depends on our ability to recognize and unleash our potential.
~ Roderick Terry, b. 1964 ~
"Hope Chest"

POWER

True power comes through cooperation and silence.
~ Ashanti Wisdom ~

The power of those whom power makes terrible to others, is, first of all,
terrible to themselves. It smiles to rage, it cajoles to deceive, it entices to
slay, it lifts up to cast down. With a certain usury of mischief, the greater
the height of dignity and honors attained, the greater is the interest of
penalty required.
~ Cyprian, 200-258 ~
Epistle to Donatus

Power comes not from the skin, but from the heart.
Set up by a powerful hand (nourishing God, denying nothing,
has given the same souls to all kinds),
virtue itself is colorless, as is wisdom.
There is no color in the soul, nor in art.
~ Francis Williams, c. 1700-c. 1774 ~
"An Ode to George Haldane"

There is in this world no such force as the force of a man determined to
rise. The human soul cannot be permanently chained.
~ W. E. B. Du Bois, 1868-1963 ~
"Race Prejudice," Speech, 1910 March 5

The only protection against injustice in man is power – physical power,
financial power, educational power, scientific power, power of every kind.
~ Marcus Garvey, 1887-1940 ~
in *Negro World*, 1922 August 5

Knowledge is power. If it is not applied properly to create, let there be no
doubt, it will destroy.
~ Haile Selassie, 1892-1975 ~

The moment you give another the power of causation, you have
transferred to him the power that rightfully belongs to you. Others are only
shadows, bearing witness to the activities taking place in you.
~ Neville, 1905-1972 ~
"All That You Behold," Lecture, 1969 April 19

Wherever I found religion in my life I found strife, the attempt of one individual or group to rule another in the name of God. The naked will to power seemed always to walk in the wake of a hymn.
~ Richard Wright, 1908-1960 ~
in *Songs of Wisdom: Quotations from Famous African Americans*, Jay David, ed., 2000

Power in defense of freedom is greater than power on behalf of tyranny.
~ Malcolm X, 1925-1965 ~

When I dare to be powerful – to use my strength in the service of my vision, then it becomes less and less important whether I am afraid.
~ Audre Lorde, 1934-1992 ~

Don't call for black power or green power. Call for brain power.
~ Barbara Jordan, 1936-1996 ~

The real power behind whatever success I have now was something I found within myself – something that's in all of us, I think, a little piece of God just waiting to be discovered.
~ Tina Turner, b. 1939 ~
I, *Tina*, 1986

Always know that there is unlimited power in a developed mind and a disciplined spirit. If your mind can conceive it and your heart can believe it, you can achieve it.
~ Jesse Jackson, b. 1941 ~
in *Brother's Keeper: Words of Inspiration for African-American Men*, Roderick Terry, ed., 1996

Peace will come when the power of love overcomes the love of power.
~ Jimi Hendrix, 1942-1970 ~

With the power of soul, anything is possible.
With the power of you, anything you wanna do.
~ Hendrix ~
"Power of Soul"

Power only means the ability to have control over your life. Power implies choice.
~ Nikki Giovanni, b, 1943 ~

It's not about the office that you hold or the money in your bank account. Real power never stems from agencies. It stems from spiritual power.
~ Cory Booker, b. 1969 ~
in *Washington Post*, 2006 July 3

PRACTICE

Anybody can observe the Sabbath, but making it holy surely takes the rest of the week.
~ Alice Walker, b. 1944 ~

Mindfulness is not only practiced when sitting. It can – and should – be brought to each and every one of our activities, regardless of how humble they might be. When walking, eating, taking out the garbage, or talking, the Dharma urges us to practice a complete and dispassionate awareness of where we are and what we are doing. Such practice is transformative.
~ Charles Johnson, b. 1948 ~
"Reading the Eightfold Path," *Dharma, Color, and Culture*, Hilda Gutiérrez Baldoquín, ed., 2004

Meditation is the path. You don't have to accept dogma. You have to spend time on the cushion.
~ Jan Willis, b. 1948 ~
in Nadya Labi, "Of Color and the Cushion," Time.com, 2000

No matter how active and energetic you are, it's always a good idea to spend some time doing some practice most of us would call spiritual.
~ Montel Williams, b. 1956 ~

Just relax. Stuff comes in time. It's the concentration that you have to exert. It's horizontal, it's not vertical. The key to practicing is to practice and concentrate over a course of years, not a bunch of time in a day. A week at a time. Then the reason you don't get tired is because you will be relaxed and calm, and you are constantly working.
~ Wynton Marsalis, b. 1961 ~
"Music's Jazz Maestro," Academy of Achievement Interview, 1991 January 8

Everything is practice, a very sacred and personal experience. There is freedom in the silence of practice, in the stillness as well as in the movement of the practice of life. The greatest teaching for me has been practicing compassion, first for myself, then for other individuals, and for all beings in all directions. It is here that I have found true freedom.
~ Marlene Jones ~
"Moving toward an End to Suffering," *Dharma, Color, and Culture*, Hilda Gutiérrez Baldoquín, ed., 2004

PREPARATION / READINESS

When the ears of the student are ready to hear, then cometh the lips to fill them with wisdom.
~ Hermes Trismegistus ~
in *The Kybalion: A Study of the Hermetic Philosophy of Ancient Egypt and Greece*, 1908

Strategy is better than strength.
~ Hausa Wisdom ~

One who doesn't look ahead falls behind.
~ Haitian Wisdom ~
Wit & Wisdom of Africa: Proverbs from Africa & The Caribbean, Patrick Ibekwe, ed., 1998

A little forethought saves afterthought.
~ Jamaican Wisdom ~
Ibid.

The only way to face the arduous tests posed by life is to be spiritually prepared for them.
~ Haile Selassie, 1892-1975 ~

It's better to be prepared for an opportunity and not have one, than to have an opportunity and not be prepared.
~ Whitney Young, Jr., 1921-1971 ~

Education is our passport to the future, for tomorrow belongs to the people who prepare for it today.
~ Malcolm X, 1925-1965 ~

"Read the book, get the education, then you can get into a conversation." That makes sense.
~ Eartha Kitt, b. 1927 ~
Interview by Blase DiStefano, "Eartha Kitt *Purr*-severes: The Feline Feminist Talks About Her Two Lives as the Child and the Woman," *OutSmart*

The challenge facing us is to equip ourselves that we will be able to take our place wherever we are in the affairs of men.
~ Barbara Jordan, 1936-1996 ~

Your future is waiting for you to act *now*. Whether you know it or not, what you're doing now is preparing you for what's next ... What you're doing may not seem important, but how you do it may turn out to be.
~ Famous Amos, b. 1937 ~
Watermelon Magic, 1996

And once you're prepared, you never know what roads will open up. And if you're prepared it does not matter. If there's a road you can pursue it. If there's no road, you can carve it through bushes.
~ Jesse Jackson, b. 1941 ~

One important key to success is self-confidence. An important key to self-confidence is preparation.
~ Arthur Ashe, 1943-1993 ~

Instead of always looking at the past, I put myself ahead twenty years and try to look at what I need to do now in order to get there then.
~ Diana Ross, b. 1944 ~

I always approach my work with clean hands. I will do a symbolic cleansing with my morning coffee, if nothing else is available. I do a lot of mental and spiritual preparation for what is essentially a journey on which I am going to make discoveries about myself and the nature of human life. It can sometimes be a painful process.
~ August Wilson, 1945-2005 ~
Interview by Bonnie Lyons & George Plimpton, *Paris Review*, No. 153, Winter 1999

The more we nourish our internal world, the more powerful we grow in the external world.
~ Susan L. Taylor, b. 1946 ~
Lessons in Living, 1995

You can't avoid life's thunderstorms; they're bound to hit you. You can, however, be prepared for them by fortifying your spirit and stocking up on food for your soul. You can teach yourself today to be resilient to the troubles of life tomorrow. You can learn to practice calmness so that when the storms do hit, you'll be strong enough to survive.
~ Keith Boykin, b. 1965 ~
Respecting the Soul: Daily Reflections for Black Lesbians and Gays, 1999

The celebration of tomorrow's harvest is dependent on the effort of today's planting ... for tomorrow soon becomes today.
~ Oliver Mbamara ~

PRESENCE

He who neglecteth the present moment, throweth away all that he hath.
As the arrow passeth through the heart, while the warrior knew not that it
was coming, so shall his life be taken away before he knoweth that he hath
it ... This instant is thine; the next is in the womb of futurity, and thou
knowest not what it may bring forth; maturity of the unborn is in the
keeping of the Law. Each future state is that thou has created in the
present.
~ Akhenaton, c. 1385-c. 1355 BCE ~

The present moment ... has several dimensions ... the present of things
past, the present of things present, and the present of things future.
~ Augustine of Hippo, 354-430 ~

Exhaust the little moment. Soon it dies.
And be it gash or gold it will not come
Again in this identical disguise.
~ Gwendolyn Brooks, 1917-2000 ~
"exhaust the little moment," *Annie Allen*, 1949

There is never time in the future in which we will work out our salvation.
The challenge is in the moment; the time is always now.
~ James Baldwin, 1924-1987 ~
Nobody Knows My Name: More Notes of a Native Son, 1961

The past is a ghost, the future a dream, and all we ever have is now.
~ Bill Cosby, b. 1937 ~
Time Flies, 1987

Time is a lie, the past is now
And all our futures are our present minutes.
~ Mervyn Morris, b. 1937 ~
"Birthday Honours," *Caribbean Literature: An Anthology*, G. R Coulthard, ed., 1966

Each moment is magical, precious and complete and will never exist again.
We forget that *now* is the moment we are in, that the next one isn't
guaranteed. And if we are blessed with another moment, any joy, creativity
or wisdom it brings will ensue from the way we live the present one.
~ Susan L. Taylor, b. 1946 ~
Lessons in Living, 1995

Memories, projections for future plans, thoughts, reveries, and the entire "mental panorama" ... leave only thirty percent of our lives lived in the present moment, the *here* and *now*. All too often, thirty percent of conscious life is wasted by our minds dwelling on events in the unrecoverable past; another thirty percent is lost pre-living the future. Put simply, we are seldom fully one hundred percent in the present.
~ Charles Johnson, b. 1948 ~
"Reading the Eightfold Path," *Dharma, Color, and Culture*, Hilda Gutiérrez Baldoquín, ed., 2004

This moment held in a tight grip was special and ordinary: for all moments are special and all moments are ordinary and who can make them so?
~ Jamaica Kincaid, b. 1949 ~
Mr. Potter, 2002

We are poised in the present moment, in which all things may change, all ignorance be transposed to knowledge; from knowledge shall come compassion, and from compassion, nobility.
~ Thomas Glave, b. 1964 ~
"Towards A Nobility of the Imagination," *Words to Our Now: Imagination and Dissent*, 2005

Winners live in the present tense. People who come up short are consumed with future or past. I want to be living in the now.
~ Alex "A-Rod" Rodriguez, b. 1975 ~

Today's present moment will be seen as the "past" when tomorrow "comes." It is in the present that the "future" is created; yet it is in the present that the expected "future" is manifested, lived, and experienced. The present moment is a continuous thing, a constant state of flux, always alive and flowing, yet always the same. The eternal now-in-the-now of every moment. A paradox of immense proportion. The state of being in which Soul exists.
~ Oliver Mbamara ~
"What Is Your Attitude of The Present?" *Why Are We Here?*, 2003

Mindfullness transports us into the single, present moment and then into the next and the next. Without space to fret about the past or ponder the future, we end up experiencing the present moment in its complete fullness. If you ever wondered where to find it, that's where life is *always* at ... Anyplace and anytime you want to experience the fullness of your life, all you have to do is bring your attention to this moment right now.
~ Angel Kyodo Williams ~
Being Black: Zen and the Art of Living with Fearlessness and Grace, 2000

PRUDENCE

Hear the words of prudence, give heed unto her counsels, and store them in thine heart; her maxims are universal, and all the virtues lean upon her; she is the guide and the mistress of human life.
~ Khemetic Wisdom ~
Temt Tchaas: Egyptian Proverbs, Muata Ashaya Ashby, ed., 1994

Grief is natural to the mortal world and is always about you; pleasure is a guest and visiteth by thy invitation. Use well thy mind and sorrow shall be passed behind you; be prudent and the visits of joy shall remain long with you.
~ Ibid.

Affairs are easier of entrance than of exit; and it is but common prudence to see our way out before we venture in.
~ Aesop, fl. c. 550 BCE ~

Prudence is love that chooses with sagacity between that which hinders it and that which helps it.
~ Augustine of Hippo, 354-430 ~
De Moribus Ecclesiae Catholicae, 387-389

Prudence is the mother of security.
~ Haitian Wisdom ~
Wit & Wisdom of Africa: Proverbs from Africa & The Caribbean, Patrick Ibekwe, ed., 1998

Count twice has defeated count once.
~ Tswana Wisdom ~
Ibid.

Cut your coat by your cloth and mark twice before you cut once.
~ Jamaican Wisdom ~
Ibid.

If you attend to what is roasting it will not be burnt.
~ Yoruba Wisdom ~
Ibid.

QUESTIONING / DOUBT

True wisdom is less presuming than folly. The wise person doubts often and changes his mind; the fool is obstinate and doubts not, knowing all but their own ignorance.
~ Khemetic Wisdom ~
Temt Tchaas: Egyptian Proverbs, Muata Ashaya Ashby, ed., 1994

The one who asks questions doesn't lose his way.
~ Akan Wisdom ~

One who asks questions cannot avoid the answer.
~ Cameroon Wisdom ~

One who does not ask a question learns nothing.
~ Swahili Wisdom ~
Wit & Wisdom of Africa: Proverbs from Africa & The Caribbean, Patrick Ibekwe, ed., 1998

You can tell whether a man is clever by his answers. You can tell whether a man is wise by his questions.
~ Naguib Mahfouz, b. 1911 ~

The greatest gift is not being afraid to question.
~ Ruby Dee, b. 1923 ~

The questions which one asks oneself begin, at least, to illuminate the world, and become one's key to the experience of others.
~ James Baldwin, 1924-1987 ~

O my body, make of me always a man who questions!
~ Frantz Fanon, 1925-1961 ~
in *Brother's Keeper: Words of Inspiration for African-American Men*, Roderick Terry, ed., 1996

If these are riddles, riddles write themselves
And where we end no starting indicates.
~ Martin Carter, 1927-1997 ~
"What We Call Wings," *Poems of Succession*, 1997

Question everything. Every stripe, every star, every word spoken.
Everything.
~ Ernest Gaines, b. 1933 ~
"The Sky Is Gray," 1963

The first sign of an educated person is that she asks more questions than
she delivers answers.
~ Johnnetta Cole, b. 1936 ~

The search for truth should always be our guiding force ... always be willing
to question past actions as well as accept constructive criticism.
~ Haki Madhubuti, b. 1942 ~
*Black Men: Obsolete, Single, Dangerous? The Afrikan American in Transition: Essays in Discovery, Solution,
and Hope, 1990*

I understand the vocation of the intellectual as trying to turn easy answers
into critical questions and ask these critical questions to those with power.
~ Cornel West, b. 1954 ~

Although visible and tangible answers may not appear immediately, we
must never stop asking questions of ourselves. It is only through this type
of self-inquiry and contemplation that we can discover our true purpose.
No one else can hear our calling.
~ Roderick Terry, b. 1964 ~
"Hope Chest"

True liberation comes when we ask not only the easy questions, but also
the tough questions with answers we may not want to hear.
~ Keith Boykin, b. 1965 ~
Respecting the Soul: Daily Reflections for Black Lesbians and Gays, 1999

When we stop questioning, we can make the mistake of adding suffering to
the world. We can't accept ignorance as an excuse. Ignorance is another
poison. We can't let ourselves off the hook by saying we didn't know
because asking the questions, no matter how difficult, is our responsibility.
Questioning is how we master the truth.
~ Angel Kyodo Williams ~
Being Black: Zen and the Art of Living with Fearlessness and Grace, 2000

REALITY

Under, and back of, the universe of time, space and change, is ever to be found the Substantial Reality – the Fundamental Truth … That which is the Fundamental Truth – the Substantial Reality – is beyond true naming, but the wise men call it The All.
~ Hermes Trismegistus ~
in *The Kybalion: A Study of the Hermetic Philosophy of Ancient Egypt and Greece*, 1908

Either you deal with what is the reality, or you can be sure that the reality is going to deal with you.
~ Alex Haley, 1921-1992 ~

Everything that we see is a shadow cast by that which we do not see.
~ Martin Luther King, Jr., 1929-1968 ~

The oral tale accepts magic as an element in life, which is no more than saying that reality is very magical.
~ Ngugi wa Thiong'o, b. 1938 ~
Interview in *Socialist Worker*, 2006 November 4, No. 2025

The dream is real, my friends. The failure to make it work is the unreality.
~ Toni Cade Bambara, 1939-1995 ~
The Salt Eaters, 1980

This life is not real. I conquered the world and it did not bring me satisfaction.
~ Muhammad Ali, b. 1942 ~

Nothing we look at is ever seen without some shift and flicker – that constant flaking of vision which we take as imperfections of the eye or simply the instability of attention itself; and we ignore this illusory screen for the solid reality behind it. But the solid reality is the illusion; the shift and flicker is all there is.
~ Samuel R. Delany, b. 1942 ~
Shadows, 1974

These notions of real and unreal – that is a construction of this particular universe. They're not so different. To choose to slip in and out of them ... is more freeing.
~ Dionne Brand, b. 1953 ~
"She's A Wanderer," Interview by Suzanne Methot, *Quill & Quire*, 1999 April

All that you are attached to, all that you love,
All that you know, someday will be gone.
Knowing this, and that the world is your mind
Which you create, play in, and suffer from,
Is known as discrimination.
Discriminate between the Real and the Unreal,
The known is unreal and will come and go
So stay with the Unknown, the Unchanging, the Truth.
~ Mooji, b. 1954 ~

I don't rack my brains worrying about the separation between fiction and reality. Fiction is our reality. Reality is our imagination.
~ Chenjerai Hove, b. 1956 ~
Prologue, *Shebeen Tales: Messages from Harare*, 1997

The things we speak, do and say to one another are literally the forces of construction and destruction, positive or negative. Reality is made by self-and-other and that other can be another person, a tree providing oxygen and shade on a summer afternoon, an ant crawling across your bare foot, or the wind blowing against your skin. Reality is about *Us* and not *I* and I alone.
~ Conrad Pegues, b. 1964 ~
"Reflections Upon the Bambara Creation Myth," in *Spirited: Affirming the Soul and Black Gay/Lesbian Identity*, G. Winston James & Lisa C. Moore, eds., 2006

Reality is a concentric circle: cause and effect – ripples pushing out into the universe. This is the secret of the world: Our interconnectedness makes the happiness of others our own.
~ Mona de Vestel, b. 1966 ~
"Buddha on the Land," in *Spirited: Affirming the Soul and Black Gay/Lesbian Identity*, G. Winston James & Lisa C. Moore, eds., 2006

Flights to distant places always arouse in me a peculiar awareness: that what we refer to as reality – not the substance, but the organization of reality – is really a strand as thin as the puffy white lines that planes leave behind as they fly.
~ Binyavanga Wainaina, b. 1971 ~
"Discovering Home," *G21*, 1995 June

RECIPROCITY / REFLECTION

While All is in THE ALL, it is equally true that THE ALL is in All. To him who understands this truth hath come great knowledge ... As above, so below; as below, so above.
~ Hermes Trismegistus ~
in *The Kybalion: A Study of the Hermetic Philosophy*, 1908

They know themselves; they know the Cosmos as well.
~ Khemetic Wisdom ~
Temt Tchaas: Egyptian Proverbs, Muata Ashaya Ashby, ed., 1994

A good deed returns to those who do it.
~ *Book of Khun-Anup (The Eloquent Peasant)* ~
in *Kemet and the African Worldview*, Maulana Karenga and Jacob Carruthers, eds., 1986

My friend, in the midst of the present upsetting conditions of life, your own healing begins by not being unkind to any other human being. The person who is not straightened out to your satisfaction still belongs to you. You are part of every other person because all alike are one in being human.
~ Augustine of Hippo, 354-430 ~

A sure way for one to lift himself up is by helping to lift someone else.
~ Booker T. Washington, 1856-1915 ~
Daily Resolves, 1896

In recognizing the humanity of our fellow beings, we pay ourselves the highest tribute.
~ Thurgood Marshall, 1908-1993 ~

God is as dependent on you as you are on Him.
~ Mahalia Jackson, 1911-1972 ~

I had a hard lesson to learn, that I could not help others free their hearts and minds of racial prejudice unless I would do all I could within myself to straighten out my own thinking and to feel and respond to kindness, to goodwill from wherever it came, whether it was the southerner, northerner, or any race.
~ Rosa Parks, 1913-2005 ~

It is a terrible, an inexorable, law that one cannot deny the humanity of another without diminishing one's own: in the face of one's victim, one sees oneself.
~ James Baldwin, 1924-1987 ~
"Fifth Avenue, Uptown," *Esquire*, 1960

People who treat other people as less than human must not be surprised when the bread they have cast on the waters comes floating back to them, poisoned.
~ Baldwin ~

The moment you have protected an individual you have protected society.
~ Kenneth Kaunda, b. 1924 ~
in *Observer* (UK), 1962

A man who makes trouble for others is also making trouble for himself.
~ Chinua Achebe, b. 1930 ~
Things Fall Apart, 1958

Anything we say about the other is what we are really saying of ourselves, because we have no way of knowing the heart of the other except through searching our own heart. The other can only be a projection of the self.
~ Earl Lovelace, b. 1935 ~
Speech, University of the West Indies, St. Augustine, Trinidad, 2002 November 1

It is essential that we understand that taking care of the planet will be done *as* we take care of ourselves. You know that you can't really make much of a difference in things until you change yourself.
~ Alice Walker, b. 1944 ~

The way you think about people often determines their behavior. So if you set the bar high, that's what you get.
~ Bill Strickland, b. 1947 ~
Sierra Club "Spirit in Nature" Address, 2004

How we are perceived by others mirrors how we feel about ourselves ... a positive self-image is also a starting point for building and maintaining strong relationships with others. When we love and respect ourselves, we are able to share these same feelings with others and establish more meaningful relationships.
~ Roderick Terry, b. 1964 ~
Brother's Keeper: Words of Inspiration for African-American Men, 1996

REGRET

Doing one's best drives away regret.
~ Malagasy Wisdom ~
Wit & Wisdom of Africa: Proverbs from Africa & The Caribbean, Patrick Ibekwe, ed., 1998

It is better to sleep on what you intend doing than to stay awake over what you have done.
~ Igbo Wisdom ~

I'm not ashamed of my grandparents for having been slaves. I am only ashamed of myself for having at one time been ashamed.
~ Ralph Ellison, 1914-1994 ~
in *In Our Own Words*, Elza Dinwiddie-Boyd, ed., 1996

If you never do something that is not good for you, you don't have to live with regret. That is not a good life.
~ Salif Keita, b. 1949 ~
"Bobo"

Don't waste your life living in regret. You are who you are supposed to be in the place you're supposed to be and at the time you're supposed to be here. Don't try to change the things you can't control. Change the things you can.
~ Keith Boykin, b. 1965 ~
Respecting the Soul: Daily Reflections for Black Lesbians and Gays, 1999

I made decisions that I regret, and I took them as learning experiences ... I'm human, not perfect, like anybody else.
~ Queen Latifah, b. 1970 ~

RELATIONSHIP

My closest relation is myself.
~ Terence, c. 190-159 BCE ~
Andria, 166 BCE

To be effective in human relations requires both skill and "feel"; it
demands the use of head and heart.
~ Howard Thurman, 1889-1981 ~
Meditations of the Heart, 1953

If a relationship is based on "what am I getting?" all is lost.
~ Ossie B. Davis, 1917-2005 ~

Wishing each other well is something you have to practice doing – wishing
each other well and believing that your light will shine also.
~ Ruby Dee, b. 1923 ~

I have always been here on this side and the other person there on that
side, and we have both tried to make the sides appear similar in the needs,
desires, and ambitions ... The likenesses will meet and make merry, but
they won't know you. They won't know the you that's hidden somewhere
in the castle of your skin.
~ George Lamming, b. 1927 ~
In the Castle of My Skin, 1953

It takes time and deeds, and this involves trust, it involves making
ourselves vulnerable to each other, to strip ourselves naked, to become
sitting ducks for each other – and if one of the ducks is shamming, then
the sincere duck will pay in pain – but the deceitful duck, I feel, will be the
loser.
~ Eldridge Cleaver, 1935-1998 ~
Soul on Ice, 1968

If you are committed to a relationship, you must stick with it through thick
and thin. Instead of looking for ways to get out, look for ways to work it
out. When you are involved in a relationship, a career, or a task, you
shouldn't look for reasons to fail, even if you failed in the past. You must
look for reasons to succeed, because you have a purpose.
~ Famous Amos, b. 1937 ~
Watermelon Magic, 1996

There is no beauty but in relationships. Nothing cut off by itself is beautiful. Never can things in destructive relationships be beautiful. All beauty is in the creative purpose of our relationships.
~ Ayi Kwei Armah, b. 1939 ~

Our relationships are our mirrors; they reflect where we are in consciousness. And if we are able to face the truth about ourselves, our relationships offer the lessons that lead to our greatest transformation.
~ Susan L. Taylor, b. 1946 ~
Lessons in Living, 1995

I do find relationships to be kaleidoscopic and infinitely changing; no relationship is ever clear or safe, no matter how intrinsically wonderful it is and all that.
~ Rita Dove, b. 1952 ~
Interview by M. Wynn Thomas, *Swansea Review*, 1995 August 12

The person who seeks to change another person in a relationship basically sets the stage for a great deal of conflict.
~ Wesley Snipes, b. 1962 ~

No matter what anyone told you, a relationship will not make you happy or whole if you're not that way already … the most important relationship to develop is the one with yourself.
~ Keith Boykin, b. 1965 ~
Respecting the Soul: Daily Reflections for Black Lesbians and Gays, 1999

It's very important for people to know that those men who are scared by women who are accomplished are the kind of men accomplished women don't want. So it's nobody's loss.
~ Chimamanda Ngozi Adichie, b. 1977 ~
in Henry Akubuiro, "My Love Life," *Nigeria Daily Sun*, 2007 January 14

We flit from one bad relationship to the next, hoping to find the sanctuary of family and belonging. We are all looking for love and we don't find it until we "become" love. We attract who and what we are. When there is too much focus on the external, the challenges of any relationship are no longer holy but temporal … It is no small wonder, therefore, that many of us falter along the way.
~ Alaric Wendell Blair ~
"I Can't Make It Without You: A Conversation on Spirituality and Relationships," in *Spirited: Affirming the Soul and Black Gay/Lesbian Identity*, G. Winston James & Lisa C. Moore, eds., 2006

RELATIVITY

The wisdom of this year is the folly of the next.
~ Yoruba Wisdom ~

Where there is no wealth there is no poverty.
~Tswana Wisdom ~
Wit & Wisdom of Africa: Proverbs from Africa & The Caribbean, Patrick Ibekwe, ed., 1998

There is neither happiness nor misery in the world; there is only the comparison of one state to another, nothing more. He who has felt the deepest grief is best able to experience supreme happiness. We must have felt what it is to die, that we may appreciate the enjoyments of life.
~ Alexandre Dumas, père, 1802-1870 ~
The Count of Monte Cristo, 1844

Looking, looking, searching, searching, and I find that I am extraordinary and then I am not so at all, I find that I am the opposite of extraordinary, and then I find that I am spectacular and then I am not so at all, spectacular, that is.
~ Jamaica Kincaid, b. 1949 ~
Mr. Potter, 2002

Only man can attain that consciousness that man search for in God, because God cannot exist without man. If there is no man, there is no God. If there is no God, there is no devil. If there is a devil, there is a God. The two of them is just the flip side of the same coin.
~ Mutabaruka, b. 1952 ~
Interview by Carter Van Pelt, 1998

We have to be just as willing to touch and acknowledge the pain as we are to feel the joy. Why? Because one doesn't exist without the other. Who needs "up" if there is no "down"? They are so linked together that they are the same thing; different perspectives on the very same thing.
~ Angel Kyodo Williams ~
Being Black: Zen and the Art of Living with Fearlessness and Grace, 2000

RELEASE

Thou must be emptied of that wherewith thou art full, that thou mayest be filled with that whereof thou art empty.
~ Augustine of Hippo, 354-430 ~

... The tree
Budding yearly must forget
How its past arose or set.
~ Countée Cullen, 1903-1946 ~
"Heritage," *My Soul's High Song: The Collected Writings of Countee Cullen, Voice of the Harlem Renaissance,* É Gerald Early, ed., 1991

We make too much of that long groan which underlines the past.
~ Derek Walcott, b. 1930 ~

Wanna fly, you got to give up the shit that weighs you down.
~ Toni Morrison, b. 1931 ~
Song of Solomon, 1977

When your dreams turn to dust, vacuum.
~ Desmond Tutu, b. 1931 ~

You can make your own decisions about the kind of person you are now. The you of your past can travel with the you of your present only at your invitation. Cancel the invitation. You will be doing yourself a big favor.
~ Famous Amos, b. 1937 ~
Watermelon Magic, 1996

There's a lot to be said for recognizing that there comes a time when terminating an interminable situation is better than digging into a dungheap and pretending it's a bed of roses.
~ Ibid. ~

Sometimes you've got to let *everything* go – purge yourself. I did that. I had nothing, but I had my freedom ... If you are unhappy with anything ... whatever is bringing you down, get rid of it. Because you'll find that when you're free, your true creativity, your true self comes out.
~ Tina Turner, b. 1939 ~
I, Tina, 1986

As far as keeping a tight rein, sometimes you just let go.; sometimes your passion can carry you to places where you lose control and then something exciting happens.
~ August Wilson, 1945-2005 ~
Interview by Bonnie Lyons & George Plimpton, *Paris Review*, No. 153, Winter 1999

Critical to our growth and happiness is learning how to live with loss; we simply cannot have everything as we wish it. Parents, children, lovers and friends part, and sometimes it is we who must leave. Our lives are full of separations that shake us up, force us to attend to our emotional selves and to learn new ways of being in the world.
~ Susan L. Taylor, b. 1946 ~
Lessons in Living, 1995

When you don't speak out, the tension is just sort of there, just about to break the surface, held and not quite let go, always just barely there. Later the heartbeat becomes salvation, particularly when you get the chant and anger vented. When the heartbeat comes through that, it becomes almost a resolution.
~ Marlon Riggs, 1957-1994 ~
in Chuck Kleinhans & Julia Lesage, "Listening to the Heartbeat: Interview with Marlon Riggs," *Jump Cut: A Review of Contemporary Media*, No. 36, 1991

You have to measure the contemporary shame and the middle class desire to shake off those shackles ... with the historical and still remnant roots of enslavement for everybody ... The desire to forget is itself replete with some of the pain of a need for cure. You really want to move on, and it'll be easier to go about it when you try to look at the sore, the pain, the chains and imagine it out of existence until you are cured.
~ Fred D'Aguiar, b. 1960 ~
Interview by Joanne Hyppolite, Fall 1997, *Anthurium: A Caribbean Studies Journal*, II.1, Spring 2004

Most things that occur in life are beyond our control. We cannot control how others feel about us. We cannot control our body structure. We cannot control the actions of our family, friends or lovers. Therefore, nothing is more critical to preserving peace of mind than being able to let go ... There is no reason to look outside of ourselves for what we already have inside. Once we understand that, we can let everything else we have been clinging to drift away – strings and all.
~ Roderick Terry, b. 1964 ~
"Hope Chest"

Unlearning the past, throwing off the tyranny of false legacies, is a new way of infusing the world with an assemblage of that which is truly one's own.

To create a new moral self is to create a self that is willing to undo the old self in many respects.
~ Jason D. Hill, b. 1965 ~
Becoming a Cosmopolitan: What It Means to Be a Human Being in the New Millennium, 2000

As we shed our false concepts and ideas about life and our false identities, then there is a feeling of being separate and adrift, because the deeper dimension of our being has not yet emerged or we are not yet conscious of it. So it feels as if we are out in the wilderness, in no-man's-land, and there's a sense of barrenness and emptiness. But in the transformational process, that's good. We're shedding, we're releasing, we're being purified.
~ Michael Beckwith ~
"Visioning," Interview by Kathy Juline, *Science of Mind Magazine*, 1996 December

All spiritual growth, 100 percent of it, is about releasing or eliminating rather than attaining something, because we're already It spiritually. We're in the process of releasing inhibitions, limitation, false concepts, and all the other baggage that prevents our greater yet-to-be self from expressing. So it's always a good sign on the path when we start to hit bottom. Something's being dissolved, transformed, redeemed.
~ Ibid.

Though I spend a great deal of time resisting discomfort, I let out a deep sigh of relief when finally I give in and simply allow it to be what it is. Then I have the energy to take care of it.
~ Merle Kodo Boyd ~
"A Child of the South in Long Black Robes," *Dharma, Color, and Culture*, Hilda Gutiérrez Baldoquín, ed., 2004

The times things have been most difficult in my life are when I don't let go of something when all the signs are that's what I should do.
~ Noluthando Crockett-Ntonga ~

Today I am cancelling mess!
Getting rid of confusion that's been hanging around like cobwebs on my
    ceiling.
I am releasing my soul from tiredness and antiquated, meaningless crap!
Stepping out of traps that have long rusted.
I'm doing like some companies do when they reorganize, forgiving debts,
    writing off losses, and establishing good credit for myself.
There are simply some things that need to be written off.
Some people too!
~ June Gatlin ~
Spirit Speaks to Sisters, 1996

RENEWAL

No one keeps his enthusiasm automatically. Enthusiasm must be nourished with new actions, new aspirations, new efforts, new vision.
~ Khemetic Wisdom ~

Out of the ruins good will come.
~ Zulu Wisdom ~

The only reconstruction worthwhile is a reconstruction of thought.
~ Kelly Miller, 1863-1939 ~
Reconstruction of Thought, 1922

We must remake the world. The task is nothing less than that. To be part of this great uniting force of our age is the crowning experience of our life.
~ Mary McLeod Bethune, 1875-1955 ~

With this renewed self-respect and self-dependence, the life of the Negro community is bound to enter a new dynamic phase, the buoyancy from within compensating for whatever pressure there may be of conditions from without.
~ Alain Locke, 1886-1954 ~
The New Negro, 1925

I don't believe in the generation gap. I believe in regeneration gaps. Each day you regenerate – or else you're not living.
~ Duke Ellington, 1899-1974 ~

Rebirth depends on inner work on one's self. No one can be reborn without changing this self. Any time that an entirely new set of reactions enters into a person's life, a change of consciousness has taken place, a spiritual rebirth has occurred.
~ Neville, 1905-1972 ~
"Fundamentals," *New Thought*, Summer 1953

We need a revolution inside of our own minds.
~ John Henrik Clarke, 1915-1998 ~

For the journey into the new millennium ... nothing short of an expansiveness of thought embracing a new vision of a groping rainbow

world, a new sense of self and new ways of knowing to underpin new ways of living, can guarantee us safe conduct into that millennium.
~ Rex Nettleford, b. 1933 ~
Address, EUA Conference, 2004 June 3-5

Old yam has to rot in order that new yam can grow. Where is the earth? Who is going to do the planting?
~ Ama Ata Aidoo, b. 1942 ~
No Sweetness Here, 1970

A new life will come forth from the womb of darkness.
~ Na'im Akbar, b. 1944 ~

When we fail to nurture ourselves, our joy is depleted and our capacity to serve diminished. Giving from an empty vessel causes stress, anger and resentment, seeds that sow disorder and disease. Attempting to meet the demands of the world without first attending to our own needs is an act of self-betrayal that can cause us to lose respect for our value and worth.
~ Susan L. Taylor, b. 1946 ~
Lessons in Living, 1995

The cultural memory is ceaselessly renewed retroactively by new discoveries. Our past, by continually modifying itself through our discoveries, invites us to new appropriations; these appropriations lead us toward a better grasp of our identity.
~ Okondo Okolo, b. 1947 ~

When we work with love we renew the spirit; that renewal is an act of self-love, it nurtures our growth.
~ bell hooks, b. 1952 ~
All About Love: New Visions, 2000

No matter how terrible we think we are, how bad we believe we have been, how low we think we have fallen, we can clean out our minds and begin again. *The only way out is truth.*
~ Iyanla Vanzant, b. 1953 ~
Acts of Faith: Daily Meditations for People of Color, 1993

Each day offers a new beginning, new promises, and a wellspring of hope. History and past experiences are not negotiable; we cannot change them. But the dawn of day gives us a fresh start to reinvent ourselves and forge new directions.
~ Roderick Terry, b. 1964 ~
Brother's Keeper: Words of Inspiration for African-American Men, 1996

RESPECT

If you are a powerful person, gain respect through knowledge and
gentleness of speech and conduct.
~Khemetic Wisdom ~
Selections from the Husia: Sacred Wisdom of Ancient Egypt, Maulana Karenga, tr., 1984

If you see one greater than you outdoors,
Walk behind him respectfully;
Give a hand to an elder sated with beer,
Respect him as his children would.
~ Amenemope, c. 11th C. BCE ~
The Instruction of Amenemope, Ch. 1, Miriam Lichtheim, tr.

Receiving honor won't make you a noble, and giving honor won't make
you a slave, so it is well to honor one another.
~ Malagasy Wisdom ~
Wit & Wisdom of Africa: Proverbs from Africa & The Caribbean, Patrick Ibekwe, ed., 1998

Respect depends on reciprocity.
~ Nyang Wisdom ~

If we lose our love and self-respect and respect for each other, this is how
we will finally die.
~ Maya Angelou, b. 1928 ~
in *Essence*, 1992 December

Respect commands itself and it can neither be given nor withheld when it
is due.
~ Eldridge Cleaver, 1935-1998 ~
"The White Race and Its Heroes," *Soul on Ice*, 1968

We must gain security in ourselves and therefore have respect and feelings
for all oppressed people.
~ Huey Newton, 1942-1989 ~

Deal with yourself as an individual worthy of respect and make everyone
else deal with you the same way.
~ Nikki Giovanni, b. 1943 ~

RESPONSIBILITY

It is the duty of man to raise up man. One is guilty of all abjection that one does not help to relieve. Only those who spread treachery, fire, and death out of hatred for the prosperity of others are undeserving of pity.
~ José Martí, 1853-1895 ~
Martí Pensamientos, Carlos Ripoll, ed.

Few things help an individual more than to place responsibility upon him, and to let him know that you trust him.
~ Booker T. Washington, 1856-1915 ~
Up From Slavery, 1901

None of us are responsible for our birth. Our responsibility is the use we make of life.
~ Joshua Henry Jones, 1886-1934 ~

We are responsible for the world in which we find ourselves, if only because we are the only sentient force which can change it.
~ James Baldwin, 1924-1987 ~
in *Brother's Keeper: Words of Inspiration for African-American Men*, Roderick Terry, ed., 1996

Wake up. The hour has come to be more responsible. Change this world by starting with yourself. The world is not going to change until you change.
~ Betty Shabazz, 1934-1997 ~

We must exchange the philosophy of excuse – what I am is beyond my control – for the philosophy of responsibility.
~ Barbara Jordan, 1936-1996 ~

We have a responsibility not only to our contemporaries but also to future generations – a responsibility to preserve resources that belong to them as well as to us, and without which none of us can survive.
~ Kofi Annan, b. 1938 ~
Address atTruman Presidential Museum & Library, 2006 December 11

To be *whole* – politically, psychically, spiritually, culturally, intellectually, aesthetically, physically, and economically – is of profound significance. It is significant because there is a correlative to this. There is a responsibility to self and to history that is developed once you are "whole," once you are well, once you acknowledge your powers.
~ Toni Cade Bambara, 1939-1995 ~

I believe in the soul. Furthermore, I believe, it is prompt accountability for one's choices, a willing acceptance of responsibility for one's thoughts, behavior, and actions that makes it powerful.
~ Alice Walker, b. 1944 ~
Afterword to Second Edition, *Grange Copeland*, 1988

Accept responsibility for your life. Know that it is you who will get you where you want to go, no one else.
~ Les Brown, b. 1945 ~

The day you take complete responsibility for your life is the day you start to the top.
~ O. J. Simpson, b.1947 ~

We create our own destiny by the way we do things. We have to take advantage of opportunities and be responsible for our choices.
~ Benjamin Carson, b. 1951 ~
in Anthony Robbins & Joseph McLendon III, *Unlimited Power: A Black Choice*, 1997

You are responsible for your life. You can't keep blaming somebody else for your dysfunction … Life is really about moving on.
~ Oprah Winfrey, b. 1954 ~

There are imperatives in one's life ... There are some things you've got to do. You don't know all the answers. You don't know all the consequences – but you've got to do something because you know it's right. There is no alternative. You cannot sit in silence. You cannot maintain neutrality. You know it's right and you've got to move.
~ Marlon Riggs, 1957-1994 ~
in Ron Simmons, "Tongues Untied," *Brother to Brother*, Essex Hemphill, ed., 1991

Life offers infinite possibilities. We must each choose our individual path in life. Our major task is to define who we are and who we will become. Do not assume a restricted or provincial place in this world. There is an urgency in our community that obliges us to take charge of our lives.
~ Roderick Terry, b. 1964 ~
Brother's Keeper: Words of Inspiration for African-American Men, 1996

Freedom is an attribute of Soul, but for every freedom of action or thought, each Soul must bear the antecedent responsibility. The theory of "action and responsibility" or "cause and effect" circumvents the perplexity that may arise from whether an action is "good" or "bad" since one gets in return what one has put into the universe regardless.
~ Oliver Mbamara ~
"The Conflict of Retaliation Versus Forgiveness," *Cafe Africana*, 2005 November

RESTRAINT

If a man refrains from provoking strife at home, he will not see its inception. Thus, everyman who wishes to master his house, must first master his emotions.
~Khemetic Wisdom ~
Selections from the Husia: Sacred Wisdom of Ancient Egypt, Maulana Karenga, tr., 1984

Proceed not to speak or act before thou hast weighed thy words, and examined the tendency of every step thou shalt take; so shall disgrace fly far from you, and in thy house shall shame be a stranger; repentance shall not visit you, nor sorrow dwell upon thy cheek.
~ Khemetic Wisdom ~
Temt Tchaas: Egyptian Proverbs, Muata Ashaya Ashby, ed., 1994

Those who have accomplished the greatest results are those who "keep under the body"; are those who never grow excited or lose self-control, but are always calm, self-possessed, patient, and polite.
~ Booker T. Washington, 1856-1915 ~
in Roderick Terry, *One Million Strong: A PhotographicTribute of the Million Man March*, 1996

I possess the courage and the grace
To bear my anger proudly and unbent ...
I must search for wisdom every hour,
Deep in my wrathful bosom sore and raw ...
I must keep my heart inviolate
Against the potent poison of your hate.
~ Claude McKay, 1889-1948 ~
"The White House"

All day long and all night through,
One thing only must I do:
Quench my pride and cool my blood,
Lest I perish in the flood.
~ Countée Cullen, 1903-1946 ~
"Heritage," l. 116–119, *My Soul's High Song: The Collected Writings of Countee Cullen*, Voice of the *Harlem Renaissance*, É Gerald Early, ed., 1991

When you clench your fist, no one can put anything in your hand, nor can you pick anything up.
~ Alex Haley, 1921-1992 ~
in *Songs of Wisdom: Quotations from Famous African Americans*, Jay David, ed., 2000

I was in prison before ... The solitude, the long moments of meditative contemplation, have given me the key to freedom.
~ Malcolm X, 1925-1965 ~

I learned in moments of humiliation to walk away with what was left of my dignity, rather than lose it all in an explosion of rage. I learned to raise my eyes to the high moral ground, and to stake my future on it.
~ Arthur Ashe, 1943-1993 ~
in Roderick Terry, *One Million Strong: A Photographic Tribute of the Million Man March*, 1996

You get angry, you kick down the wall and punch in the window, and it makes you into a big man. But I came to understand that when you react like that, it actually is a sign of weakness, because it means that other people and the environment can control you.
~ Benjamin Carson, b. 1951 ~

To pursue morality in the best sense, means you ain't gonna make as much money as you could've otherwise made, even if you're rich. There are some things you ain't gonna do.
~ Michael Eric Dyson, b. 1958 ~
in Angela Bronner, "'Come Hell or High Water,' 11 Questions for Michael Eric Dyson on Hurricane Katrina and Other Issues of the Day," *AOL Black Voices*, 2006 January 18

It becomes of greater concern when the mind becomes the master ... Soul has to awaken from Its slumber and take control or the mind could go wild like an uncontrollable wildfire. This is why the masters always urge the spiritual student to recognize his identity as Soul.
~ Oliver Mbamara ~
"Will You Keep Your New Year Resolution?" *Cafe Africana*, 2003

RETREAT / WITHDRAWAL

The one peaceful and trustworthy tranquility, the one solid and firm and
constant security, is this, for a man to withdraw from these eddies of a
distracting world, and, anchored on the ground of the harbor of salvation,
to lift his eyes from earth to heaven; and having been admitted to the gift
of God, and being already very near to his God in mind, he may boast, that
whatever in human affairs others esteem lofty and grand, lies altogether
beneath his consciousness.
~ Cyprian, 200-258 ~
Epistle to Donatus

Sometimes you need more courage to retreat than to advance.
~ Haitian Wisdom ~
Wit & Wisdom of Africa: Proverbs from Africa & The Caribbean, Patrick Ibekwe, ed., 1998

Hibernation is a covert preparation for more overt action.
~ Ralph Ellison, 1914-1994 ~

You should always know when you're shifting gears in life. You should
leave your era; it should never leave you.
~ Leontyne Price, b. 1927 ~

Each of us needs to withdraw from the cares which will not withdraw from
us. We need hours of aimless wandering, or spates of time sitting on park
benches, observing the mysterious world of ants and the canopy of
treetops. If we step away for a time, we are not, as many may think and
some will accuse, being irresponsible, but rather we are preparing ourselves
to more ably perform our duties and discharge our obligations.
~ Maya Angelou, b. 1928 ~
Wouldn't Take Nothing for My Journey Now, 1993

For two or three years I was away from all social interaction. There was no
music. There was no television. It was a very introspective and complicated
time because I had to really confront my fears and master every demonic
thought about inferiority, about insecurity or the fear of being black, young
and gifted in this Western culture. It took a considerable amount of
courage, faith and risk to gain the confidence to be myself.
~ Lauryn Hill, b. 1975 ~
in Joan Morgan, "They Call Me Ms. Hill," *Essence,* 2006 January

REVENGE

Why seeketh revenge, O man! With what purpose is it that thou pursuest it? Thinkest thou to pain thine adversary by it? Know that thou thyself feelest its greatest torments ... Be always more ready to forgive, than to return an injury; they who watch for an opportunity for revenge, lieth in waste against themselves, and draweth down mischief on their own head.
~ Khemetic Wisdom ~
Temt Tchaas: Egyptian Proverbs, Muata Ashaya Ashby, ed., 1994

The root of revenge is the weakness of the Soul; the most abject and timorous are the most addicted to it.
~ Ibid.

There is nothing so easy as to revenge an offence; but nothing so honorable as to pardon it.
~ Akhenaton, c. 1385-c. 1355 BCE ~

Think not thou art revenged of thine enemy when thou slayest him; thou puttest him beyond thy reach, thou givest him quiet, and takest from thyself all means of hurting him.
~ Akhenaton ~

A blow is repaid by the like of it, and all that is achieved is a hitting.
~ Khemetic Wisdom ~
Wit & Wisdom of Africa: Proverbs from Africa & The Caribbean, Patrick Ibekwe, ed., 1998

To forget a wrong is the best revenge.
~ Swahili Wisdom ~
Ibid.

Be above revenge; – if any have taken advantage either of your guilt or distress, punish them with forgiveness – and not only so – but, if you can serve them any future time, do it – you have experienced mercy and long-sufferance in your own person – therefore gratefully remember it, and show mercy likewise.
~ Ignatius Sancho, 1729-1780 ~
Letter XIII to Mr S, 1772 October 11 in *The Letters of the Late Ignatius Sancho, an African*, Vol. I, 1782

To take revenge is often to sacrifice oneself.
~ Bakongo Wisdom ~

It's harder to defeat
Than it is to spell,
Revenge is not sweet,
It's bitter as Hell.
~ Duke Ellington, 1899-1974 ~
"Don't Get Down on Your Knees to Pray Until You Have Forgiven Everyone," *Sacred Concert*, 1965

That old law about "an eye for an eye" leaves everybody blind. The time is always right to do the right thing.
~ Martin Luther King, Jr., 1929-1968 ~

Man must evolve for all human conflict a method which rejects revenge, aggression and retaliation. The foundation of such a method is love.
~ King ~

Some people would rather get even instead of get ahead.
~ Les Brown, b. 1945 ~

The man who wakes up today carrying with him the bitterness of yesterday finds himself burdened and preoccupied with the anger, loss, and rancor which influences his day and slows down his progress in life and as an individual. He wastes precious time and energy drained on how to get back at someone. The irony of it all is that even after the act of vengeance is carried out, it rarely ever gives the vengeful person any relief or peace of mind. Actually, the only thing that may come out of it is that the offended person may retaliate in similar terms, and thus, the cycle of negativity continues while consuming the involved persons with hate, anger, revulsion, animosity, acrimony, and more.
~ Oliver Mbamara ~
"The Conflict of Retaliation Versus Forgiveness," *Cafe Africana*, 2005 November

SEEKING

Searching for one's self in the world is the pursuit of an illusion.
~ Khemetic Wisdom ~
Temt Tchaas: Egyptian Proverbs, Muata Ashaya Ashby, ed., 1994

Nothing is so difficult but that it may be found out by seeking.
~ Terence, c. 190-159 BCE ~

Perhaps ... our lot on earth is to seek and to search. Now and again we find just enough to enable us to carry on. I now doubt that any of us will completely find and be found in this life.
~ Jean Toomer, 1894-1967 ~
in *Words to Make My Children Live*, Deirdre Mullane, ed., 1995

The idyllic condition cannot be arrived at and held on to eternally. It is in the search itself that one finds ecstasy.
~ Maya Angelou, b. 1928 ~
Wouldn't Take Nothing for My Journey Now, 1993

I sometimes realize that there is something on the earth that is free of everything but what created it, and that is the one thing I have been trying to find.
~ Ornette Coleman, b. 1930 ~

All beings search and long for lasting happiness, peace, truth and understanding. Our life can be the expression and celebration of that discovery. But without real understanding of who we truly are, we take ourselves to be mere body-mind entities, unaware of our deeper nature as Pure Consciousness. This limited view leaves us enmeshed in a world of confusion, fear and conflict – a most unhappy state.
~ Mooji, b. 1954 ~

The longer you look for something "special" that is beyond yourself and the tools that you already have available to you, the less likely you'll be to find what is there.
~ Angel Kyodo Williams ~
Being Black: Zen and the Art of Living with Fearlessness and Grace, 2000

SELF

The personhood of man, therefore, is an inter-involvement of rich inter-communication or dialogue. Man, though he feels lonely, is always in encounter with himself. The more he presses this dialogue of the self, the deeper he goes into the self itself. Sooner or later he encounters the Totally Other within the self. This is a radical departure from the sharp cleavage between the subjective and the objective world which one finds in classical idealism. There is an inner reality which is as surely objective as any outer reality.
~ Augustine of Hippo, 354-430 ~
in Wayne E. Oates, *Religious Dimensions of Personality*, 1957

In doing good one does it to oneself; in doing evil one does it to oneself.
~ Tamashek Wisdom ~
Wit & Wisdom of Africa: Proverbs from Africa & The Caribbean, Patrick Ibekwe, ed., 1998

Men can starve from a lack of self-realization as much as they can from a lack of bread.
~ Richard Wright, 1908-1960 ~
Native Son, 1940

The consciousness of self is not the closing of a door to communication. Philosophic thought teaches us, on the contrary, that it is its guarantee.
~ Frantz Fanon, 1925-1961 ~
Speech to Congress of Black African Writers, *Wretched of the Earth*, Constance Farrington, tr., 1959

You can never leave home. You take it with you wherever you go.
~ Maya Angelou, b. 1928 ~

The time will come
when, with elation,
you will greet yourself arriving
at your own door, in your own mirror,
and each will smile at the other's welcome.
~ Derek Walcott, b. 1930 ~
"Love after Love," *Collected Poems 1948-1984*, 1986

Ego has always been a paradox – it is the point from which you see, but it also makes you blind.
~ Bill Russell, b. 1934 ~

Despite the myriad influences via the colonial conditioning of yesteryear and cultural penetration in these electronic times, the human being is able to retain a capacity for self-reflection and self-realization. That sense of self must be manifested in our capacity to distinguish through our actions what in us is autonomous from what is determined.
~ Rex Nettleford, b. 1933 ~
Address, EUA Conference, 2004 June 3-5

As we are social beings, the self is also the society which makes us. So, at the time, you only think of yourself, but you also think of a part of the self which is formed, which responds.
~ Maryse Condé, b. 1937 ~
"One Day, People Are Going to Manage Simply to Say : I Am What I am," Interview by Catherine Dana, *Africultures*, 2002 October 21

Revolution begins with the self, in the self. The individual, the basic revolutionary unit, must be purged of poison and lies that assault the ego and threaten the heart.
~ Toni Cade Bambara, 1939-1995 ~

This thing we call "self" is, depending on the spiritual angle from which it is viewed, everything. And nothing.
~ Charles Johnson, b. 1948 ~
"Reading the Eightfold Path," *Dharma, Color, and Culture*, Hilda Gutiérrez Baldoquín, ed., 2004

The self that we find ourselves in possession of at any moment need not be the self that we are saddled with for life. The attributes that form the primary substance of the moral self – the values and beliefs that determine the kinds of commitments and worldview held – may be, and in a great many cases ought to be, radically changed.
~ Jason D. Hill, b. 1965 ~
Becoming a Cosmopolitan: What It Means to Be a Human Being in the New Millennium, 2000

You have to honor your own intrinsic value and protect yourself, as well. Practicing good for yourself is both allowed and encouraged. Your own healthfulness and well-being is critical in your effort to master life. Taking care of yourself is a wonderful place to begin the practicing of good. You have to tend to all aspects of your well-being – physical, mental, psychic, emotional, and of course, spiritual. There is no point in going out into the world broken and unbalanced. Everything begins at home. This is not selfishness, it's common sense.
~ Angel Kyodo Williams ~
Being Black: Zen and the Art of Living with Fearlessness and Grace, 2000

SELF-RELIANCE

If you travel on a road made by your own hands each day, you will arrive at the place where you would want to be.
~ Khemetic Wisdom ~
Temt Tchaas: Egyptian Proverbs, Muata Ashaya Ashby, ed., 1994

The gods help those who help themselves.
~ Aesop, fl. c. 550 BCE ~
"Hercules and the Wagoner"

Train one for yourself; other people's dogs will not bark for you.
~ Ovambo Wisdom ~
Wit & Wisdom of Africa: Proverbs from Africa & The Caribbean, Patrick Ibekwe, ed., 1998

We dared to be free, let us dare to be so by ourselves and for ourselves, let us emulate the growing child: his own weight breaks the edge that has become useless and hampers its walk.
~ Jean-Jacques Dessalines, 1758-1806 ~
Haiti Independence Proclamation, 1804 January 1, Noe Dorestant, tr.

Hope not between crumbling walls
Of mankind's gratitude to find repose,
But rather,
Build within thy own soul
Fortresses!
~ Georgia Douglas Johnson, 1886-1967 ~
Lesson, 1924

Lift up yourselves ... take yourselves out of the mire and hitch your hopes to the stars.
~ Marcus Garvey, 1887-1940 ~
Philosophy and Opinions of Marcus Garvey, Vol. I, Amy Jacques Garvey, ed., 1923

According to the commonest principles of human action, no man will do as much for you as you will do for yourself.
~ Garvey ~

Let us not waste time in breathless appeals to the strong while we are weak, but lend our time, energy, and effort to the accumulation of strength among ourselves by which we will voluntarily attract the attention of others.
~ Garvey ~
in Roderick Terry, *One Million Strong: A PhotographicTribute of the Million Man March*, 1996

Unless man becomes independent in his knowledge and capacity, what help he gets from others is little, but if he is self-dependent, he may be able to extend help to others.
~ Haile Selassie, 1892-1975 ~

Even Jesus when he got hung upon the cross ... was calling for help. Now if he couldn't help himself how is he going to help you? ... Our position is not to ask dead people to come back and help us; our position is to find ways and means to help ourselves.
~ Yosef ben-Jochannan, b. 1918 ~

Gifts which increase, or act as a catalyst, to our own efforts are valuable. Gifts which could have the effect of weakening or distorting our own efforts should not be accepted until we have asked ourselves a number of questions.
~ Julius Nyerere, 1922-1999 ~
The Arusha Declaration, 1967, Ayanda Madyibi, tr.

One must learn to care for oneself first, so that one can then dare to care for someone else. That's what it takes to make the caged bird sing.
~ Maya Angelou, b. 1928 ~

If you expect somebody else to guide you, you'll be lost.
~ James Earl Jones, b. 1931 ~
in *Brother's Keeper: Words of Inspiration for African-American Men*, Roderick Terry, ed., 1996

At some point you can't continue to ask for help; you have to act. Then, whether or not there's a God behind you, there's a kind of freedom. You establish that you are not an automaton, that somebody else isn't pulling the strings.
~ John Edgar Wideman, b. 1941 ~
Interview by Laura Miller, *Salon*

SENSIBILITY / SENSUALITY

The place is in accord with the season, and the pleasant aspect of the gardens harmonizes with the gentle breezes of a mild autumn in soothing and cheering the senses. In such a place as this it is delightful to pass the day in discourse ... And that no profane intruder may interrupt our converse, nor any unrestrained clatter of a noisy household disturb it, let us seek this bower. The neighbouring thickets ensure us solitude, and the vagrant trailings of the vine branches creeping in pendent mazes among the reeds that support them have made for us a porch of vines and a leafy shelter. Pleasantly here we clothe our thoughts in words; and while we gratify our eyes with the agreeable outlook upon trees and vines, the mind is at once instructed by what we hear, and nourished by what we see.
~ Cyprian, 200-258 ~
Epistle to Donatus

The heart's eye sees many things.
~ Swahili Wisdom ~
Wit & Wisdom of Africa: Proverbs from Africa & The Caribbean, Patrick Ibekwe, ed., 1998

There is a wisdom in the body that is older and more reliable than clocks and calendars.
~ John Harold Johnson, 1918-2005 ~
Succeeding Against Odds, 1989

To be sensual, I think, is to respect and rejoice in the force of life, of life itself, and to be *present* in all that one does, from the effort of loving to the breaking of bread.
~ James Baldwin, 1924-1987 ~
The Fire Next Time, 1962

Here – in this here place, we flesh; flesh that weeps, laughs; flesh that dances on bare feet in grass. Love it. Love it hard ... *You* got to love it, *you*.
~ Toni Morrison, b. 1931 ~
Beloved, 1987

The erotic is not a question only of what we do; it is a question of how acutely and fully we can feel in the doing.
~ Audre Lorde, 1934-1992 ~

If you don't take care of your body, where will you live?
~ Unknown ~

I am a person who for all my life has been very aware of my body. I have
always used it as a gauge of things, as a measure for things ... you had to be
willing, with your body – with the reality and truth of your body – to back
up what you were saying ... basketball and other contact sports are all
about testing, pushing, within arbitrary frameworks.
~ John Edgar Wideman, b. 1941 ~
in Lisa Baker, "Storytelling and Democracy," *African American Review*, 2000 Summer

A loud voice is not always angry; a soft voice not always to be dismissed;
and a well-placed silence can be the indisputable last word ... there are
reliable ways to "listen" to someone without using your ears. Watching the
twitch of a mouth belie ... Feeling the quiver through a tensed arm ...
Smelling the mellow scent of love ... and tasting such love.
~ Gloria Naylor, b. 1950 ~
"Finding Our Voice: 11 Black Women Writers Speak," *Essence*, 1995 May

The storyteller's speech is the sound from his throat, but it's also his sweat,
the rolling of his eyes, his belly, the gestures he draws with his hands, his
smell, that of his listeners, the sound of the ka-drum and all the silences.
Plus, you have to add the night, the rain if it rains, and the world's silent
vibrations.
~ Patrick Chamoiseau, b. 1953 ~
Solibo Magnificent, Rose-Myriam Réjouis & Val Vinokurov, trs., 1998

Communing with nature is a critical link to living a vital, full and creative
life. All one has to do is see the beauty of a rainbow, smell the fragrance of
a rose, feel the warmth of the sun, listen to the howl of the wind or taste
the sweetness of honeysuckle to know that nature is a source of abundance
... we discover the presence of a power greater than ourselves. The forces of
nature are omnipresent – they exist wherever we are ... A brilliant sunset
or a whiff of lavender in the air can be a transforming experience ... as
simple as peeling an orange, tossing a pebble into a lake and watching the
ripples appear in the water, or enjoying a fresh breeze. By communing with
nature, we develop a better sense of ourselves and join forces with the flow
of the universe. The restorative and healing powers of nature provide the
sustenance we need to understand that our lives are an integral part of the
greater whole.
~ Roderick Terry, b. 1964 ~
"Hope Chest"

SEX / SEXUALITY

Youth who are not corrupted by base desires are not blamed, and those who control their sexual appetite, their name does not send forth an unpleasant odor.
~Khemetic Wisdom ~
Selections from the Husia: Sacred Wisdom of Ancient Egypt, Maulana Karenga, tr., 1984

It seems less degrading to give one's self, than to submit to compulsion. There is something akin to freedom in having a lover who has no control over you, except that which he gains by kindness and attachment.
~ Harriet Jacobs, 1813-1897 ~
Incidents in the Life of A Slave Girl, 1861

A kiss that is never tasted, is forever and ever wasted.
~ Billie Holiday, 1915-1959 ~

It's ill-becoming for an old broad to sing about how bad she wants it. But occasionally we do.
~ Lena Horne, b. 1917 ~

The face of a lover is an unknown, precisely because it is invested with so much of oneself. It is a mystery, containing, like all mysteries, the possibility of torment.
~ James Baldwin, 1924-1987 ~

The safest sex is on the shore of abstinence. The next is with one faithful partner. If you insist on wading out into the turbulent waters of multiple sex partners – wear a life jacket.
~ Joseph Lowery, b. 1924 ~
in *Jet*, 1989 March

The most exciting men in my life have been the men who have never taken me to bed. One can lose a great friend by going to bed with them.
~ Eartha Kitt, b. 1927 ~
in *Songs of Wisdom: Quotations from Famous African Americans*, Jay David, ed., 2000

I can't see anything wrong with sex between consenting anybodies.
~ Marvin Gaye, 1939-1984 ~

Responsibility is one of those ten-dollar words tossed around us as lightly as love and free sex. Think about that – free sex! Nothing is free these days, and certainly not sex.
~ Nikki Giovanni, b. 1943 ~

Sex is the "secret" that two people hide between them or the voyeur keeps concealed, and the things that you hide are the things that define you.
~ Nuruddin Farah, b. 1945 ~

Who I am is about discovering, accepting and appreciating all of me, my spirituality as well as my sexuality. The two go hand-in-hand. As my spirituality deepens and broadens, so does my sexuality.
~ Anthony Farmer, b. 1960 ~
"Shamanism: My Path to Self-Discovery," in *Spirited: Affirming the Soul and Black Gay/Lesbian Identity*, G. Winston James & Lisa C. Moore, eds., 2006

If you're an artist, there's no reason not to make art out of anything. Sex is a big part of the human experience. It's something that we're hardwired to think about. Why would you avoid making art about something that is so all-encompassingly important to human beings?
~ Nalo Hopkinson, b. 1960 ~
Interview by Kellie Magnus, *Caribbean Review of Books*, Issue 73

I want kids to understand that safe sex is the way to go. Sometimes we think that only gay people can get HIV, or that it's not going to happen to me. Here I am. And I'm saying it can happen to anybody, even Magic Johnson.
~ Magic Johnson, b. 1960 ~

The power and energy that comes from sexuality carries a price tag. It's called responsibility … When it comes to sex, each of us bears responsibility for the consequences of our individual actions and behavior.
~ Keith Boykin, b. 1965 ~
Respecting the Soul: Daily Reflections for Black Lesbians and Gays, 1999

SHADOW

Turn your face to the sun and the shadows fall behind you.
~ Maori Wisdom ~

When the moon is not full, the stars are bright.
~ Hausa Wisdom ~

The price one pays for pursuing any profession or calling, is an intimate knowledge of its ugly side.
~ James Baldwin, 1924-1987 ~
Nobody Knows My Name: More Notes of a Native Son, 1961

Everything we see is a shadow cast by that which we do not see.
~ Martin Luther King, Jr., 1929-1968 ~

The indigenous mind ... gives ample space to the invisible because the invisible holds the key to the wisdom of the universe. Eventually such awareness becomes an honoring of the shadowy and hidden parts of ourselves, those parts of ourselves that are invisible.
~ Malidoma Somé, b. 1956 ~
The Healing Wisdom of Africa, 1999

That sense of barrenness or darkness just means undeveloped capacity, something that has not yet been developed but is in the process of developing so a deeper dimension of our being can emerge. As we do our spiritual work, we go through these periods of darkness, of barrenness, of wilderness, which is all part of refining and eliminating the false concepts and false identities.
~ Michael Beckwith ~
"Visioning," Interview by Kathy Juline, *Science of Mind Magazine*, 1996 December

We all have to examine the shadow we all carry as part of this society before we can heal our unintended racism. Each of us has to skillfully do our individual work in this area so that we can work on the collective. Otherwise we'll just keep on causing suffering for ourselves and others.
~ Ralph M. Steele ~
"A Teaching on the Second Noble Truth," *Dharma, Color, and Culture*, Hilda Gutiérrez Baldoquín, ed., 2004

SILENCE / STILLNESS

I wonder whether words out of a mouth
are less than silence, or if silences
tell more than declarations make obscure.
~ Martin Carter, 1927-1997 ~
"All to Endure," *Poems of Succession*, 1997

To return to your original state of being,
You must become a master of stillness.
Activity for health's sake,
Never carried to the point of strain,
Must alternate with perfect stillness.
Sitting motionless as a rock,
Turn next to stillness of mind.
Close the gates of the senses.
Fix your mind upon one object or,
Even better, enter a state
Of objectless awareness.
Turn the mind in upon itself
And contemplate the inner radiance.
~ Unknown ~

What are the words you do not yet have? What do you need to say? What
are the tyrannies you swallow day by day and attempt to make your own,
until you will sicken and die of them, still in silence?
~ Audre Lorde, 1934-1992 ~
"The Transformation of Silence into Language and Action," *Sister Outsider: Essays and Speeches*, 1984

Learning how to be still, to really be still and let life happen – that stillness
becomes a radiance.
~ Morgan Freeman, b. 1937 ~

Silence, *fiaga*, is the principal condition of the inner life. Fiaga is the
mother of the word, or *diomon* ... To keep silent is to cultivate one's inner
dimension.
~ Yaya Diallo, b. 1946 ~
in Yaya Diallo & Mitchell Hall, *The Healing Drum: African Wisdom Teachings*, 1989

We need quiet time to examine our lives openly and honestly ... spending quiet time alone gives your mind an opportunity to renew itself and create order.
~ Susan L. Taylor, b. 1946 ~

Silence is speech ... because from the word you build the village, but from silence you construct the world.
~ Patrick Chamoiseau, b. 1953 ~
Solibo Magnificent, Rose-Myriam Réjouis & Val Vinokurov, trs., 1998

There is a power in silence that energizes the mind, body and soul ...
There is wisdom in silence ... There is love in silence ... Silence is an art, a tool of the wise. When we perfect the art of silence, chances are we will get a whole lot more done.
~ Iyanla Vanzant, b. 1953 ~
Acts of Faith: Daily Meditations for People of Color, 1993

The power of quiet is great. It generates the same feelings in everything one encounters. It vibrates with the cosmic feeling of oneness. It is everywhere, available to anyone at any time. It is us, the force within that makes us stable, trusting, and loving. It is contemplation contemplating. Peace is letting go – returning to the silence that cannot enter the realm of words because it is too pure to be contained in words.
~ Malidoma Somé, b. 1956 ~
Of Water and the Spirit, 1994

When delusion raises confusion in my mind, pitting my African American identity against my universal identity, creating the illusion that they are different, it is the practice of zazen[3] that brings me back to reality. Its stillness can appear passive. It can appear to be the opposite of the action I was raised to see as the solution to injustice and suffering, but gradually I have come to see zazen as one of the most radical actions I can take ... Sitting still, it is impossible to escape the busyness, the amorality of one's own mind. What gradually becomes clear is the way the mind works, bouncing from one thought to another, evoking first one emotion then another. Still and silent, accepting all thoughts, emotions, and sensations no matter how painful or disturbing, zazen is the experience of taking a long unblinking look at oneself.
~ Merle Kodo Boyd ~
"A Child of the South in Long Black Robes," *Dharma, Color, and Culture*, Hilda Gutiérrez Baldoquín, ed., 2004

---

[3] Zen sitting meditation

SIMPLICITY

Complexity is the decadence of society; simplicity is the path of reality and salvation.
~ Khemetic Wisdom ~
Temt Tchaas: Egyptian Proverbs, Muata Ashaya Ashby, ed., 1994

Making the simple complicated is commonplace; making the complicated simple, awesomely simple, that's creativity.
~ Charles Mingus, Jr., 1922-1979 ~

Great leaders are almost always great simplifiers, who can cut through argument, debate and doubt, to offer a solution everybody can understand.
~ Colin Powell, b. 1937 ~

Expect nothing. Live frugally on surprise.
~ Alice Walker, b. 1944 ~

Keep it simple. Life is not that complicated.
~ Denzel Washington, b. 1954 ~

Life does not have to be complicated. If the daily rituals of living have become an uphill climb, take measures to simplify your life. Simplicity is an essential path all of us must take to restore order and balance in our lives. Too much clutter clouds our thought process and distracts us from our real purpose. Simplicity, on the other hand, provides us the clarity, serenity and mental strength we need to meet everyday challenges ... It requires sacrifice, courage and a commitment to let go of our mental and physical attachments, some of which we have spent a lifetime developing.
~ Roderick Terry, b. 1964 ~
"Hope Chest"

Just try to find simple pleasures and get ready to get on up out of here.
~ Queen Latifah, b. 1970 ~
Interview by Ellen Leventry, "It Was Just a Gang for God," Belief.net

The less I have, the freer I am to do whatever I want to do.
~ Lauryn Hill, b. 1975 ~

SINCERITY / AUTHENTICITY

Men who are in earnest are not afraid of the consequences.
~ Marcus Garvey, 1887-1940 ~
Philosophy and Opinions of Marcus Garvey, Vol. I, Amy Jacques Garvey, ed., 1923

Be, in reality, all that you appear to be. Don't give yourself the impression of being anything but yourself. That is precisely what you have got to deal with, live with, and manage for better or worse, the rest of your life.
~ T. M. Alexander, Sr., 1919-2001 ~
in Roderick Terry, *One Million Strong: A PhotographicTribute of the Million Man March*, 1996

Love takes off masks that we fear we cannot live without and know we cannot live within.
~ James Baldwin, 1924-1987 ~

I do not believe that a beautiful relationship has to always end in carnage. I do not believe that we have to be fraudulent and pretentious, because that is the source of future difficulties and ultimate failure. If we project fraudulent, pretentious images, or if we fantasize each other into distorted caricatures of what we really are, then, when we awake from the trance and see beyond the sham and front, all will dissolve, all will die and transform into bitterness and hate.
~ Eldridge Cleaver, 1935-1998 ~
Soul on Ice, 1968

If we're not willing to be personally open and honest about who we are, we can't expect people who deal with us to respect us.
~ Keith Boykin, b. 1965 ~
in *St. Petersburg Times*, 1998 September 16

The only way to be truly honest is to stay completely in the moment that we are already in. And then the next, and the next. Every single being's truth and the truth of every given situation are all happening at the same time, moment to moment to moment, radiating out into every direction, dynamically creating new truths as they go.
~ Angel Kyodo Williams ~
Being Black: Zen and the Art of Living with Fearlessness and Grace, 2000

SKILL / TALENT / RESOURCE

Do not be arrogant because of your knowledge, but confer with the ignorant man as with the learned, for the limit of skill has not been attained, and there is no craftsman who has fully acquired his mastery.
~ Ptahotep, c. 2350 BCE ~
in *Kemet and the African Worldview*, Maulana Karenga and Jacob Carruthers, eds., 1986

The sound of the drum depends on the drummer.
~ Shona Wisdom ~
Wit & Wisdom of Africa: Proverbs from Africa & The Caribbean, Patrick Ibekwe, ed., 1998

One who is naturally gifted in anything becomes expert in it.
~ Hausa Wisdom ~
Ibid.

Talent is a gift that brings with it an obligation to serve the world, and not ourselves, for it is not of our making. To use for our exclusive benefit what is not ours is theft. Culture, which makes talent shine, is not completely ours either, nor can we place it solely at our disposal. Rather, it belongs mainly to our country, which gave it to us, and to humanity, from which we receive it as a birthright.
~ José Martí, 1853-1895 ~
Martí Pensamientos, Carlos Ripoll, ed.

All classes of a people under social pressure are permeated with a common experience; they are emotionally welded as others cannot be. With them, even ordinary living has epic depth and lyric intensity, and this, their material handicap, is their spiritual advantage.
~ Alain Locke, 1886-1954 ~
"Youth Speaks," *Survey Graphic* Harlem Number, 1925 March

We start with gifts. Merit comes from what we make of them.
~ Jean Toomer, 1894-1967 ~
Essentials: Definitions and Aphorisms, VI, 1931

Every one has a gift for something, even if it is the gift of being a good friend.
~ Marian Anderson, 1902-1993 ~

Beyond talent lie all the usual words: discipline, love, luck – but, most of all, endurance.
~ James Baldwin, 1924-1987 ~

Tremendous amounts of talent are being lost to our society just because that talent wears a skirt.
~ Shirley Chisholm, 1924-2005 ~
in *Songs of Wisdom: Quotations from Famous African Americans*, Jay David, ed., 2000

Quite often people do not know what they have. It's only when they try to examine themselves in a particular situation that they discover that they have this resource.
~ George Lamming, b. 1927 ~
Interview, 1989

Once you understand what your work is and you do not try to avert your eyes from it, but invest energy in getting that work done, the universe will send you what you need. You simply have to know how to be still and receive it.
~ Toni Cade Bambara, 1939-1995 ~

Life is a journey, often difficult and sometimes incredibly cruel, but we are well equipped for it if only we tap into our talents and gifts and allow them to blossom.
~ Les Brown, b. 1945 ~

Black minds and talent have skills to control a spacecraft or scalpel with the same finesse and dexterity with which they control a basketball.
~ Ronald McNair, 1950-1986 ~
in *Songs of Wisdom: Quotations from Famous African Americans*, Jay David, ed., 2000

If we recognize our talents and use them appropriately, and choose a field that uses those talents, we will rise to the top of our field.
~ Benjamin Carson, b. 1951 ~

Remember, your purpose is to act on the resources God gives you. If God gives you a bucket of fish, you have to distribute those fish. If you don't, they're going to rot, attract a bunch of flies and start stinking up your soul.
~ Russell Simmons, b. 1957 ~
Do You!: 12 Laws to Access the Power in You to Achieve Happiness and Success, 2007

SOLITUDE

It is better to be alone than to have bad company.
~ Oromo Wisdom ~
Wit & Wisdom of Africa: Proverbs from Africa & The Caribbean, Patrick Ibekwe, ed., 1998

He who lives alone has no quarrel.
~ Kikuyu Wisdom ~
Ibid.

I was in prison before entering here ... The solitude, the long moments of meditative contemplation, have given me the key to my freedom.
~ Malcolm X, 1925-1965 ~

There comes a point when you really have to spend time with yourself to know who you are.
~ Bernice Johnson Reagon, b. 1942 ~

We cannot avoid being alone, so we'd better learn to love our own company. We learn our greatest life lessons alone. We discover the truth of who we are alone.
~ Susan L. Taylor, b. 1946 ~
Lessons in Living, 1995

Taking time to experience ourselves in solitude is one way that we can regain a sense of the divine that can feel the spirit moving in our lives. Solitude is essential to the spiritual for it is there that we cannot only communicate with divine spirits but also listen to our inner voice. One way to transform the lonely feeling that overwhelms some of us is to enter that lonely place and find there a stillness that enables us to hear the soul speak.
~ bell hooks, b. 1952 ~
Sisters of the Yam: Black Women and Self-Recovery, 1993

Sitting in a sacred place means you must sit alone.
~ Marilyn "Omi Funke" Torres ~

SOLUTION

Every door has its own key.
~ Swahili Wisdom ~
Wit & Wisdom of Africa: Proverbs from Africa & The Caribbean, Patrick Ibekwe, ed., 1998

Loving your enemy is manifest in putting your arms not around the man but around the social situation, to take power from those who misuse it – at which point they can become human too.
~ Bayard Rustin, 1912-1987 ~
in Sally Belfrage, Freedom Summer, 1965

Darkness cannot drive out darkness; only light can do that. Hate cannot drive out hate; only love can do that.
~ Martin Luther King, Jr., 1929-1968 ~

I'm still in a state of uncertainty, but I'm not worried anymore. I'm not looking for the answers, because I believe now that we will never know. I believe now that what we have to do is make our passage through life as meaningful and as useful as possible.
~ Chinua Achebe, b. 1930 ~
Interview by Bradford Morrow, 1991

If you're not part of the solution, you're part of the problem.
~ Eldridge Cleaver, 1935-1998 ~

The answer to a better world is lots of local groups putting out lots of local energy into solving the immediate local problems by which oppression manifests itself ... Only then will the solutions link up, support, and stabilize larger patterns of liberation.
~ Samuel R. Delany, b. 1942 ~
"The Possibility of Possibilities," interview by Joseph Beam, In the Life, 1986

Let's stop looking outside ourselves for answers to our problems. We are the solution.
~ Susan L. Taylor, b. 1946 ~
in Essence, 1990 April

There's no single answer that will solve all of our future problems. There's no magic bullet. Instead there are thousands of answers – at least. You can be one of them if you choose to be.
~ Octavia Butler, 1947-2006 ~
"A Few Rules for Predicting The Future"

Nature and spirituality and all the things that allow us to be biological and organic I think happens to be the cure for a lot of what's troubling this country. It may be the cure for what's troubling the planet.
~ Bill Strickland, b. 1947 ~
Sierra Club "Spirit in Nature" Address, 2004

There are times in our lives when we feel there is no way up or out ... It is exactly in these times that you must turn to the infinite power within yourself. You must know that the answer is exactly where you are. The strength you need, the answer you want, the solution that will turn the situation around is you.
~ Iyanla Vanzant, b. 1953 ~
Acts of Faith: Daily Meditations for People of Color, 1993

Whites are as befuddled about race as we are, and they're as scared of us as we are of them. Many of them are seeking solutions, just like us.
~ Nathan McCall, b. 1955 ~
Makes Me Wanna Holler: A Young Black Man in America, 1994

We must learn from each other, listen to each other, correct each other and struggle with each other if the destiny of our people is to be secure. And we must fight for the best that is within our reach, even if that means disagreeing with icons and resisting the myopia of mighty men.
~ Michael Eric Dyson, b. 1958 ~
Is Bill Cosby Right?, 2005

When we are confronted with problems and hardship in life, we have a tendency to look to outside sources for guidance. However, we should recognize that solutions to day-to-day trials can be found within ourselves. We must seek our own counsel rather than always seeking the advice of others.
~ Roderick Terry, b. 1964 ~
Brother's Keeper: Words of Inspiration for African-American Men, 1996

SPIRITUALITY

The spirit is life and the body is for living.
~ Khemetic Wisdom ~
Temt Tchaas: Egyptian Proverbs, Muata Ashaya Ashby, ed., 1994

My inner life is mine, and I shall defend and maintain its integrity against all the powers of hell.
~ James Weldon Johnson, 1871-1938 ~

To spiritually regulate oneself is another form of the higher education that fits man for a nobler place in life.
~ Marcus Garvey, 1887-1940 ~

I believe in hearing the inaudible and touching the intangible and seeing the invisible.
~ Adam Clayton Powell, Jr., 1908-1972 ~

You can't regiment spirit, and it is the spirit that counts.
~ Romare Bearden, 1914-1988 ~

Nothing can dim the light which shines from within.
~ Maya Angelou, b. 1928 ~

If you let the world define you, you are dead, and that is all there is to it. If you let spirit define you, you have a life that even death itself cannot intimidate or extinguish.
~ Peter J. Gomes, b. 1942 ~

The spiritual life is not an alternative to the life you're living. The spiritual life is the only life worth living, and it begins to provide the basis for your thinking and your feeling and your being.
~ Gomes ~
"Words for the Heart," Interview by David Gergen, 1996 December 25

The most sacred place isn't the church, the mosque, or the temple, it's the temple of the body. That's where spirit lives.
~ Susan L. Taylor, b. 1946 ~

It isn't until you come to a spiritual understanding of who you are – not necessarily a religious feeling, but deep down, the spirit within – that you can begin to take control ... there is no life without a spiritual life ... more and more, people are becoming aware of the spiritual dynamics of life. And for me, it's always about, "Why are you really here? What is your purpose really about? All the stuff that's really going on, what does it really mean?" I think we've all just kind of gotten lost in believing that things of the exterior, all the things that we acquire, mean more.
~ Oprah Winfrey, b. 1954 ~
in *Songs of Wisdom: Quotations from Famous African Americans*, Jay David, ed., 2000

A physical body alone cannot have any sort of direction in this life, so it is important to recognize that the body is an extension of the spirit, and the spirit is an extension of the body, and that the two are inseparable, with a communication that goes both ways. This is nothing supernatural, it is just what is ... for many indigenous cultures, the supernatural is part of our everyday lives. To us the material is just the spiritual taking on form. The secular is religion in a lower key, a rest area from the tension of religious and spiritual practice.
~ Malidoma Somé, b. 1956 ~
The Healing Wisdom of Africa, 1999

Spiritual growth requires meditation and nurturing. To tap into your spiritual self, be still. Learn to listen to yourself, and to follow your inner voice.
~ Roderick Terry, b. 1964 ~
Brother's Keeper: Words of Inspiration for African-American Men, 1996

Our most effective vehicles for the journey to spirituality are our relationships with others. The hope of a viable relationship is perhaps one of the most prevalent cultural motivations in a person's life – as is the quest for a spiritual and halcyon life.
~ Alaric Wendell Blair ~
"I Can't Make It Without You: A Conversation on Spirituality and Relationships," in *Spirited: Affirming the Soul and Black Gay/Lesbian Identity*, G. Winston James & Lisa C. Moore, eds., 2006

The thing that brought me to spiritual practice was a concern for me. That's not only okay, it's how it is for everyone, and it should be. It's our personal, individual concern that makes spiritual practice human. No matter who we are, where we come from, or what our cultural conditioning is, it's natural that practical results for our own lives are what we want from any spiritual practice we choose.
~ Angel Kyodo Williams ~
Being Black: Zen and the Art of Living with Fearlessness and Grace, 2000

SPONTANEITY

Accept what is felt before it is spoken, what has not been accumulated with tardy painstaking during the lapse of years, but has been inhaled in one breath of ripening grace.
~ Cyprian, 200-258 ~
Epistle to Donatus

I do find a certain fascination with the unpredictable. The transitory years we wade through are what they are – what we make of them.
~ Gordon Parks, 1912-2006 ~
Voices in the Mirror, 1990

A consciousness about what we're doing might help us see that uniformity, that singularity, that oneness of purpose, may not be the best ... Rather, the image is one of improvisation ... taking what is there at any given moment and creatively finding ways to make it all work. Composing our lives.
~ Johnnetta Cole, b. 1936 ~
"Spelman's First Female President," Academy of Achievement Interview, 1996 June 28

There's so much spontaneity involved, what do you practice? How do you practice teamwork? How do you practice sharing? How do you practice daring? How do you practice being nonjudgmental?
~ Herbie Hancock, b. 1940 ~

My way of working is sort of stream of consciousness ... Every moment is important ... Improvisation is my guiding philosophy. Dancing back and forth between public and private, arts and jobs, right brain and left brain.
~ Bill Strickland, b. 1947 ~
in John Brant, "What One Man Can Do," *Inc Magazine*, 2005 September

It just takes whim, essentially. I think you just follow a moment, a clear moment. It takes clarity instead of courage. With courage it seems you have to drum something up, you have to come to it with painful means. What I mean is that sparkling moment we all have. That real, bright, sparkling moment ... and if you just kind of launch into that ... everything will be all right!
~ Dionne Brand, b. 1953~
Interview by Nuzhat Abbas, *Herizons*, 1999 September 22

STRENGTH

Magic is knowledge and strength; without strength, nothing worthwhile can be achieved; without knowledge, strength is uncontrolled.
~ Khemetic Wisdom ~
Temt Tchaas: Egyptian Proverbs, Muata Ashaya Ashby, ed., 1994

Another heart might bend or break, but a strong heart in the midst of difficulties is an ally to its owner.
~ *Book of Khakheper-Ra-Soneb* ~
in *Kemet and the African Worldview*, Maulana Karenga and Jacob Carruthers, eds., 1986

There are two ways of exerting one's strength: one is pushing down, the other is pulling up.
~ Booker T. Washington, 1856-1915 ~

There is no such force as the force of a man determined to rise. The human soul cannot be permanently chained.
~ W. E. B. Du Bois, 1868-1963 ~

We are strong in spirit, strong in determination; we are unbroken in every direction; we stand firm facing the world, determined to carve out and find a place for the four hundred millions of our suffering people.
~ Marcus Garvey, 1887-1940 ~
"The Negro is Dying Out," *Philosophy and Opinions of Marcus Garvey, Vol. 2*, Amy Jacques Garvey, ed., 1925

There is an indomitable quality within the human spirit that cannot be destroyed; a face deep within the human personality that is impregnable to all assaults. They rest so deeply that prejudice, oppression, lynching, riots, time, or weariness can never corrode or destroy them.
~ Chester Himes, 1909-1984 ~
Beyond the Angry Black, 1966

Go within every day and find the inner strength so that the world will not blow your candle out.
~ Katherine Dunham, 1910-2006 ~
American Visions, 1987 February

If one is continually surviving the worst that life can bring, one eventually ceases to be controlled by a fear of what life can bring; whatever it brings must be borne.
~ James Baldwin, 1924-1987 ~
Native Son, 1940

There's water and there's breath, speech is breath, breath is strength, strength is the body's idea of life, of its life.
~ Patrick Chamoiseau, b. 1953 ~
Solibo Magnificent, Rose-Myriam Réjouis & Val Vinokurov, trs., 1998

I'd learned about the strength of the mind and seen that mental toughness, more than brawn, determines who survives and who buckles.
~ Nathan McCall, b. 1955 ~
Makes Me Wanna Holler: A Young Black Man in America, 1994

Although at times we may be inclined to look beyond ourselves for answers and understanding ... our greatest strengths are embedded within our own heads, hearts and souls.
~ Roderick Terry, b. 1964 ~
"Hope Chest"

And then a hero comes along
With the strength to carry on
And you cast your fears aside
And you know you can survive
So when you feel like hope is gone
Look inside you and be strong
And you'll finally see the truth
That a hero lies in you.
~ Mariah Carey, b. 1969 ~
"Hero," 1993

I was a young woman with an evolved mind who was not afraid of her beauty or her sexuality. For some people that's uncomfortable. They didn't understand how *female* and *strong* work together. Or young and wise. Or *black* and *divine*.
~ Lauryn Hill, b. 1975 ~
in Joan Morgan, "They Call Me Ms. Hill," Essence, 2006 January

STRUGGLE

If there is no struggle, there is no progress. Those who profess to favor freedom, and yet deprecate agitation, are men who want crops without plowing up the ground. They want rain without thunder and lightning. They want the ocean without the awful roar of its many waters. The struggle may be a moral one, or it may be a physical one, or it may be both moral and physical, but it must be a struggle. Power concedes nothing without a demand.
~ Frederick Douglass, 1817-1895 ~
Address on West India Emancipation, 1857 August 4

There must always be the continuing struggle to make the increasing knowledge of the world bear some fruit in increasing understanding and in the production of human happiness.
~ Charles R. Drew, 1904-1950 ~

The battles that count aren't the ones for gold medals. The struggle within yourself – the invisible, inevitable battles inside all of us – that's where it's at.
~ Jesse Owens, 1913-1980 ~
Blackthink, 1970

The struggle continues but at a higher level, a more human place, above the race and color which ... in themselves, are not worth the pain and suffering they have called down on humanity in our time.
~ Peter Abrahams, b. 1919 ~
in Charles R. Larson, "Self-Exile From Wretchedness," World and I, 2002 March 1

Achievement is never completely won. I find it now, fighting the same battles, again and again. I've had to accept the fact: freedom is never won. You are always in the process of winning it. You have to do it again.
~ Lloyd Richards, 1919-2006 ~
"Broadway's Groundbreaking Director," Academy of Achievement Interview, 1991 February 15

Struggle is a never ending process. Freedom is never really won you earn it and win it in every generation.
~ Coretta Scott King, 1927-2006 ~

Equality is not offered,
It must be conquered.
To emancipate the women
Is to rid the society
Of its blemishes, its deformities.
~ Ahmed Sékou Touré, 1922-1984 ~
"Woman of Africa"

Change does not roll in on the wheels of inevitability, but comes through continuous struggle. And so we must straighten our backs and work for our freedom. A man can't ride you unless your back is bent.
~ Martin Luther King, Jr., 1929-1968 ~

Like a kung fu movie, we are leaping and kicking and fighting on all fronts. We cannot sever any of our parts, place them on the back burner. We have to join all fights, all struggles at the same time ... either the whole group swims, or we all drown.
~ Rosemary Brown, 1930-2003 ~
in Michele Landsberg, "Farewell to a Political Kung Fu Fighter," *Toronto Star*, 2003 June 15

Battling racism and battling heterosexism and battling apartheid share the same urgency inside me as battling cancer ... Each victory must be applauded, because it is so easy not to battle at all, to just accept and call that acceptance inevitable.
~ Audre Lorde, 1934-1992 ~
A *Burst of Light*, 1988

The real language of humankind: the language of struggle. It is the universal language underlying all speech and words of our history. Struggle. Struggle makes history. Struggle makes us. In struggle is our history, our language and our being.
~ Ngugi wa Thiong'o, b. 1938 ~
Decolonising the Mind, 1986

Whether I live or die is immaterial. It is enough to know that there are people who commit time, money and energy to fight this one evil among so many others predominating worldwide. If they do not succeed today, they will succeed tomorrow. We must keep on striving to make the world a better place for all of mankind – each one contributing his bit, in his or her own way.
~ Ken Saro-Wiwa, 1941-1995 ~

If you stop struggling, then you stop life.
~ Huey Newton, 1942-1989 ~
in Digby Diehl, *Supertalk*, 1974

SUBMISSION / SURRENDER

The pleasure of those who injure you lies in your pain. Therefore they will suffer if you take away their pleasure by not feeling pain.
~ Tertullian, c. 160-240 ~

Happy is he who can give himself up.
~ Naguib Mahfouz, b. 1911 ~

Believe it or not, you can gain great power when you let go. Your power comes when you let go of your need to have all the answers, when you relinquish your need to control the future, and when you lose your anxiety about the outcome.
~ Keith Boykin, b. 1965 ~
Respecting the Soul: Daily Reflections for Black Lesbians and Gays, 1999

One knows through the deepest part of one's intuitive, nonreflexive being the presence of the authentic and the genuine. The need to hand oneself over to a superior is deep and stems from the moral epicenter of one's soul … This act is greater than passive submission, however. It is a form of radical intersubjectivity. It is freedom granted to oneself to be deeply touched by another, and to allow the spontaneous gestures and responses that blossom from the encounter to shape a new identity.
~ Jason D. Hill, b. 1965 ~
"Moral Hierarchy: The Key to Evolving Consciousness," *What Is Enlightenment? Magazine*, Issue 31

It is the perfection within you that draws the perfection that is in others – to the point where we see what's "right" with another and not what's "wrong." We then begin to celebrate similarities and differences and we lower our defenses to allow love to happen. Only when we reveal our vulnerabilities can we heal.
~ Alaric Wendell Blair ~
"I Can't Make It Without You: A Conversation on Spirituality and Relationships," in *Spirited: Affirming the Soul and Black Gay/Lesbian Identity*, G. Winston James & Lisa C. Moore, eds., 2006

I am like the lost feather that has surrendered its freedom of direction unto the movement and guidance of the wind's current, ready and willing to travel in any direction, trusting in the comfort of the wind's navigation, which may seem uncertain and without direction at the moment yet in the end, justified in its destination.
~ Oliver Mbamara ~

SUCCESS

If the social order judges success by material gain, the most successful will be the most corruptible and selfish.
~ Khemetic Wisdom ~
Temt Tchaas: Egyptian Proverbs, Muata Ashaya Ashby, ed., 1994

Success is to be measured not so much by the position that one has reached in life as by the obstacles which one has overcome while trying to succeed.
~ Booker T. Washington, 1856-1915 ~
Up From Slavery, 1901

Most people search high and low for the key to success. If they only knew, the key to their dreams lies within.
~ George Washington Carver, 1864-1943 ~

There is no royal flower-strewn path to success. And if there is, I have not found it, for if I have accomplished anything in life it is because I have been willing to work hard.
~ Madame C. J. Walker, 1867-1919 ~

There is no secret to success except hard work and getting something indefinable which we call the "breaks."
~ Countée Cullen, 1903-1946 ~
"Rendezvous with Life," Interview by James Baldwin in *The Magpie*, Winter 1942, Vol. 26, No. 1

If you set out to be successful, then you already are.
~ Katherine Dunham, 1910-2006 ~
in *Songs of Wisdom: Quotations from Famous African Americans*, Jay David, ed., 2000

Success can be wracking and reproachful, to you and those close to you. It can entangle you with legends that are consuming and all but impossible to live up to.
~ Gordon Parks, 1912-2006 ~
Voices in the Mirror, 1990

If you can somehow think and dream of success in small steps, every time you make a step, every time you accomplish a small goal, it gives you confidence to go on from there.
~ John Harold Johnson, 1918-2005 ~

The ultimate of being successful is the luxury of giving yourself the time to do what you want to do.
~ Leontyne Price, b. 1927 ~

We are prone to judge success by the index of our salaries or the size of our automobiles, rather than by the quality of our service and relationship to humanity.
~ Martin Luther King, Jr., 1929-1968 ~

I try to choose the ethical route even when defeat rather than success may wait at the end of the road. In fact, just as I know victory based solely on might is no victory, it is also hard for me to imagine truly fulfilling success that isn't the result of ethically founded, sustained endeavor.
~ Derrick Bell, b. 1930 ~
Ethical Ambition: Living A Life of Meaning and Worth, 2002

Success does not come to you. You must go to it ... You must be open-minded and actively involved in creating your successes. Make your own choices rather than allowing others to choose for you.
~ Famous Amos, b. 1937 ~
Watermelon Magic, 1996

There are no secrets to success: Don't waste time looking for them. Success is the result of preparation, hard work, learning from failure, loyalty to those for whom you work, and persistence.
~ Colin Powell, b. 1937 ~

Success is a journey not a destination. The doing is usually more important than the outcome. Not everyone can be Number 1.
~ Arthur Ashe, 1943-1993 ~

The things you want are always possible; it is just that the way to get them is not always apparent. The only real obstacle in your path to a fulfilling life is you, and that can be a considerable obstacle because you carry the baggage of insecurities and past experience.
~ Les Brown, b. 1945 ~

You can get confused when your sense of responsibility to the world isn't necessarily doing what you love. You don't realize that the real success in your life is based upon doing what you love to do.
~ Walter Mosley, b. 1952 ~

I remind young people everywhere I go, one of the worst things the older generation did was to tell them for twenty-five years "Be successful, be

successful, be successful" as opposed to "Be great, be great, be great".
There's a qualititative difference.
~ Cornel West, b. 1954 ~
Democracy Matters Speech, 2004 October 1

We're born with success. It is only others who point out our failures, and
what they attribute to us as failure. I think the idea that you know who
your inner self is on a daily basis ... to keep in touch with that, I think
that's the first ingredient for success.
~ Whoopi Goldberg, b. 1955 ~
"The One-Woman Show," Academy of Achievement Interview, 1994 June 17

If you have achieved any level of success, then pour it into someone else.
Success is not success without a successor.
~ T. D. Jakes, b. 1957 ~

The thing that makes me happiest, that's what I do for a living. And when
you have that, there's nothing you can complain about.
~ Spike Lee, b. 1957 ~

Piling up zeros in your bank account, or cars in your driveway, won't in and
of itself make you successful. Rather, true success is based on a constant
flow of giving and recieving. In fact, if you look up *affluence* in the
dictionary, you'll see its root is a Latin phrase meaning "to flow with
abundance". So in order to be truly affluent, you must always let what you
have recieved flow back into the world.
~ Russell Simmons, b. 1957 ~
Do You!: 12 Laws to Access the Power in You to Achieve Happiness and Success, 2007

Success can also cause misery. The trick is not to be surprised when you
discover it doesn't bring you all the happiness and answers you thought it
would.
~ Prince, b. 1958 ~

Our characterization of success evolves as we do. Regardless of how we
define success, it does not come overnight. Like a child, success requires
nurturing. It is the result of hard work, persistence, determination,
sacrifice, commitment and faith. Although there is no guarantee that our
road to success will be paved in gold, all of us have the inner capacity to
reach our chosen destination ... Success is a state of mind, not just an
outcome.
~ Roderick Terry, b. 1964 ~
"Hope Chest"

SUFFERING

Suffering in search of truth gives true meaning to the truth.
~ Khemetic Wisdom ~
Temt Tchaas: Egyptian Proverbs, Muata Ashaya Ashby, ed., 1994

To suffer, is a necessity entailed upon thy nature, wouldst thou that
miracles should protect thee from its lessons? Or shalt thou repine, because
it happeneth unto thee, when lo! it happeneth unto all? Suffering is the
golden cross upon which the rose of the Soul unfoldeth.
~ Akhenaton, c. 1385-c. 1355 BCE ~

He conquers once who suffers at once; but he who continues always
battling with punishments, and is not overcome with suffering, is daily
crowned.
~ Cyprian, 200-258 ~
Epistle XV to Moyses and Maximus, and the Rest of the Confessors

Suffering doesn't kill, it teaches sense.
~ Mamprussi Wisdom ~
Wit & Wisdom of Africa: Proverbs from Africa & The Caribbean, Patrick Ibekwe, ed., 1998

Life without pain ain't worth living.
~ August Wilson, 1945-2005 ~

People who are always miserable have invested their time in holding on to
their pain.
~ Susan L. Taylor, b. 1946 ~

Suffering, then, arises from the belief in a separate, unchanging "identity"
for things. That is the foundation for attachment and craving. Put another
way, we cling to our static ideas about things, not the fluid things
themselves, which are impermanent and cannot be held onto. (Nothing
can endure change and remain unchanged.) In a universe of moment-by-
moment transformations all predications are risky; they *must* be highly
provisional, tentative.
~ Charles Johnson, b. 1948 ~
"Reading the Eightfold Path," *Dharma, Color, and Culture*, Hilda Gutiérrez Baldoquín, ed., 2004

The man who suffers much knows much.
~ Ewe Wisdom ~

To be capable of love one has to be capable of suffering and of
acknowledging one's suffering. We all suffer, rich and poor. The fact is that
when people have material privilege at the enormous expense of others,
they live in a state of terror as well. It's the unease of having to protect
your gain.
~ bell hooks, b. 1952 ~
in *Tricycle: The Buddhist Review*, 1992 Fall

Always, no matter how dark the day, live on, no matter how sad the
circumstances, laugh on, and most of all, my friend, no matter how
winding the journey, always go on. We will all have pleasure and pain,
sunshine and rain; we will all laugh ourselves to tears one day and cry
ourselves to sleep the next. These are the processes of the soul. I would
rather have either than to be left numb and indifferent. The pleasure or
pain of the soul is an indication that whatever is wrong can be repaired.
~ T. D. Jakes, b. 1957 ~

A person in pain is being spoken to by that part of himself that knows only
how to communicate this way.
~ Malidoma Somé, b. 1956 ~

And one day our suffering
Will turn into the wonders of the earth ...
That is why our music is so sweet.
It makes the air remember.
~ Ben Okri, b. 1959 ~
An African Elegy, 1992

The cause of our suffering is not allowing the impermanence of life and
death, the good and the bad, to flow. When we freeze up at the bad, we'll
never overcome the fear of looking at our shadow. The cause of suffering
is not being aware of the interconnectedness of the internal and external,
not accepting, not being ready for the transitions of life, not being
relentlessly mindful.
~ Ralph M. Steele ~
"A Teaching on the Second Noble Truth," *Dharma, Color, and Culture*, Hilda Gutiérrez Baldoquín, ed.,
2004

SURVIVAL

Go beyond surviving. There is no achievement in surviving. We must prevail.
~ John Henrik Clarke, 1915-1998 ~

If one is continually surviving the worst that life can bring, one eventually ceases to be controlled by a fear of what life can bring; whatever it brings must be borne ... If we had not loved each other none of us would have survived.
~ James Baldwin, 1924-1987 ~
The Fire Next Time, 1962

You just realize that survival is day to day and you start to grasp your own spirit, you start to grasp the depth of the human spirit, and you start to understand your own ability to cope no matter what.
~ Melba Beals, b. 1941 ~
in *Voices of Freedom*, Henry Hampton, ed., 1990

As long as hope remains and meaning is preserved, the possibility of overcoming oppression stays alive.
~ Cornel West, b. 1954 ~
in Roderick Terry, *One Million Strong: A PhotographicTribute of the Million Man March*, 1996

The survival instinct within us is a powerful tool. It enables us to endure unbearable things as long as we escape long enough to express that where we are is not where we are going.
~ T. D. Jakes, b. 1957 ~

With a lone person, there is not just triumph in the survival story, there is triumph in the telling of it. There is a joy at having survived, a sense of disbelief that you survived at all and that you have a new life. But there is also the burden of survival.
~ Edwidge Danticat, b. 1969 ~
in *LA Weekly*

SYNTHESIS

The African, the West Indian, the Negro American ... Proscription and prejudice have thrown these dissimilar elements into a common area of contact and interaction. Within this area, race sympathy and unity have determined a further fusing of sentiment and experience. So what began in terms of segregation becomes more and more, as its elements mix and react, the laboratory of a great race-welding.
~ Alain Locke, 1886-1954 ~
The New Negro, 1925

The African ... conceives the world, beyond the diversity of its forms, as a fundamentally mobile, yet unique, reality that seeks synthesis ... sensitive to the external world, to the material aspect of beings and things ... to the tangible qualities of things – shape, color, smell, weight, etc. ... (he) considers these things merely as signs that have to be interpreted and transcended in order to reach the reality of human beings ... This reality is *being* in the ontological sense of the word, and it is life force. Thus, the whole universe appears as an infinitely small, and at the same time, an infinitely large, network.
~ Léopold Senghor, 1906-2001 ~
Négritude: a Humanism of the Twentieth Century, 1970

The hybridization of which we are the outcome has achievements and positive values to its credit wherein the West and Europe also had their share. There was, as I say, a positive side, the effects of which were only belatedly felt by the non-Europeans but which are undeniable and in which we are simultaneously agents and partners – and, I should add, sometimes the beneficiaries as well.
~ Aimé Césaire, b. 1913 ~
"The Liberating Power of Words," Interview by Annick Thebia Melsan in *UNESCO Courier*, 1997 May

The imagination is integrative. That's how you make the new – by putting something else with what you've got.
~ Ralph Ellison, 1914-1994 ~

In the realm of thought, man may claim to be the brain of the world; but in real life where every action affects spiritual and physical existence, the world is always the brain of mankind; for it is at this level that you will find

the sum total of the powers and units of thought, and the dynamic forces of development and improvement; and it is there that energies are merged and the sum of man's intellectual values is finally added together.
~ Ahmed Sékou Touré, 1922-1984 ~
Speech, 2nd Congress of African Writers

I think that words have a magic, that human situations create a magic, that you can capture that extra dimension by placing ideas side by side.
~ Chinua Achebe, b. 1930 ~
Interview by Bradford Morrow, 1991

I have always wanted to be both man and woman, to incorporate the strongest and richest parts of my mother and father within/into me – to share valleys and mountains upon my body the way the earth does in hills and peaks.
~ Audre Lorde, 1934-1992 ~
Zami: A New Spelling of My Name, 1983

We are the products of many cultures, traditions and memories; that mutual respect allows us to study and learn from other cultures ... we gain strength by combining the foreign with the familiar.
~ Kofi Annan, b. 1938 ~
Nobel Lecture, Oslo, 2001 December 10

We are moving rapidly toward the obsolescence and eventual disappearance of a single traditional model and its replacement by others that are hybrids.
~ Gilberto Gil, b. 1942 ~
"Gilberto Gil Hears the Future, Some Rights Reserved," New York Times, 2007 March 11

The Feminine is Wisdom, and it is also the Soul. Since each and every person is born with an internal as well as an eternal Feminine, just as everyone is born with an internal and eternal Masculine, this is not a problem except for those who insist on forcing humans into gender roles. Which makes it easier for them to be controlled.
~ Alice Walker, b. 1944 ~
"This Was Not an Area of Large Plantations," in Dharma, Color, and Culture, Hilda Gutiérrez Baldoquín, ed., 2004

I accepted nature as it is, in the depths of its gentleness. I went elsewhere and I saw scientific life. I got to know other societies. Then I made a fusion and I saw that I was born where I should have been.
~ Salif Keita, b. 1949 ~
in David Dacks, "The Golden Voice of Mali," Exclaim.ca, 2006 July

TACT / DISCRETION

Speak not too much, for men are deaf to the man of many words; be silent rather, then thou shalt please, therefore speak not. Before all things guard thy speech, for a man's ruin lies in his tongue. The body is a storehouse, full of all manner of answers. Choose therefore the right one and speak well, and let the wrong answer remain imprisoned in the body.
~ Khemetic Wisdom ~
Temt Tchaas: Egyptian Proverbs, Muata Ashaya Ashby, ed., 1994

Keep your tongue from answering your superior,
And take care not to insult him.
Let him not cast his speech to catch you,
Nor give free rein to your answer.
Converse with a man of your own measure,
And take care not to offend him.
~ Amenemope, c. 11th C. BCE ~
The Instruction of Amenemope, Ch. 1, Miriam Lichtheim, tr.

A heart that does not reflect will speak a thoughtless word.
~ Ganda Wisdom ~
Wit & Wisdom of Africa: Proverbs from Africa & The Caribbean, Patrick Ibekwe, ed., 1998

Home affairs are not talked about on the public square.
~ Kenyan Wisdom ~
Ibid.

Rabbit says, "Drink everything, eat everything, but don't tell everything."
~ Martinican Wisdom ~
Ibid.

Every mouth has two lips. The high lip gives to praise, the low lip gives to gossip. When we do not guard what we say or to whom we say it, we can never be sure which lip will repeat the words.
~ Iyanla Vanzant, b. 1953 ~

TEACHING

It is not enough that the teachers of teachers should be trained in technical normal methods; they must also, as far as possible, be broad-minded, cultured men and women.
~ W. E. B. Du Bois, 1868-1963 ~

We have got lots of folks who are colleged, but too few who are educated.
~ Langston Hughes, 1902-1967 ~

Life, indeed, is the true school, and our schools, whether of general education or vocational training, should be auxiliaries of life.
~ Ahmed Sékou Touré, 1922-1984 ~
Education and Nation-Building in Africa, L. G. Cowan, et al., eds., 1965

Contrary, to still commonly held beliefs, the writing of poetry, the composition of a piece of music, the creation of a play, the painting of pictures and so on are all forms of action and not modes of escape from reality. They are valid routes to cognition which the educational system and higher education ignore at their peril.
~ Rex Nettleford, b. 1933 ~
Address, EUA Conference, 2004 June 3-5

It is necessary to teach by living and speaking those truths which we believe and know beyond understanding. Because in this way alone we can survive, by taking part in a process of life that is creative and continuing, that is growth.
~ Audre Lorde, 1934-1992 ~
The Cancer Journals, 1980

A great teacher is one who realizes that he himself is also a student and whose goal is not to dictate the answers, but to stimulate his students' creativity enough so that they go out and find the answers themselves.
~ Herbie Hancock, b. 1940 ~

When you are lucky enough to teach, you are also the one to learn the most. In the process of transmission of knowledge, you are forced to question yourself, to ask yourself questions that would never have come to your mind if you had been alone.
~ Gaston Kaboré, b. 1951 ~
Masterclass with Gaston Kaboré, Cannes Film Festival 2007, Céline Dewaele, tr.

THINKING / THOUGHT

The Universe is mental – held in the Mind of The All.
~ Hermes Trismegistus ~
in *The Kybalion: A Study of the Hermetic Philosophy of Ancient Egypt and Greece*, 1908

His road of thought is what makes every man what he is.
~ Zora Neale Hurston, 1891-1960 ~

Human thought, like God, makes the world in its own image.
~ Adam Clayton Powell, Jr., 1908-1972 ~
Keep the Faith, Baby!, 1967

Rarely do we find men who willingly engage in hard, solid thinking. There is an almost universal quest for easy answers and half-baked solutions. Nothing pains some people more than having to think.
~ Martin Luther King, Jr., 1929-1968 ~

I cannot fathom why people might get into drugs, because for me the real joy of life is to experience thought and to turn thought into action, I mean really creative thought. To see some new, amazing thought being turned into some new, amazing moment on the screen, I mean you can't buy that.
~ Trevor Rhone, b. 1940 ~
Interview by Kinisha O'Neill, *Jamaica Daily Gleaner*, 2003 March 31

Thoughts have power; thoughts are energy. And you can make your world or break it by your own thinking.
~ Susan L. Taylor, b. 1946 ~
in Maya Angelou, *And Still I Rise*, 1978

Thoughts are the seeds of our intentions, so they are the original source of every action we perform. Even if an action doesn't follow the thought right away, the thought will hang around until it can reveal itself in some way. Thoughts find themselves with a voice and become speech. In turn, speech eventually gives fuel to action.
~ Angel Kyodo Williams ~
Being Black: Zen and the Art of Living with Fearlessness and Grace, 2000

TIME

'Tis time, my friend, 'tis time!
For rest the heart is aching;
Days follow days in flight, and every day is taking
Fragments of being, while together you and I
Make plans to live. Look, all is dust, and we shall die.
~ Aleksandr Pushkin, 1799-1837 ~
"'Tis time, my friend," l. 1-5, 1834, C.M. Bowra, tr., 1943

Time is an invisible web on which everything may be embroidered.
~ Joaquim Machado de Assis, 1839-1908 ~
Esau and Jacob, Dain Borges, ed., Elizabeth Lowe, tr., 1965

We kill time; time buries us.
~ Machado de Assis ~
Epitaph for a Small Winner, 1952

The more the men of our time we are
the more our time is. But always
we have been somewhere else.
~ Martin Carter, 1927-1997 ~
"Our Time," *Poems of Affinity*, 1980

We must use time creatively, and forever realize that the time is always
ripe to do right.
~ Martin Luther King, Jr., 1929-1968 ~
Letter from a Birmingham Jail, 1963 January 16

Great Time is the ancestral time. It's non-linear. It is, if anything, like a
river, like the sea – and we kind of swim through it ... it's always been here,
it always will be here. It's like an ocean. So as you pass through it, you are
not going in one direction, you are floating. You are immersed in it. It is
the medium which holds everything and always has. So there is no
beginning, no end.
~ John Edgar Wideman, b. 1941 ~
in Lisa Baker, "Storytelling and Democracy," *African American Review*, 2000 Summer

They call Time an old man. But Time don't age, ain't old. Every day is
new. Don't nothin' age but us and what we make ... Time takes care of
everything ... and it will take care of you.
~ J. California Cooper, b. 1966 ~

TODAY

Day's short as ever, time's long as it's been.
~ Geechee Wisdom ~

Yesterday is history. Tomorrow is a mystery. And today? Today is a gift.
That's why we call it The Present.
~ Babatunde Olatunji, 1927-2003 ~

I live a day at a time. Each day I look for a kernel of excitement. In the
morning I say: "What is my exciting thing for today?" Then, I do the day.
Don't ask me about tomorrow.
~ Barbara Jordan, 1936-1996 ~

It's always today. If you're not living to the fullest today, you never will. If
you're not having fun now because you're waiting for a better time or you
think you need more something or someone, you're never going to have
fun.
~ Famous Amos, b. 1937 ~
Watermelon Magic, 1996

Memories, important yesterdays, were once todays. Treasure and notice
today.
~ Gloria Gaither, b. 1942 ~

You don't own the future; you don't own the past. Today is all you have.
~ Les Brown, b. 1945 ~

We must realize that the attitude with which we greet the day says a great
deal about what the day will be like. We make our days pleasant or
miserable ... the day will give us exactly what we give it.
~ Iyanla Vanzant, b. 1953 ~
Acts of Faith: Daily Meditations for People of Color, 1993

We are so obsessed with the future that we cannot enjoy the reality of
today. Ordinary days are treated like mundane occurrences that have no
significance ... In life, *every* day counts. Try not to be so anxious about
tomorrow that you fail to notice what is happening in your life today.
~ Roderick Terry, b. 1964 ~
"Hope Chest"

TOLERANCE

Bear with a fool; there is foolishness in you too.
~ Ovambo Wisdom ~
Wit & Wisdom of Africa: Proverbs from Africa & The Caribbean, Patrick Ibekwe, ed., 1998

It is better to build bridges than walls.
~ Swahili Wisdom ~
Ibid.

One does not like heat and the other does not like cold; make it tepid and still be friends.
~ Malagasy Wisdom ~
Ibid.

If you wish to keep peace, sometimes you have to make concessions.
~ Haitian Wisdom ~
Ibid.

I am forced to own, that I am for universal toleration. Let us convert by our example, and conquer by our meekness and brotherly love!
~ Ignatius Sancho, 1729-1780 ~
Letter to John Spink, 1780 June 6 in The Letters of the Late Ignatius Sancho, an African, Vol. I, 1782

All the religions have become mixed up together in this country ... They all have to be respected. That's my way of doing things.
~ Esteban Montejo, 1856-1965 ~
in Miguel Barnet, Biography of a Runaway Slave, W. Nick Hill, tr., 1994

Intolerance can grow only in the soil of ignorance; from its branches grow all manner of obstacles to human progress.
~ Walter Francis White, 1893-1955 ~
The Rope and the Faggot, 1929

Men are punished not always for what they do, but often for what people think they will do, or for what they are. Remember that and you will find it easier to forgive them.
~ Abioseh Nicol, 1924-1994 ~

One thing is clear to me: We as human beings must be willing to accept people who are different from ourselves.
~ Barbara Jordan, 1936-1996 ~

The only way to make sure people you agree with can speak is to support the rights of people you don't agree with.
~ Eleanor Holmes Norton, b. 1937 ~

Most of us have overlapping identities which unite us with very different groups. We *can* love what we are, without hating what – and who – we are *not*. We can thrive in our own tradition, even as we learn from others.
~ Kofi Annan, b. 1938 ~
Nobel Lecture, Oslo, 2001 December 10

Does tolerance have a chance? Only if we want it to. Only when we want it to. Tolerance, like any aspect of peace, is forever a work in progress, never completed, and, if we're as intelligent as we like to think we are, never abandoned.
~ Octavia Butler, 1947-2006 ~

The inability to accept or even tolerate those who are different from us … encourages suspicion, fear, and resentment. Thus it is an illness of the collective psyche when different cultures don't understand one another. The history of mankind is plagued by this psychic disease that has caused much pain and disappointment in the world.
~ Malidoma Somé, b. 1956 ~
The Healing Wisdom of Africa, 1999

Life is filled with variable circumstances and differing perspectives, hence man will always differ with one another in many ways. Therefore, is it not folly to think that life will always go along smoothly amongst people of different background and orientation? Whether we find ourselves together in a relationship, business association, partnership, or in any other circumstance as momentary colleagues or partners, we could have the best of times while they last by realizing that the other person or entity may not be perfect and may sometimes offend us or differ from our perspective.
~ Oliver Mbamara ~
"The Conflict of Retaliation Versus Forgiveness," Cafe Africana, 2005 November

It's not true that we have to tolerate people because they are here. They are not *just here*. Nobody is "just." We are here sharing space. We are sharing resources, the air that we breathe. So rather than "just here," we are co-existing, co-living, co-being here. And as the planet gets smaller, it becomes more and more clear that none of us are free-floating and inconsequential.
~ Angel Kyodo Williams ~
Being Black: Zen and the Art of Living with Fearlessness and Grace, 2000

TRANSFORMATION

Mind (as well as metals and elements) may be transmuted from state to state; degree to degree; condition to condition; pole to pole; vibration to vibration.
~ Hermes Trismegistus ~
in *The Kybalion: A Study of the Hermetic Philosophy of Ancient Egypt and Greece*, 1908

The younger generation is vibrant with a new psychology; the new spirit is awake in the masses, and under the very eyes of the professional observers is transforming what has been a perennial problem into the progressive phases of contemporary Negro life ... A transformed and transforming psychology permeates the masses.
~ Alain Locke, 1886-1954 ~
The New Negro, 1925

I merely took the energy it takes to pout and wrote some blues.
~ Duke Ellington, 1899-1974 ~

We have been oppressed a great deal, we have been exploited a great deal and we have been disregarded a great deal. It is our weakness that has led to our being oppressed, exploited and disregarded. Now we want a revolution – a revolution which brings an end to our weakness, so that we are never again exploited, oppressed, or humiliated.
~ Julius Nyerere, 1922-1999 ~
The Arusha Declaration, 1967, Ayanda Madyibi, tr.

Only through an inner spiritual transformation do we gain the strength to fight vigorously the evils of the world in a humble and loving spirit.
~ Martin Luther King, Jr., 1929-1968 ~
in *Brother's Keeper: Words of Inspiration for African-American Men*, Roderick Terry, ed., 1996

In the transformation of silence into language and action, it is vitally necessary for each one of us to establish or examine her function in that transformation and to recognize her role as vital within that transformation.
~ Audre Lorde, 1934-1992 ~
Sister Outsider: Essays and Speeches, 1984

To dare transition is the ultimate test of the human spirit.
~ Wole Soyinka, b. 1934 ~

The human being is transformed by where his mind goes, not where his body goes.
~ Na'im Akbar, b. 1944 ~

It may sometimes seem as if our baptisms are all of fire, but in the fire we forge new strengths ... Time and again we emerge from this chrysalis changed, remade, born again. This is the pattern for all life, the end of each journey marking the beginning of new and different ones.
~ Susan L. Taylor, b. 1946 ~
Lessons in Living, 1995

The new standard of civilized life ... now demands our urgent labor, a new world order, if you will, that subverts traditional conceptions of social order: a standard which in effect subverts the meaning of the word "standard" itself. For the new order must be comprised of multiple standards: shifting, open-ended, dynamically transforming, so as to engender ways of thinking and living that privilege no one set of cultural differences over another but affirm virtue in all.
~ Marlon Riggs, 1957-1994 ~
Introduction, *Standards*, V5N1, 1992

It's hard to hand over the reins and embrace the transition, but it must be done. This doesn't mean that old prophets and sages are of no use; it means they must learn to coexist with an upcoming phalanx of rebels with new spirits and vision. Even if they wear dreads and baggy pants or speak in ways foreign to the elders.
~ Michael Eric Dyson, b. 1958 ~
Is Bill Cosby Right?, 2005

I do think paradigm shifts will happen. I don't know what will bring it about, or when, but the one thing humanity does consistently (other than to die) is to change.
~ Nalo Hopkinson, b. 1960 ~
"Filling the Sky With Islands: An Interview with Nalo Hopkinson," by Chris Aylott, Space.com

What must underlie successful epidemics, in the end, is a bedrock belief that change is possible, that people can radically transform their behavior or beliefs in the face of the right kind of impetus.
~ Malcolm Gladwell, b. 1963 ~
The Tipping Point: How Little Things Can Make a Big Difference, 2000

TRUST

One who does not trust others cannot be trusted.
~ Swahili Wisdom ~

Not realizing that "he surrounds himself with the true image of himself"
and that "what he is, that only can he see," … he is shocked when he
discovers that it has always been his own deceitfulness that made him
suspicious of others. Self-observation would reveal this deceitful one in all
of us; and this one must be accepted before there can be any
transformation of ourselves.
~ Neville, 1905-1972 ~
"Fundamentals," *New Thought*, Summer 1953

If you don't trust yourself to be involved in transforming that which needs
to be changed, then you end up waiting for someone else to come along
and do the work for you. This leads to a constant state of dependence on
some external authority, when the means to achieving what you want sits
within yourself.
~ Malidoma Somé, b. 1956 ~
The Healing Wisdom of Africa, 1999

There is an aversion to intimacy when I tell myself that I can't trust anyone
and therefore I am not safe – which, at a deeper level, means I don't trust
myself.
~ Hilda Gutiérrez Baldoquín ~
"Don't Waste Time," *Dharma, Color, and Culture*, Hilda Gutiérrez Baldoquín, ed., 2004

Trust is learning to trust oneself even if we make mistakes. Learning from
these mistakes can create positive growth. Trusting oneself builds self
esteem.
~ Ralph M. Steele ~
An Introduction to Vipassana Meditation, 1995

When you are aware of what you are doing, placing your trust in someone
or something takes a lot of courage. It's an act of bravery. It acknowledges
that you are not alone in the world and that there is a connection between
you and all things.
~ Angel Kyodo Williams ~
Being Black: Zen and the Art of Living with Fearlessness and Grace, 2000

TRUTH

Truth is but one; thy doubts are of thine own raising. It that made virtues what they are, planted also in thee a knowledge of their pre-eminence. Act as Soul dictates to thee, and the end shall be always right.
~ Khemetic Wisdom ~
Temt Tchaas: Egyptian Proverbs, Muata Ashaya Ashby, ed., 1994

To the person who seeks it, truth is immediately revealed. Indeed he who investigates with the pure intelligence set by the creator in the heart of each man and scrutinizes the order and laws of creation will discover the truth.
~ Zara Yacob, 1599-1692 ~
The Treatise of Zara Yacob, Claude Sumner, tr., 1985

Truth burns up error.
~ Sojourner Truth, 1797-1883 ~

Truth is not encompassing one person alone. Your mother's truth becomes a part of yours, so generational truths have a way of sifting down because anyhow it forms you, and so you have to deal with some of these issues that form you in order to clear your mind, even of pressures that you don't know are there.
~ Rosa Guy, b. 1925 ~
Banyan Interview

There is a world of difference between truth and facts. Facts can obscure the truth.
~ Maya Angelou, b. 1928 ~

Whether this contest is being performed along ideological lines or along religious lines, ultimately, really what we have is truth versus power. Truth for me is freedom, is self-destination. Power is domination, control, and therefore a very selective form of truth which is a lie. And the polarity between these two, in fact, forms for me the axis of human striving.
~ Wole Soyinka, b. 1934 ~
Interview by Harry Kreisler, 1998 April 16

We have rarely been encouraged and equipped to appreciate the fact that the truth works, that it releases the Spirit and that it is a joyous thing.
~ Toni Cade Bambara, 1939-1995 ~

I think the truth keeps you alive and young in your heart and your mind, where it counts.
~ Richard Pryor, 1940-2005 ~

If you raise up truth, it's magnetic. It has a way of drawing people.
~ Jesse Jackson, b. 1941 ~

If now isn't a good time for the truth, I don't see when we'll get to it.
~ Nikki Giovanni, b.1943 ~

There's the almost-true, the sometimes-true, and the half-true. That's what telling a life is like, braiding all of that like one plaits the white Indies currant's hair to make a hut. And the true-true comes out of that braid.
~ Patrick Chamoiseau, b. 1953 ~
Texaco, Rose-Myriam Réjouis & Val Vinokurov, trs., 1992

Most of us handle the truth like a fragile package. We do not know whether to caress it gently or place it aside; whether to guard it with our lives or set it free; whether to live with it or deny it; whether to whisper it softly or proclaim it to the world. The truth can also be a heavy and burdensome load to carry. It can hurt and disappoint us, ruin good intentions or bring the wrath of others upon us. Regardless of the consequences, start today to embrace the truth.
~ Roderick Terry, b. 1964 ~
"Hope Chest"

Truth is a negotiation: not a statement or a theory; truth is negotiated by point of view; it is as fluid as life, and is never "found".
~ Binyavanga Wainaina, b. 1971 ~
"Hell is in Bed with Mrs Pepra," Writers on Writing

How much we learn when we pause for a while, put our purported wisdom aside, and calmly let things be while ready to accept the truth with an objective mind. The man who is ready for the reality of truth will find it in many ways and through many channels while the man who is stuck with his dogma or conclusion will have to work out his situation first and no amount of seeking would find the truth until the walls of dogma are broken and his conclusions are no longer prejudicial. For only then will he see that the truth has always been before him while he has been looking at it turned upside down.
~ Oliver Mbamara ~
"Will You Keep Your New Year Resolution?" *Cafe Africana*, 2003

UNCONSCIOUS / SUBCONSCIOUS

The poetry of a people comes from the deep recesses of the unconscious, the irrational and the collective body of our ancestral memories.
~ Margaret Walker, 1915-1998 ~
in *Black World*, 1971 December

We must ultimately express in form those thoughts, emotions and impulses we store in the subconscious mind. That part of us does not think. It does not reason, balance, judge or reject. It is the fertile ground that accepts any and everything we plant in our minds.
~ Iyanla Vanzant, b. 1953 ~
Acts of Faith: Daily Meditations for People of Color, 1993

There's a subconscious racism that's been driven on blacks so hard that it's become part of their attitude about everything. But you cannot become part of the oppression. I want to hear black people say, "I can do anything!"
~ Arsenio Hall, b. 1955 ~
in *Songs of Wisdom: Quotations from Famous African Americans*, Jay David, ed., 2000

Truth, fiction, fantasy, fact, history, mythology really interweave to inform our character, psyche, values and beliefs ... they inform us and work within us to make us who and what we are as individuals and as a culture, as a group, race, and nationality.
~ Marlon Riggs, 1957-1994 ~
in Chuck Kleinhans & Julia Lesage, "Listening to the Heartbeat: Interview with Marlon Riggs," *Jump Cut: A Review of Contemporary Media*, No. 36, 1991

Whenever we shift our attention to the intricacies of breathing, we automatically widen our path of awareness and capacity for enlightenment. Every breath we take has the potential to unlock an immense reservoir of creativity, intelligence, truth, imagination and wisdom that lies deep within our subconscious mind, where the soul and spirit dwell.
~ Roderick Terry, b. 1964 ~
"Hope Chest"

From the conscious mind comes intellect; from the unconscious, wisdom.
~ Unknown ~

UNDERSTANDING

The study of nature is the first rung on the ladder to understanding.
~ Khemetic Wisdom ~
Temt Tchaas: Egyptian Proverbs, Muata Ashaya Ashby, ed., 1994

A wise man is he who understands his speech
When we say understand it
The wise man always understands it
But when we do not understand it
We say it is of no account.
~ *Ifa Odu* ~
in James Johnson, *Yoruba Heathenism*

For knowledge about all the things that we understand, we do not apply to
somebody speaking audible words outside us, but to the truth which
governs the mind itself inside us.
~ Augustine of Hippo, 354-430 ~
The Teacher Within

One problem thoroughly understood is of more value than a score poorly
mastered.
~ Booker T. Washington, 1856-1915 ~

We can only reflect our own experience, but we would hope that we would
be understood by others, universally beyond the source.
~ Jacob Lawrence, 1917-2000 ~

You have to understand what motivates people; that even the racist has a
problem which can be understood if you see where they are coming from.
~ Horace Ové, b. 1939 ~
in Kim Janssen, "Horace's Life in Black Power," *New Journal Enterprises*, 2005

What heals ancestors is understanding them. And understanding as well
that it is not in heaven or in hell that the ancestors are healed. *They can
only be healed inside of us.*
~ Alice Walker, b. 1944 ~
"This Was Not an Area of Large Plantations," in *Dharma, Color, and Culture*, Hilda Gutiérrez
Baldoquín, ed., 2004

VALUE / WORTH

I daresay you will ever remember that the truest worth is that of the mind –
the blest rectitude of the heart – the conscience unsullied with guilt – the
undaunted noble eye, enriched with innocence, and shining with social
glee – peace dancing in the heart – and health smiling in the face.
~ Ignatius Sancho, 1729-1780 ~
Letter I to Mr JWE, 1768 February 14 in *The Letters of the Late Ignatius Sancho, an African*, Vol. I, 1782

Have you grown to the point where you can unflinchingly stand up for the
right, for that which is honorable, honest, truthful, whether it makes you
popular or unpopular? Have you grown to the point where absolutely and
unreservedly you make truth and honor your standard of thinking and
speaking?
~ Booker T. Washington, 1856-1915 ~

Do not think that life consists of dress and show. Remember that
everyone's life is measured by the power that that individual has to make
the world better – this is all life is.
~ Washington ~

Human dignity is more precious than prestige.
~ Claude McKay, 1889-1948 ~

No one can figure out your worth but you.
~ Pearl Bailey, 1918-1990 ~
The Raw Pearl, 1968

No race has a monopoly on vice or virtue, and the worth of an individual is
not related to the color of his skin.
~ Whitney Young, Jr., 1921-1971 ~

The means by which we live have outdistanced the ends for which we live.
Our scientific power has outrun our spiritual power. We have guided
missiles and misguided men.
~ Martin Luther King, Jr., 1929-1968 ~
Strength to Love, 1963

If we are to go forward, we must go back and rediscover those precious values – that all reality hinges on moral foundations and that all reality has spiritual control.
~ King ~

Your best shot at happiness, self-worth, and personal satisfaction – the things that constitute real success – is not in earning as much as you can but in performing as well as you can something that you consider worthwhile. Whether that is healing the sick, giving hope to the hopeless, adding to the beauty of the world, or saving the world from nuclear holocaust, I cannot tell you.
~ William Raspberry, b. 1935 ~

The basic tenet of black consciousness is that the black man must reject all value systems that seek to make him a foreigner in the country of his birth and reduce his basic human dignity.
~ Steve Biko, 1946-1977 ~
Statement as witness, 1976 May 3

Our culture needs to recognize that having $20 million in the bank is not an absolute requirement for being happy. We have got to be more attuned to the idea that the life experience has its own value.
~ Bill Strickland, b. 1947 ~
in Sara Terry, "Genius at Work," *Fast Company*, No. 17, 1998 August

If we aren't willing to pay a price for our values, if we aren't willing to make some sacrifices in order to realize them, then we should ask ourselves whether we truly believe in them at all.
~ Barack Obama, b. 1961 ~
The Audacity of Hope: Thoughts on Reclaiming the American Dream, 2006

No matter what the popular culture tells us, we have to measure ourselves by our dignity, not by our dollars; by our manners, not by our Mercedes; and by our souls, not by our soles.
~ Keith Boykin, b. 1965 ~
Respecting the Soul: Daily Reflections for Black Lesbians and Gays, 1999

Mindfulness also means understanding how one's values can cause disharmony in the mind/body system and lead to habitual behaviors that promote suffering. Mindfulness leads us to understand that our health depends on how we live our lives.
~ Ralph M. Steele ~
An Introduction to Vipassana Meditation, 1995

VICE

Vices are their own punishment.
~ Aesop, fl. c. 550 BCE ~

We make a ladder of our vices, if we trample those same vices underfoot.
~ Augustine of Hippo, 354-430 ~
De Ascensione

He who does not see his own vices should not take notice of the faults of
his companions.
~ Swahili Wisdom ~
Wit & Wisdom of Africa: Proverbs from Africa & The Caribbean, Patrick Ibekwe, ed., 1998

It is best to let an offence repeat itself at least three times: the first may be
an accident; the second a mistake; but the third is likely to be intentional.
~ Kongo Wisdom ~
Ibid.

Without evil the All would be incomplete. For most or even all forms of
evil serve the Universe … Vice itself has many useful sides.
~ Plotinus, 205-270 ~

Go very light on the vices, such as carrying on in society – the social
ramble ain't restful.
~ Satchel Paige, 1900-1982 ~
Formula for Staying Young, 1953

The first and worst of all frauds is to cheat one's self. All sin is easy after
that.
~ Pearl Bailey, 1918-1990 ~

Most fear stems from sin; to limit one's sins, one must assuredly limit one's
fear, thereby bringing more peace to one's spirit.
~ Marvin Gaye, 1939-1984 ~

VISION / VISUALIZATION

No longer is there a spectator outside gazing on an outside spectacle; the clear-eyed hold the vision within themselves, though for the most part, they have no idea that it is within but look towards it as to something beyond them and see it as an object of vision caught by a direction of will. All that one sees as a spectacle is still external; one must bring the vision within and see no longer in that mode of separation but as we know ourselves; thus a man filled with a god – possessed by Apollo or by one of the Muses – need no longer look outside for his vision of the divine being; it is but finding the strength to see divinity within.
~ Plotinus, 205-270 ~
The Enneads, S. McKenna, tr., 1956

To see once is to see twice.
~ Zulu Wisdom ~
Wit & Wisdom of Africa: Proverbs from Africa & The Caribbean, Patrick Ibekwe, ed., 1998

Who does not see by himself, does not see even when it is shown to him.
~ Swahili Wisdom ~
Ibid.

With our short sight we affect to take a comprehensive view of eternity. Our horizon is the universe.
~ Paul Laurence Dunbar, 1873-1906 ~
The Uncalled, 1908

Most people think I am a dreamer ... We need visions for larger things, for the unfolding and reviewing of worthwhile things.
~ Mary McLeod Bethune, 1875-1955 ~

Sometimes in the amazing ignorance
I hear things and see things
I never knew I saw and heard before
Sometimes in the ignorance
I feel the meaning
Invincible invisible wisdom,
And I commune with intuitive instinct
With the force that made life be.

Sometimes in my amazing ignorance
Others see me only as they care to see
I am to them as they think
According the standard I should not be
And that is the difference between I and them
Because I see them as they are to is
And not the seeming isness of the was.
~ Sun Ra, 1914-1993 ~
"The Differences"

What Rimbaud calls "le voyant," the seer, is the one who sees what others
don't, that is, hidden aspects of existence, of the world, etcetera. And
consequently, this function is at the very heart of human expression, and it
conditions everything.
~ Édouard Glissant, b. 1928 ~
Interview by Michael Dash, *Renaissance Noire*, Hillina Seife, tr., 2006 March 22

The achievement is never up to the vision. What the eye sees can never be
reached by the stone the hand throws. The stone always falls short. I've
learned to live with that. I don't make too much about it. The language of
the dream is always superior to the language when you wake up and try to
recapture the dream. One need not waste one's life lamenting that. One
must be grateful for what one has achieved, and always try to do better, or
at least try not to rest.
~ Chinua Achebe, b. 1930 ~
Interview by Bradford Morrow, 1991

Above all, where there is no vision we lose the sense of our great power to
transcend history and create a new future for ourselves with others ...
Therefore the quest is not a luxury; life itself demands it of us.
~ Vincent Harding, b. 1931 ~
There is a River: The Black Struggle for Freedom in America, 1981

What you see is what you get.
~ Flip Wilson, 1933-1998 ~

Our visions are essential to create that which has never been, and we must
each learn to use all of who we are to achieve those visions.
~ Audre Lorde, 1934-1992 ~
Callaloo, 1990 August 29

What could be any more correct for any people than to see with their own
eyes?
~ Molefi Kete Asante, b. 1942 ~

It is not the eye that understands, but the mind.
~ Hausa Wisdom ~
Wit & Wisdom of Africa: Proverbs from Africa & The Caribbean, Patrick Ibekwe, ed., 1998

When children ask me, "How does one make a film?" I always say that you have to have freedom to make a film, and to have freedom, you need confidence. I tell them to close their eyes, to look at the stars, and look into their hearts, and then to open their eyes and see if the film they want to make is there, in front of their eyes.
~ Djibril Diop Mambety, 1945-1998 ~
in N. Frank Ukadike, "The Hyena's Last Laugh: A Conversation with Djibril Diop Mambety," *Transition 78*, Vol. 8, No. 2, 1999

When we use our eyes to project what we want into the world, we send forth the creative power of the soul's force. When we use positive perception to interpret what we see, we avoid falling prey to doom and gloom. If we can look beyond today, its challenges and obstacles, we can create a better tomorrow. If we can see, it must come to be.
~ Iyanla Vanzant, b. 1953 ~
Acts of Faith: Daily Meditations for People of Color, 1993

Who you think you are is who you will become. Life moves in the direction of your most dominant thoughts.
~ Roderick Terry, b. 1964 ~
"Hope Chest"

Seeing is always only noticing. We pass our eyes upon the landscapes of our familiars and choose what to acknowledge.
~ Binyavanga Wainaina, b. 1971 ~
"Discovering Home," *G21*, 1995

Visualization is a beginning phase in metaphysics in which we mentally conceive of something we want. We imagine doing it or having it and we generate the feelings that would accompany the experience. Visualization involves having an idea of what we want to accomplish or how we want to live our life, then imaging that goal as already achieved and establishing the necessary mental and emotional vibrations to bring it forth and manifest it. Visualization is a beautiful and wonderful stage in our evolution, and it's very important. When we do visioning, on the other hand, we align in consciousness with our divine purpose, which is to love and to express a greater degree of life. Then we open ourselves to catch a sense of how that expression is supposed to occur through us.
~ Michael Beckwith ~
"Visioning," Interview by Kathy Juline, *Science of Mind Magazine*, 1996 December

WAR / AGGRESSION / VIOLENCE

Force against force equals more force.
~ Ashanti Wisdom ~

When two elephants struggle, it is the grass that suffers.
~ Kikuyu Wisdom ~

Not to fight is better than fighting and making it up.
~ Angass Wisdom ~
Wit & Wisdom of Africa: Proverbs from Africa & The Caribbean, Patrick Ibekwe, ed., 1998

The whole world is wet with mutual blood; and murder, which in the case of an individual is admitted to be a crime, is called a virtue when it is committed wholesale. Impunity is claimed for the wicked deeds, not on the plea that they are guiltless, but because the cruelty is perpetrated on a grand scale.
~ Cyprian, 200-258 ~
Epistle to Donatus

Violence of language leads to violence of action. Angry men seldom fight if their tongues do not lead the fray.
~ Charles V. Roman, 1864-1934 ~
"Dark Pages in the White Man's Civilization," *American Civilization and the Negro*, 1916

Violence seldom accomplishes permanent and desired results. Herein lies the futility of war.
~ A. Philip Randolph, 1889-1979 ~
The Truth About Lynching, 1922

Non-violence is a powerful and just weapon. It is a weapon unique in history, which cuts without wounding, and ennobles the man who wields it. It is a sword that heals ... Non-violent resistance is not a method for cowards; it does resist.
~ Martin Luther King, Jr., 1929-1968 ~
The Words of Martin Luther King, Jr., Coretta Scott King, ed., 1983

Non-violence is the answer to the crucial political and moral questions of
our time: the need for man to overcome oppression and violence. Man
must evolve for all human conflict a method which rejects revenge,
aggression and retaliation. The foundation of such a method is love.
~ King ~

The ultimate weakness of violence is that it is a descending spiral,
begetting the very thing it seeks to destroy. Instead of diminishing evil, it
multiplies it. Through violence you may murder the liar, but you cannot
murder the lie, nor establish the truth. Through violence you murder the
hater, but you do not murder hate. In fact, violence merely increases hate
… Returning violence for violence multiplies violence, adding deeper
darkness to a night already devoid of stars. Darkness cannot drive out
darkness; only light can do that. Hate cannot drive out hate; only love can
do that.
~ King ~

Violence is immoral because it thrives on hatred rather than love. It
destroys community and makes brotherhood impossible. It leaves society in
monologue rather than dialogue. Violence ends by defeating itself. It
creates bitterness in the survivors and brutality in the destroyers.
~ King ~
The Words of Martin Luther King, Jr., Coretta Scott King, ed., 1983

Oppressive language does more than represent violence; it is violence; does
more than represent the limits of knowledge; it limits knowledge.
~ Toni Morrison, b. 1931 ~
Nobel Prize Address, 1993 December 7

The easiest thing to do is to destroy someone. If you have a toxic tongue,
then you have toxins in your body. It means that if you destroy with your
tongue, you can kill somebody.
~ Sonia Sanchez, b. 1934 ~

It is better to win the peace and to lose the war.
~ Bob Marley, 1946-1981 ~

Violence is not only physical. It is also psychological and verbal. It begins
in the mind.
~ Charles Johnson, b. 1948 ~
"Reading the Eightfold Path," *Dharma, Color, and Culture*, Hilda Gutiérrez Baldoquín, ed., 2004

WEALTH / PROSPERITY

To be satisfied with a little, is the greatest wisdom; and he that increaseth his riches, increaseth his cares; but a contented mind is a hidden treasure, and trouble findeth it not.
~ Akhenaton, c. 1385-c. 1355 BCE ~

An immoderate desire for riches is a poison lodged in the mind. It contaminates and destroys everything that was good in it. It is no sooner rooted there than all virtue, all honesty, all natural affection, fly before the face of it.
~ Khemetic Wisdom ~
Temt Tchaas: Egyptian Proverbs, Muata Ashaya Ashby, ed., 1994

Wealth takes charge of its owner.
~ Khemetic Wisdom ~
Wit & Wisdom of Africa: Proverbs from Africa & The Caribbean, Patrick Ibekwe, ed., 1998

Better is praise with the love of men
Than wealth in the storehouse;
Better is bread with a happy heart
Than wealth with vexation.
~ Amenemope, c. 11th C. BCE ~
The Instruction of Amenemope, Ch. 7, Miriam Lichtheim, tr.

Abundance in the world becomes great with good faith.
~ Moroccan Wisdom ~

Those, moreover, whom you consider rich, who add forests to forests, and who, excluding the poor from their neighbourhood, stretch out their fields far and wide into space without any limits, who possess immense heaps of silver and gold and mighty sums of money, either in built-up heaps or in buried stores, – even in the midst of their riches those are torn to pieces by the anxiety of vague thought, lest the robber should spoil, lest the murderer should attack, lest the envy of some wealthier neighbour should become hostile, and harass them with malicious lawsuits. Such a one enjoys no security either in his food or in his sleep.
~ Cyprian, 200-258 ~
Epistle to Donatus

Manage good is better than big wage.
~ Jamaican Wisdom ~
Wit & Wisdom of Africa: Proverbs from Africa & The Caribbean, Patrick Ibekwe, ed., 1998

More and more convinced of the futility of all our eagerness after worldly riches, my prayer and hope is only for bread, and to be enabled to pay what I owe.
~ Ignatius Sancho, 1729-1780 ~
Letter XXXVII to Mr K, 1776 August 28 in *The Letters of the Late Ignatius Sancho, an African*, Vol. I, 1782

If the wealth of a person cannot be for the general welfare, what would he gain for himself but grudge and hatred?
~ Haile Selassie, 1892-1975 ~

Money, it turned out, was exactly like sex, you thought of nothing else if you didn't have it and thought of other things if you did.
~ James Baldwin, 1924-1987 ~
Nobody Knows My Name: More Notes of a Native Son, 1961

We are perhaps poor in money but so rich by situation and hope.
~ Djibril Diop Mambety, 1945-1998 ~
Interview by Rachel Rawlins, *Africa Film & TV Magazine*, 1993

Don't gain the world and lose your soul,
happiness is better than silver and gold.
~ Bob Marley, 1946-1981 ~

Your wealth can be stolen, but the precious riches buried deep in your soul cannot.
~ Minnie Riperton, 1948-1979 ~

Abundance means a sense of fullness, which cannot be measured by the yardstick of the material goods we possess or the amount of money in a bank account. Abundance, in that sense of fullness, has a power that takes us away from worry.
~ Malidoma Somé, b. 1956 ~
The Healing Wisdom of Africa, 1999

Money is not the most important thing in life. The acquisition of money is not a worthy end in itself, but is a worthy means to achieving more fundamental life-objectives.
~ Ian McDonald ~
in *Jamaica Daily Gleaner*, 2006 July 11

WISDOM

The lips of the wise are as the doors of a cabinet; no sooner are they opened, but the treasures are poured before you. Like unto trees of gold arranged in beds of silver, are wise sentences uttered in due season.
~ Khemetic Wisdom ~
Temt Tchaas: Egyptian Proverbs, Muata Ashaya Ashby, ed., 1994

If then you do not make yourself equal to God, you cannot apprehend God; for like is known by like.
~ Hermes Trismegistus ~

True wisdom is less presuming than folly. The wise man doubteth often, and changeth his mind; the fool is obstinate, and doubteth not; he knoweth all things but his own ignorance.
~ Akhenaton, c. 1385-c. 1355 BCE ~

Wisdom is something we acquire through learning; it is not something we buy.
~ Akan Wisdom ~

Wisdom does not live in only one house.
~ Ashanti Wisdom ~

We have Reason given us for our rudder – Religion is our sheet anchor – our fixed star Hope – Conscience our faithful monitor – and Happiness the grand reward; – we all in this manner can preach up trite maxims: –ask any jackass the way to happiness – and like me they will give vent to picked up common-place sayings – but mark how they act – why just as you and I do – content with acknowledging a slight acquaintance with Wisdom, but ashamed of appearing to act under her sacred guidance.
~ Ignatius Sancho, 1729-1780 ~
Letter VII to Mr M, 1770 March 21 in *The Letters of the Late Ignatius Sancho, an African*, Vol. I, 1782

Never confuse knowledge with wisdom. By wisdom I mean wrestling with how to live.
~ Cornel West, b. 1954 ~

Wisdom is not gained by traveling afar, but by standing still; not by thought, but by absence of thought.
~ Unknown ~

WONDER / MYSTERY

Casteth he his eye towards the clouds, findeth he not the heavens full of wonders? Looketh he down to the earth, doth not the worm proclaim "Less than omnipotence could not have formed me!"
~ Akhenaton, c. 1385-c. 1355 BCE ~

Miracles happen, not in opposition to Nature, but in opposition to what we know of Nature.
~ Augustine of Hippo, 354-430 ~

People travel to wonder at the height of the mountains, at the huge waves of the seas, at the long course of the rivers, at the vast compass of the ocean, at the circular motion of the stars, and yet they pass by themselves without wondering.
~ Augustine ~

A man who doesn't believe in miracles may believe in them tomorrow. Proofs occur every day, some more convincing than others, but all quite reasonable.
~ Esteban Montejo, 1856-1965 ~
in Miguel Barnet, *Biography of a Runaway Slave*, W. Nick Hill, tr., 1994

When I touch that flower, I am not merely touching that flower. I am touching infinity. That little flower existed long before there were human beings on this earth. It will contrive to exist for thousands, yes, millions of years to come.
~ George Washington Carver, 1864-1943 ~

The more I wonder ... the more I love.
~ Alice Walker, b. 1944 ~

the mystery is there you can see
the truth lives within you and me
~ Mutabaruka, b. 1952 ~
The Next Poems, 2005

There is wonder here
And there is surprise
In everything the unseen moves.
The ocean is full of songs.
The sky is not an enemy.
Destiny is our friend.
~ Ben Okri, b. 1959 ~
An African Elegy, 1992

There has to be a head and energy for theory ... and another head that
continually forgets the past and treats the mundane as extraordinary. To
keep this sense alive ... I go back to reading things like Lewis Carroll and
other material that will encourage me to be a mad hatter. You have to
connect all those things in a mysterious way.
~ Fred D'Aguiar, b. 1960 ~
Interview by Joanne Hyppolite, Fall 1997, *Anthurium: A Caribbean Studies Journal*, II.1, Spring 2004

Fantasy pays homage to folklore and folklore talks a lot about archetypes.
Fantasy explores those archetypes and also explores the way we tell stories
to explain things like why there's a moon in the sky or things that we have
no explanation for, but we believe. Fantasy explores what we believe.
~ Nalo Hopkinson, b. 1960 ~
Interview by Kellie Magnus, *Caribbean Review of Books*, Issue 73

Whether bird watching, star gazing or mountain climbing, each of us ought
to have some relationship with the energies, forces and wonders of nature.
Communing with nature is a critical link to living a vital, full and creative
life.
~ Roderick Terry, b. 1964 ~
"Hope Chest"

There is a sense of mystery everywhere, in everything that surrounds us –
there is a sense of the continuity of your ancestors, or just of a world
beyond the one we're in, and that there are other forces that interact in
our lives other than the ones we see. That's something I've always felt: a
kind of continuity in my life; that I'm not here, just here; that I didn't just
sprout ... We're deeper. There's more to us than the surface and I've always
taken that for granted.
~ Edwidge Danticat, b. 1969 ~

If there is a miracle in the idea of life it is this: that we are able to exist for
a time – in defiance of chaos.
~ Binyavanga Wainaina, b. 1971 ~
"Discovering Home," *G21*, 1995

WORK

Where our work is, there let our joy be.
~ Tertullian, c. 160-240 ~
De cultu feminarum

Work is good provided you do not forget to live.
~ Bantu Wisdom ~

It is work that puts one man ahead of another.
~ Nupe Wisdom ~

Only toiling can support one; Idleness cannot bring dividend.
Whoever refuses to work, such a person does not deserve to eat.
~ *Eji Ogbe* ~

Love to work with your hands as much as your life allows, and be expert in
this work that you may gain a profit from it; don't be ashamed to work with
your hands, because it is God's precept; without working of their hands all
human creatures perish and their whole life is destroyed.
~ Walda Heywat, 17th C. ~
The Treatise of Walda Heywat, Claude Sumner, tr. 1985

Nothing ever comes to one that is worth having, except as a result of hard
work.
~ Booker T. Washington, 1856-1915 ~

There is as much dignity in tilling a field as in writing a poem.
~ Washington ~
Address, Atlanta International Exposition, 1895 September 18

The return from your work must be the satisfaction which that work brings
you and the world's need of that work. With this, life is heaven, or as near
heaven as you can get. Without this – with work which you despise, which
bores you, and which the world does not need – this life is hell.
~ W. E. B. Du Bois, 1868-1963 ~
"To His Newborn Great-Grandson," Address on his ninetieth birthday, 1958

I have come to know by experience that work is the nearest thing to
happiness that I can find.
~ Zora Neale Hurston, 1891-1960 ~

There is neither shame nor disgrace in a day's work well and truly done, whatever the task and whatever the rank or status of the worker. The farmer and the laborer who have toiled diligently throughout the day have earned their bread and honest sleep. But the man, whatever his rank, who has spent his time in idleness, whose hand has been turned to little of profit or value during his working hours has earned only the scorn and disdain of his fellowmen whom he has cheated.
~ Haile Selassie, 1892-1975 ~
Important Utterances of H.I.M. Emperor Haile Selassie I, Jah Rastafari, Volume 1, 1963-1972, 1994

People who make a living doing something they don't enjoy wouldn't even be happy with a one-day work week.
~ Duke Ellington, 1899-1974 ~

Each of us must earn our own existence. And how does anyone earn anything? Through perseverance, hard work, and desire.
~ Thurgood Marshall, 1908-1993 ~
in Roderick Terry, *One Million Strong: A PhotographicTribute of the Million Man March*, 1996

All labor that uplifts humanity has dignity and importance and should be undertaken with painstaking excellence.
~ Martin Luther King, Jr., 1929-1968 ~

The principal horror of any system which defines the good in terms of profit rather than in terms of human need to the exclusion of the psychic and emotional components of that need – is that it robs our work of its erotic value, its erotic power and life appeal and fulfillment. Such a system reduces work to a travesty of necessities, a duty by which we earn bread or oblivion for ourselves and those we love. But this is tantamount to blinding a painter and then telling her to improve her work and enjoy the act of painting. It is not only next to impossible, it is also profoundly cruel.
~ Audre Lorde, 1934-1992 ~

That's what you really have to look for in life, something that you like, and something that you think you're pretty good at. And if you can put those two things together, then you're on the right track, and just drive on ... then do it for all it's worth. Be the very best you can be.
~ Colin Powell, b. 1937 ~
"America's Premier Soldier-Statesman," Academy of Achievement Interview, 1998 May 23

Enjoy your sweat because hard work doesn't guarantee success, but without it you don't have a chance.
~ Alex "A-Rod" Rodriguez, b. 1975 ~

WORRY

If the heart worries, there is no lack of tears.
~ Oromo Wisdom ~
Wit & Wisdom of Africa: Proverbs from Africa & The Caribbean, Patrick Ibekwe, ed., 1998

Pound's worth of fret never paid a quattie's[4] worth of debt.
~ Jamaican Wisdom ~

There are two kinds of worries – those you can do something about and those you can't. Don't spend any time on the latter.
~ Duke Ellington, 1899-1974 ~

Every life has some trouble
When you worry you make it double.
~ Bobby McFerrin, b. 1950 ~

Worrying is a form of atheism. I don't understand people who call themselves Christian or Buddhist or Moslem or whatever and worry. Because you cannot believe in a power greater than yourself and worry. It does not compute.
~ Oprah Winfrey, b. 1954 ~

Worry is a future tense emotion acted out in the present, with no basis other than an overactive imagination and fear. We have the capacity to cope with the challenges of each day. It is when we project fear into our future that we become overwhelmed with worry.
~ Roderick Terry, b. 1964 ~
"Hope Chest"

I call this airplane theory: If you're scared to fly, worry about it on the ground while you're standing next to a phone and you can get on a train or bus. Once the plane takes off, relax. There's nothing you can do.
~ Will Smith, b. 1968 ~

---

[4] Colonial era coinage worth one and a half pence, or penny-ha'penny

ZEAL / ZEST

A child able to run doesn't know to hide.
~ Mamprussi Wisdom ~
Wit & Wisdom of Africa: Proverbs from Africa & The Caribbean, Patrick Ibekwe, ed., 1998

One thing alone I charge you. As you live, believe in life!
~ W. E. B. Du Bois, 1868-1963 ~

Do not ask yourself what the world needs. Ask yourself what makes you come alive, and then go do that. Because what the world needs is people who have come alive.
~ Howard Thurman, 1889-1981 ~

To love life is to be whole in all one's parts; and to be whole in all one's parts is to be free and unafraid.
~ Thurman ~
in Roderick Terry, *One Million Strong: A PhotographicTribute of the Million Man March*, 1996

Fires can't be made with dead embers, nor can enthusiasm be stirred by spiritless men. Enthusiasm in our daily work lightens effort and turns even labor into pleasant tasks.
~ James Baldwin, 1924-1987 ~

You better live every day like your last because one day you're going to be right.
~ Ray Charles, 1930-2004 ~

If the way you approach your goal is right for you, then you won't have self doubt. Undiminished enthusiasm always stays with you.
~ James Earl Jones, b. 1931 ~
"The Voice of Triumph," Academy of Achievement Interview, 1996 June 29

When we approach life with passion and enthusiasm, we expose hidden dimensions of our lives that allow us to connect with others in a more meaningful way. The energy created allows us to experience the fullness of life. Follow your passion.
~ Roderick Terry, b. 1964 ~
"Hope Chest"

LAST WORD

I entreat any wise and inquisitive man
who may come after I am dead to add
his thought to mine. Behold, I have
begun an inquiry such as has not been
attempted before. You can complete
what I have begun so that the people
of our country will become wise with
the help of God and arrive at the
science of truth.
~ Zara Yacob, 1599-1692 ~
The Treatise of Zara Yacob, Claude Sumner, tr., 1985

BIOGRAPHICAL INDEX

About the Authors

Larry Chang is a life counselor and teacher of
I-sight, a synthesis of the perennial philosophy,
the dharma and transpersonal psychology. He
has collected and uses many quotations in his
work, which he shares in this and a previous
anthology, *Wisdom for the Soul: Five Millennia
of Prescriptions for Spiritual Healing*. He has
been, in turn and simultaneously, an artist,
designer, editor, activist, trader, consultant,
restauranteur and publisher. An exile from
Jamaica, he was granted asylum based on
sexual orientation by the US, where he now
lives in Washington, DC.

*One could say of me that in this book I
have only made up a bunch of other men's
flowers, providing of my own only the
string to tie them together.*
~ Montaigne ~

Hailing from Pine Bluff, Arkansas,
Roderick Terry is an attorney, author and
photographer, currently resident in
Washington, D.C. His previous publications
are *Brother's Keeper: Words of Inspiration for
African-American Men* and *One Million Strong:
A Photographic Tribute of the Million Man
March*.

About the Type

GOUDY OLD STYLE

Designed by Frederick Goudy, 1915
Inspired by the Froeben capitals believed to
have been cut by Peter Schoeffer the Younger,
son of Gutenberg's apprentice, this design is
neither strictly a Venetian nor an Aldine,
although it is placed in the Venetian group
due to its archaic approach and lack of the
Aldine model. The design owes more to
Goudy than to Schoeffer.

Additional copies may be ordered
from
GNOSOPHIA Publishers
P O Box 3183, Washington, DC
20010-0183
www.wisdomforthesoul.org
orders@wisdomforthesoul.org

Selected quotations are available
on cards in a variety of assortments.

*Have you ever observed that we pay much
more attention to a wise passage when it is
quoted than when we read it in the
original author?*

~ *Philip G. Hamerton, 1834-1894* ~